Feeling Sexy

A Christian Woman's Guide to
Sexual Confidence & Desire

By: Josh & Cassie Spurlock

Publishing

Table of Contents

Introduction

The Bra Drawer Revelation

*R*achel hadn't planned on crying over her underwear drawer that Tuesday morning.

She'd been running late already. Her preschooler had just sneezed a trail of yogurt across the kitchen, and her oldest was asking existential questions about dinosaurs and Noah's Ark while brushing his teeth with what she hoped wasn't Desitin.

Somewhere between wiping the counter (with a sock, naturally) and yelling upstairs, "We are leaving in five minutes whether your shoes are on or not!"—she'd opened her bra drawer looking for her one decent bra. The one that didn't pinch or squeak or make her feel like she was being gently suffocated by holy Lycra.

And there it was: a lacey little number from her honeymoon. Deep plum. Labeled "exotic plum passion" or something equally optimistic. It had been buried under nursing bras, sports bras, and that one beige thing she swore she'd toss six months ago.

She picked it up.

Then she sat down.

Then she cried.

Not big, dramatic, Lifetime-movie tears. Just the quiet kind that sneak up on you when your soul's trying to say, Hey, remember me? I used to feel sexy. I used to want things. I used to laugh and flirt and let him see me with the lights on.

Rachel wasn't even sure what she was grieving, exactly. Her body? Her confidence? The part of her that used to want sex, not just feel guilty for avoiding it?

She wasn't mad at her husband. He was patient, kind, trying his best.

She just didn't know where she'd gone. And whether she could come back.

Then her toddler screamed from the bathroom, "MOM! I POOPED BUT I DIDN'T NEED TO!"

She sighed. Stood up. Stuffed the plum bra back in the drawer.

But not all the way.

She left a little lace peeking out—like a whisper of hope.

Maybe she couldn't fix everything overnight.

But maybe, just maybe, she could start here.

So... What If You Could Feel Sexy Again?

Or maybe for the first time?

Maybe you're here because you want to want sex more often. Or because you're tired of feeling awkward, unsure, or disconnected in the bedroom. Maybe you've read the marriage books, tried the oils, and even *attempted* to get excited about lace (but really just ended up itchy and slightly annoyed). Maybe you love your husband deeply—but your desire feels like a distant memory, buried under laundry piles, past wounds, or the plain old exhaustion of life.

Friend, you're not broken. You're not a prude. You're not failing.

You're a woman with a body designed by God Himself for joy, pleasure, and intimacy. And guess what? That design hasn't changed—even if your circumstances, hormones, or confidence have.

This book is for you—the Christian woman who wants to feel sexy, not someday, but in your real, right-now body and marriage. It's for the woman who's tired of silence and shame, and ready for something different—something healing, holy, and maybe even a little spicy.

Inside these pages, we'll laugh together. Probably blush together. Maybe even cry a little. We'll talk honestly about sex, desire, shame, trauma, pleasure, play, and the good kind of surrender. We'll explore what it means to reconnect with your body, awaken your desire, and become a sexually confident woman—not by faking it or trying harder, but by healing from the inside out.

You'll learn about the *Thrive-Drive* hardwired into your soul, how your nervous system plays a role in sexual response, and why Jesus is the most pro-orgasm person in the universe (yep, we said it). We'll talk Scripture. We'll talk science. And we'll talk vibrators. All in the same breath.

Because sex was never meant to be a source of shame for God's daughters. It was meant to be a source of joy, connection, and delight.

So take a deep breath. Pour a cup of coffee (or wine—no judgment). And lean in.

This journey is for you. You're ready.

And the best part? *You don't have to walk it alone.* Let's begin.

Chapter 1: You Are Normal

The Spanx and the Snickerdoodle

*E*mily *stood frozen in her closet, clutching a crumpled pair of Spanx in one hand and a half-eaten snickerdoodle in the other. The Sunday morning worship playlist was still playing in the background, trying its best to summon something sacred while her toddler smeared banana on the bathroom mirror.*

She sighed.

"Lord, I love You. But also, if You could've made the female body a little more... stretch-resistant, that would've been great."

Today was her church's "marriage and intimacy" Sunday—she knew because it was boldly announced on the email she deleted twice. Her husband, bless him, was already in the kitchen cheerfully packing goldfish into Ziplocks like it was a holy calling. Meanwhile, Emily was locked in a spiritual battle with her mirror.

She hadn't worn anything other than leggings in weeks. Her postpartum body was still sticking around... two years later. Every time she even thought about sex, a mental slideshow of insecurity started playing: sagging belly, jiggly thighs, labia she wasn't totally convinced were "normal," and boobs that had apparently joined a union and gone on strike.

She tried on the dress anyway. It fit. Kind of.

Then came the spiral.

"Should I even still be struggling with this? I'm a grown woman. A Christian. I know I'm supposed to believe I'm fearfully and wonderfully made... but I'm sure the psalmist had better abs."

Cue shame. Cue fake smile. Cue hugging everyone at church like she wasn't holding her body hostage in her own mind.

Later that evening, after the kids were in bed and the dishes were mostly done, she curled up with her tea, exhausted from trying to be fine all day. Her husband leaned over, kissed her shoulder, and whispered, "You're beautiful."

She smiled. Sort of. But inside, a quiet ache answered back: I wish I could believe that.

The Struggle is REAL

Let's get one thing out in the open: if you've ever felt insecure about your body, confused about your sexual desire, or totally out of sync with your husband in the bedroom—you're not alone. In fact, you're in the majority.

Struggling with body image, confidence, or low desire isn't some weird anomaly—it's shockingly normal. Most women experience it at some point (or many points) in their lives. And no, you're not broken. You're human, and you're living in a world that's broken.

The truth is, we're all shaped by the fallen world around us. From the ads we see to the messages we got growing up (and even some from church), our sense of self—especially as women—can get tangled up in shame, comparison, and confusion. That tangled-up version? That's what we call the false self.

The false self is the part of us that formed in response to pain—where our wounds, missing experiences (gaps), and immature habits all live. It's the version of you that hustles to be enough, hides what you really feel, or fakes "fine" when you're anything but. It's the part that says, "I shouldn't be struggling with this," or "Other women probably don't deal with this."

But hear me: they do. And so do we.

And while that struggle might be common, it's not your final destination. Because here's the good news—we don't have to stay stuck in the false self. God has a redemptive plan, and that includes restoring you to your true self—the woman He designed: sexually confident, free to feel, free to connect, and yes, free to enjoy pleasure.

False Self & Fake Joy

You didn't come out of the womb worried about your body or anxious about sex. Insecurity, shame, disconnection— these aren't built-in. They're learned. And they're learned through our stories.

That means whatever you're feeling right now—however confusing or frustrating it might be—makes sense. You just might not understand the "why" yet. That's what this chapter (and this whole book) is here to help you uncover.

Enter: the false self.

The false self is the version of you that got shaped by pain. She formed as you navigated wounds (things that shouldn't have happened but did), gaps (things that should've happened but didn't), and the immature habits you picked up to survive it all. Those habits can look like insecurity, body shame, avoiding sex, or never fully stepping into your sexual identity as a confident, God-designed woman.

One of the sneakiest of those habits? Fake joy.

Fake joy is the socially acceptable mask we wear when our soul feels anything but joyful. It's the "praise hands" in church while your heart's silently screaming. It's the big smile that says, "I'm great!" when you're actually running on empty. It's the staying busy with good things so you don't have to feel the hard things.

It's also the glass of wine you reach for to calm your nerves... or the way you scroll endlessly through Instagram to numb out... or the obsessive focus on dieting (or giving up on it completely) because you feel like your body is never quite right. Fake joy doesn't always look bad. In fact, sometimes it looks like you're winning. But deep down, you know—it's just keeping you distracted from the ache.

And here's the thing: all that unresolved stuff—the buried emotions, the stories we've never made sense of, the feelings we've never processed—it doesn't just stay hidden. It leaks. Especially into our sexual desire.

Fake joy and the false self suck the life out of your sex drive and feed the very insecurities that keep you disconnected from your body and your husband.

And let's not miss this: we didn't just pick this stuff up on our own. We inherited it. Many of the hang-ups we carry about sex and our bodies were passed down—often unintentionally—by the false selves and fake joy of the people who influenced us. And if we don't address it, we'll pass it right along to the next generation, too.

But there's good news—you're not stuck. Healing is possible. And it starts by getting real about where we've *been*, so we can discover who we really *are*.

Bringing Sexy Back

Just because something is common doesn't mean it's how things are supposed to be.

Yes, it's normal to struggle with desire. Yes, it's common to feel disconnected from your body or unsure of how to claim your sexual confidence. But "normal" isn't the same as God's best for you.

God has a redemptive plan—and it includes your sexuality.

He wants to take you on a healing journey. One that restores you to your true self—not the self shaped by shame or fear or false messages, but the woman He designed from the beginning: whole, holy, sexually confident, and fully alive.

This journey doesn't ignore your wounds, gaps, or immature habits. It heals them. It fills in what was missing. It gently but powerfully transforms the ways you've learned to cope into new, life-giving ways of being. This is the work of maturing into your true self.

And guess what's waiting for you on the other side of that healing?

True happiness. Not the fleeting kind that depends on mood or circumstances—but the kind that the Bible describes as peace, joy, and deep satisfaction in life... all anchored in hope. It's what the NICC (Neuroscience Informed Christian Counseling®) model calls a "homeostatic state"— a steady, grounded way of being where your soul can rest, your body can enjoy, and your sexual desire has room to thrive.

Yes, friend—God wants that for you. And yes, it's possible.

Your Sexy Body

Let's say this loud for the women in the back: your body is normal.

Unless you're experiencing pain, what you're feeling in your body—and how your body is shaped—is within the beautiful, God-designed range of normal. And yes, that includes your genitals, your sexual responses, your curves (or lack thereof), your skin, your stretch marks, and every inch in between.

There is immense diversity in how female bodies look, function, and experience pleasure. That diversity isn't a mistake—it's intentional. Incredible sex lives happen in bodies of all shapes, sizes, and levels of experience. Your body isn't disqualified from intimacy or pleasure because it doesn't look like a filtered Instagram model or a magazine cover.

But the enemy has a strategy. And it's working overtime.

His goal? To steal joy from your marriage, kill your desire, and destroy your confidence. And one of his most effective tools is comparison.

Research backs this up: people who constantly compare themselves to others are significantly less happy—even if they think they're "winning" the comparison. Why? Because comparison kills joy. It feeds insecurity and suffocates intimacy.

When we start believing our bodies aren't "okay," or that our experience is somehow not enough, we fall into a trap.

That trap sells billions of dollars in makeup, diet books, gym memberships, and beauty products—but it doesn't lead to more happiness, more confidence, or more desire. It just keeps us stuck in a loop of "not enough."

So let's be real for a second. Whatever the shape or size of your breasts, nipples, areola, booty, waist, labia, or clitoris—unless you're in physical pain, your body is within the normal spectrum of female design. You can have a rich, satisfying, God-honoring sex life in the body you have right now.

That doesn't mean you have to stop growing or give up on changes you'd like to make—but it does mean this: acceptance is the starting point. Not shame. Not striving. Not "when I finally lose the weight." Acceptance.

Loving the body you live in today, as it is, is one of the most powerful, biblical, and even rebellious acts you can choose in a culture obsessed with perfection.

This book is here to help you do just that—to walk you step-by-step through the process of healing your story, untangling shame, building practical skills, and learning to live as the sexually confident, desire-filled woman God created you to be.

Wrapping It Up

So friend, let's take a deep breath together.

We've named some big truths in this chapter: It's normal to struggle with body image, sexual desire, and confidence—and that "normal" often flows from our false self, shaped by wounds, gaps, and immature coping habits like fake joy. But just because it's common doesn't mean it's your forever.

God's not done with you. He's not surprised by your struggles. And He's inviting you on a redemptive journey—one that leads to healing, wholeness, and sexual confidence rooted in your true self.

Your body, your desire, your story? They're not too far gone. They're good, and they matter deeply to the One who created them.

As we move into the next chapter, we're going to zoom in on one of the most powerful tools God gives us for reclaiming our sexual confidence: body acceptance. Even if there are things you'd love to change, you can start learning to love and honor the body you're in today.

Because how you see your body is directly tied to how you show up in your sexual story. And learning to see yourself through God's eyes? That's where the real transformation begins.

Let's go there—together.

Chapter 2: Kissing The Mirror

The Bra in the Microwave

Rachel didn't mean to put her bra in the microwave. It just... happened.

She was running late (again), trying to get herself and her kids dressed for church while her husband, God bless him, hummed happily from the bathroom like they weren't living in a domestic war zone. One kid had spilled orange juice down the front of her only clean blouse. The other was crying because she couldn't find her other sparkly shoe, which Rachel was 98% sure the dog had chewed.

In a moment of chaotic genius, Rachel remembered a TikTok that said you could "refresh" wrinkled clothes in the microwave. Except it wasn't a shirt in her hand. It was a lightly padded, definitely stretched out, seen-better-days bra.

She caught it before sparks flew, but barely. "Well," she muttered, tossing the scorched strap onto the kitchen counter, "that's probably symbolic of something."

By the time they got to church, her nerves were fried and her smile was fake. Sitting in the pew, she felt like a fraud. Her pastor was preaching about joy and renewal, and all she could think was how exhausted she felt. Not just physically tired—soul tired. Tired of trying to hold it all together. Tired of comparing herself to women who looked like they actually enjoyed *their lives. Tired of feeling like her body, her marriage, and her faith were all supposed to feel different... better... fixed.*

She shifted uncomfortably, adjusting the backup bra that never quite fit right and thought, "Why do I always feel so behind? Why does "feeling good" feel like such a mystery?"

Later that night, she stood in front of her bathroom mirror, makeup smeared, her hair in a messy knot that had lost the "cute" part somewhere around noon. She looked herself in the eyes. Not with judgment, but with something new. Curiosity.

"What if it's not about fixing everything at once? What if it's about finding out what happened... and healing that first?"

She didn't have answers yet. But for the first time in a long time, she had a starting place. And maybe—just maybe—that was enough.

Woman in the Mirror

You didn't start out unsure of yourself.

Before the stretch marks, the shame, the youth group talks that left more questions than answers—you were knit together by God with purpose, precision, and delight.

From the moment of conception, you were given not one, but two kinds of DNA.

Your **physical DNA** came preloaded with the blueprint for your body—eye color, skin tone, the curve of your hips, the way your breasts would form, your metabolism, even the shape of your labia. It's all there, a stunning biological design authored by the same God who carved mountains and painted sunsets.

But that's only half the story.

You also received what we call your **Soul DNA**—the divine design for who you are on the inside. Your temperament. Your gifts and talents. Your God-given wiring for relationships, creativity, purpose, and joy. All the ingredients for reflecting the image of God in a way only *you* can. This blueprint contains your true self—the mature, secure, deeply connected woman you were always meant to become, rooted in Christ and radiant with His love.

In a perfect world, both kinds of DNA would unfold just as God designed.

Physically, you'd get all the nourishment, movement, and care your body needed to develop freely. Soulfully, you'd receive all the life-giving experiences necessary to mature emotionally, relationally, and spiritually. No trauma. No shame. No awkward messages about sex or whispers that your body is "too much" or "not enough."

But that's not the world we grew up in.

Even if you had amazing parents—and praise God if you did—they weren't Jesus. Which means they were imperfect, just like everyone else around you. And those imperfections left marks.

Some things happened that shouldn't have—those are your **wounds**. And some things didn't happen that you desperately needed—those are your **gaps**. Both have a lasting impact.

They shape how we see ourselves. How we understand our worth. How we experience our bodies. And especially how we show up (or shut down) sexually.

Over time, we develop a **false self**—a version of us shaped more by pain and protection than by God's original design. And that false self still echoes in how we feel when we look in the mirror... how we carry our bodies... how freely (or not) we respond to touch, desire, and pleasure.

The good news? That's not the end of your story.

God is still working. And that woman in the mirror? She's not a lost cause. She's a masterpiece in progress.

What Happened To You

Let's ask a tender but telling question: Was your mom comfortable in her own skin? Did she feel confident in her sexuality? Was she able to model body acceptance, pleasure, and healthy desire?

If your answer is "not really" or even "definitely not," that had an effect on you. There's no way around it.

Our mothers—or whoever played that primary nurturing role—are our first template for womanhood. We watched them. We absorbed their beliefs, their energy, their silences. Whether they struggled with their body image, felt awkward about sex, or avoided the topic entirely, it shaped how we see ourselves as women. Not always because they said something direct—but because of what they didn't say. These things are more caught than taught.

And when it comes to sex and the body, silence is never neutral. It's shaming. We don't talk about what we think is shameful. So when no one talked about your developing body, your desires, or your questions about sex, the message landed anyway: "This must be something I should feel weird about."

Of course, it's not just our parents who shaped us.

We were marinated in messages from TV, magazines, church sermons, worship songs, and billboards. Some of those messages pointed us toward the beauty and truth of who God made us to be. But many didn't. Many left wounds or created gaps—distorting our view of our worth, our bodies, and our sexuality.

Then there's the crowd of classmates, youth group friends, and locker room comparisons. The girls who developed earlier. The ones the boys chased. The social food chain that seemed to rank every part of us, including our desirability.

And then—for far too many women—there are the sexual experiences we didn't ask for.

Somewhere between 1 in 5 and 1 in 3 women experience sexual abuse or harassment before age 18. That includes overt abuse, but also:

- Unwanted advances
- Boyfriends who pushed too far
- Exposure to pornography or sexual content before you were ready
- Playing "doctor" with older kids
- Confusing touch that felt wrong but also triggered arousal
- Moments you didn't have language for, so you buried them

Even if no one "told" you what to feel, your nervous system remembered. Your brain made associations between your body, your sexuality, and those early, overwhelming experiences. And those memories—some clear, some vague—are still influencing how you feel today. About sex. About yourself. About what's possible.

Hear this: none of that was your fault.

Even if you made some immature choices along the way (as we all do), the shaping experiences of your story were never something you chose. But they *are* something you can heal from.

That's why this journey matters so much. Healing from what happened to you is part of reclaiming the abundant life Jesus came to give. It's how we redeem what's been damaged and grow into the confident, sexually free woman God designed you to be.

Ditch the Fake Joy

As the wise and slightly snarky saying goes: poop happens.

We live in a broken world, and that means things go sideways—sometimes in small ways, sometimes in gut-wrenching, identity-shaking ways. So what do we do with that?

First, we've got to face the truth: while your body may have its own set of issues (don't worry, we'll get to those), your *soul* plays a huge role in how you feel about your body, your sexuality, and your capacity for pleasure and confidence.

You cannot ignore what's happened to you—what shaped you—and expect to magically mature into joy, freedom, and sexual confidence. I know. It's not fair. And I wish I could tell you there's a shortcut. But friend, we both know life isn't fair. Still, here's the good news: God is good. And He's made a redemptive path forward.

What happened to you? *Not your fault.*

But as a grown-up woman who deeply longs for wholeness, confidence, and intimacy... the responsibility to pursue healing? That *is* yours. No one else can walk this road for you. And that takes courage. Holy courage.

The first brave step? Look in the mirror—not just the one on your wall, but the mirror of your soul—and choose **compassionate curiosity** over criticism.

No more "shoulding" all over yourself.

"I should feel more desire."

"I should love my body by now."

"I should be over this."

"I shouldn't still struggle with this stuff."

Sister, "should" doesn't heal. "Should" shames.

What heals is this: getting honest about what *is*. Not what you wish was true. Not what other people seem to experience. Not the filtered version of your story. The real stuff.

And when you meet that real stuff with grace—when you stop faking fine and start asking, "What's going on under the surface here?"—you create space for corrective, **life-giving experiences**. Those are the moments that heal wounds, fill gaps, and start maturing you into your true self.

That's why we have to ditch the fake joy.

Stop numbing out with distractions. Stop pretending everything's alright when it's not. Stop holding it all together with a shaky smile and a packed schedule. It's okay if you're not okay. That's where healing begins.

And friend, it's so worth it.

Find A Buddy

Let's be real. The idea of being vulnerable about your deepest, most awkward insecurities and painful stories probably sounds about as appealing as getting poked in the eye with a sand-covered spoon.

We get it.

But remember—this journey isn't about wishful thinking. It's about embracing reality as it is. And the reality is: you weren't wounded in isolation, and you won't heal in isolation either.

Wounds happen in relationship. Healing happens there too.

That's why the real game-changer isn't just more *information*—it's **transformation**. And transformation doesn't come from reading alone. (Yes, even if this book is super helpful. We hope it is!) It comes from whole-brain, right-brain, relational experiences. It comes from people.

So yes, sister—you're going to need some humans to walk this road with you.

Not just your husband (though he matters too!). You need *others*—two key categories of people, in fact:

1. Your Sage Circle

These are your mentors—the wise ones you invite into your life. Think of them as your personal board of directors for healing and growth.

A mentor isn't someone who's perfect (spoiler alert: no one is). It's someone who's just further along in one or more areas of life than you. They might be a trusted family member, a spiritual parent, a coach, a spiritual director, a pastor, or a professional therapist. They might even be an author or podcast host who speaks into your soul regularly. Those folks count too.

But you also need mentors you can look in the eye. People who can sit with you knee to knee, help regulate your nervous system, and speak truth in love when you're tempted to spiral. These are the people who walk with you—not just teach you.

2. Your Iron Sharpeners

These are your peers who are doing their own hard work—leaning into their healing, asking the tough questions, and growing toward their true self.

They're not perfect either, but they're not content to stay stuck. They're the girlfriends who will pray with you, laugh with you, call you out (gently), and send you an enthusiastic emoji pep talk when you're on the verge of giving up. These people are gold.

So, where do you start?

Ask a friend (or two) to read this book with you. Meet up for coffee, talk through what's hitting home, and cheer each other on as you grow in sexual confidence. Start rocking your husband's world—and your own—as you claim your God-given sexual power.

And if you want to connect with a whole community of women doing the same? Join the **Omazing® Intimacy online community** and meet sisters from around the world on this same redemptive path.

Need deeper help? You might also benefit from a therapist—especially one trained in **Neuroscience Informed Christian Counseling®**. The sex therapists at MyCounselor.Online® are experts in guiding women like you through healing, growth, and freedom.

Because healing? It's a team sport. And you don't have to do this alone.

Compassionate Curiosity and Corrective Experiences

Here's a beautiful truth you might need to hear today: God is *not* neutral about your healing.

He knew the world you'd be born into—a world cracked by sin, laced with pain, and brimming with confusion about bodies, sex, and worth. And He didn't shrug His shoulders or leave you to figure it out alone. He made *provision* for your redemption—*every* part of you, including your sexuality.

Inside you is what we call the **Thrive-Drive**—the breath of God animating your body and soul, moving you toward healing, growth, and maturity. It's the sacred force that propels your physical body to recover when you're injured. Cut your finger? Immediately, white blood cells race to fight off infection, platelets rush in to stop the bleeding, and new skin cells begin their quiet work of repair.

No conscious effort required. Your body was *designed* by Jesus to heal.

And that healing instinct doesn't stop at paper cuts and bruises. It's hardwired into your **soul**, too.

Your Thrive-Drive is the Spirit of God in you, whispering: "There's more. You were made for more. Let's heal what's been broken." It alerts you to your spiritual and emotional needs and nudges you toward the people and experiences that can meet them. God uses the body of Christ—your **Sages** and **Iron Sharpeners**—to pour out His grace in ways that restore what sin has tried to steal.

Here's how that healing happens: through **compassionate curiosity** and **corrective experiences**.

When you approach your wounds—not with shame or judgment—but with kindness and curiosity (the way you'd treat a hurting friend), your Thrive-Drive starts spotlighting the places in you that are ready to heal. It points to:

- **Wounds:** unresolved pain from things that *shouldn't* have happened.

- **Gaps:** missed experiences that *should* have shaped you.

- **Immature habits:** old survival strategies that once protected you, but now limit you.

And the Spirit doesn't do this to shame you. That's the accuser's voice. God brings things forward to *heal you.*

When you choose to be vulnerable—sharing your story with someone safe, letting your heart show—it creates the opportunity for transformation. In a space of emotional safety, the unresolved pain surfaces. Through relationship, or in guided prayer (like the Approach), you get to feel the feelings all the way through. You reprocess the experience in a new, safe context—creating what neuroscience calls a **mismatching experience**.

This process rewires old beliefs, dissolves the lies you've carried ("I'm not enough," "My body is gross," "I don't deserve pleasure"), and replaces them with peace, clarity, and truth. You literally *feel* the healing—often through relief, release, and an overwhelming sense of gratitude.

It's a miracle. A Jesus-powered, nervous-system-integrated miracle.

And in those same safe spaces, you'll also begin to receive what was missing—new, life-giving input about your body, your worth, your sexuality. These are the **corrective life-**

giving experiences that fill your gaps and help mature your soul toward your true self.

If your Iron Sharpeners don't know how to help create these experiences yet—no worries! We've got resources to teach you how to support each other in this journey.

Because here's the deal: information alone won't heal the wounds driving your insecurity. It's **relational, emotionally alive experiences** that unlock the healing process Jesus wired into your body.

And that's the foundation for becoming your bold, radiant, super sexy self.

Your Super Sexy Self

Here's the truth that ties this whole chapter together: healing your wounds is the foundation for becoming your super sexy self.

You simply can't build sexual confidence, healthy desire, and pleasure mastery on top of unresolved pain. If you try, it's like trying to build a house on a sinkhole—it might look okay for a minute, but eventually, things start to crack.

As you work through this journey, some of those wounds will surface. That's not a failure—it's a sign that healing is ready to happen. But if you ignore those wounds and try to "fake it till you make it," you'll be stuck in a cycle of frustration. Real, lasting change doesn't come through force. It comes through wholeness.

And one of the most important pieces of healing? Grief.

Grief is how we emotionally accept what we can't change. You can't go back and undo what happened to you. You can't rewrite the parts of your story that were marked by silence, shame, or struggle. And let's be honest—your ability to change your body is limited, too. Diets, exercise, makeup, Spanx, even plastic surgery—they may help shape things on the outside, but they can't fix what's underneath.

Here's the surprising gift of grief: when you let yourself mourn the gap between what is and what you wish was, it frees up the emotional energy you need to *actually* change the things you can. It makes room for peace and even joy in the process.

Now, to be clear: It's *okay* to want to improve your body. Dress it up, contour it, strengthen it, tone it—go for it! But it's *not* okay to believe you're "not enough" unless you do.

That's not your Heavenly Father's heart for you.

He sees your beauty right now. He delights in your body, your femininity, your desire. But until your heart agrees with His, your efforts will always feel just a little… hollow.

Here's where things get wild: your most powerful sex organ isn't between your legs—it's between your ears.

Yep. Your brain is where sexual confidence, desire, arousal, and even orgasm begin. Your body may *feel* those things, but your mind is the command center. And if your mental and emotional wiring is stuck in shame, self-hatred, or unresolved trauma, it'll block the signals your body needs to respond.

That's why healing the emotional wounds behind your body dissatisfaction is *essential*. You weren't born loathing your thighs or doubting your desirability. Those beliefs were formed through painful experiences—and they can be *reformed* through healing.

All the self-talk in the world won't stick if you haven't done the deep work. But once you have? Speaking truth in love to

yourself becomes a powerful reinforcement of the transformation that's taking root.

So be kind to your mind. Heal your story. And let your brain
become the launchpad for a body—and a life—alive with
pleasure, confidence, and holy desire.

Wrapping It Up

You've done some brave work in this chapter—looking
honestly at your story, getting curious about your wounds
and gaps, and learning how healing really happens.

We talked about how your sense of self—including your
sexual self—was shaped by your experiences. Not just the
big moments, but the quiet silences, the subtle shames, and
the messages you absorbed without even realizing it. We
named the power of **compassionate curiosity**, the im-
portance of safe people, and the healing wisdom built into
your **Thrive-Drive**—God's own breath in you, pulling you
toward wholeness.

And we reminded you that your brain—yes, your brain—is
your most powerful sex organ. Healing your thoughts, beliefs, and past experiences is key to unlocking the sexual
confidence and desire you were made to enjoy.

Now it's your turn to reflect:

- What's surfacing for you right now?
- What stories or experiences feel like they need a lit-
tle more compassion and curiosity?
- Who can be part of your healing team?

And most of all—are you willing to believe that the woman
God created you to be is not only possible... but already beginning to emerge?

Next up, we're going to talk about the *Inventor* of sex—yep, God Himself—and the jaw-droppingly good design He had in mind when He made *you* sexy on purpose.

Let's keep going. It's about to get even better.

Chapter 3: Sex God

Holy Sexy Jesus

*L*auren had been a Christian her whole life, but she still couldn't say the word "clitoris" without whispering it like she was confessing a felony.

She sat on the edge of the bathtub, her church hoodie half-zipped and makeup smudged under her eyes from toddler tantrums and bedtime battles. Her husband had just texted, "Kids down. You coming up?" with a winky face that made her smile and panic all at once.

She wanted to. She really did. But "in the mood" felt like a foreign country, and she didn't have a passport.

Plus, she'd just seen a reel from that Christian influencer couple who do date nights in matching outfits and probably have silent, sacred orgasms while praying Psalm 23. Meanwhile, she was still trying to remember if she shaved her legs this week... or last.

She looked at herself in the mirror—mascara smears, stained sweatshirt, hair in what she optimistically called a "lived-in bun." She sighed and muttered under her breath, "Holy sexy Jesus... what is this phase of life?"

And that's when it hit her.

Not the desire. Not yet.

But the realization that she'd been waiting for someone to give her permission. Permission to feel pleasure. Permission to stop apologizing for liking things that made her body come alive. Permission to explore, enjoy, and not compare.

She grabbed her phone and Googled, "Is God okay with Christians doing sexy things in marriage?" The search results made her laugh and groan in equal measure.

Then she looked back at her reflection, softer this time, and whispered, "Maybe He's more okay with it than I've ever been taught."

She took a breath. Unzipped the hoodie. And walked upstairs— not with a performance mindset, but with curiosity.

Not because she had all the answers, but because something deep inside her finally believed she was allowed to ask the questions.

Our Erotic God

Let's start with a little truth bomb: you didn't invent sex. Your grandma didn't. The patriarchy didn't. And it definitely wasn't the internet's idea.

Sex is God's idea. And not just functional, baby-making sex—God dreamed up **pleasurable**, **playful**, **whole-person**, deeply **erotic** sex. Penises, vaginas, clitorises, nipples that respond to touch, orgasms that leave you breathless, that electric pulse of desire that can make your whole body feel alive... every last detail was God's design.

Seriously—if God wanted humans to reproduce like plants, He could've had us release pollen into the wind. Or lay eggs like fish and let the guy come by later and hose it down. Efficient, sure. Intimate? Not so much.

But that's not the way He did it.

God created us **in His image**—erotic, embodied, relational beings who get to experience one of life's most mind-blowingly pleasurable acts *not just for procreation*, but for connection, celebration, and delight. We're wired to crave intimacy, to be drawn toward touch, to respond with arousal and pleasure even when we're not "in heat." That's not an accident. It's sacred design.

And what if—just go with me here—God made sex as a reflection of the kind of relationship He wants with *us*?

The Bible is filled with imagery of God as the bridegroom, passionately pursuing His people, longing for intimacy, connection, and union. Not a cold, distant deity—but a Lover of your soul. A God who wants to come so close that He actually lives inside you—transforming your life with joy, peace, and yes, *pleasure*.

Graphic? Maybe. But so is the Bible. Read Song of Songs. The divine romance isn't tame—and neither is the God who wrote it.

Our Creator is **not embarrassed by eroticism**. He is the Author of it. He exists beyond gender but chose to express Himself in the masculine throughout Scripture—and then made humans in His image, *male and female.* He created gender. He created sex. And He called it **very good**.

And let's not forget the very first command God gave His freshly sculpted humans: "Be fruitful and multiply." Translation? Go have sex. *A lot.* Fill the earth with life—and by the way, enjoy it.

You probably didn't hear that version in Sunday School. But it's true.

God is not only okay with your erotic pleasure—He designed your body for it. Because He is an erotic God. And He delights in your delight.

God Likes Women More

Okay, hear us out: when it comes to sexual design, there's a pretty compelling case that God might just be especially fond of women.

For all the talk about men being the "more sexual" gender, a closer look at how God wired the female body tells a much richer story—one that suggests He went above and beyond in crafting women for deep, multidimensional pleasure.

Let's talk about the **hardware**.

Men have a single pleasure center—the penis. It's straightforward, functional, and, let's be honest, a bit of a one-note instrument.

But women? God gifted them the **clitoris**—a structure with over 10,000 nerve endings (double that of the penis), designed *solely* for pleasure. No reproductive function. No hidden utility. Just unfiltered, divine delight.

Who does that?

Who creates an entire organ for joy, if not a God who delights in delighting His daughters?

And then there's stamina. Most men need a "recovery period" after orgasm—anywhere from 10 to 30 minutes, sometimes longer. But women? Their bodies are capable of multiple orgasms with no mandatory reboot. They can ride wave after wave of pleasure without ever leaving the ocean. It's as if God said, "One blessing? Please. Let's go for the abundance package."

Let's not overlook the **design perks** either. Men's plumbing is external—straightforward but not exactly elegant. Women? The vagina is self-cleaning, self-lubricating, and pH-balanced. Think of it as a luxury suite: high-end design, no upgrades needed.

And get this—female desire doesn't expire.

While male libido tends to peak early and slowly coast into the sunset, many women report that their sexual confidence, satisfaction, and desire actually *increase* with age. With wisdom comes freedom, and with freedom comes fire. That's not just a biological fluke—it sounds like divine design to us.

And the way women experience sex? It's not just physical.

Female sexuality is this beautiful blend of body, soul, spirit, and mind. It's connection-driven. Emotionally rich. Mentally engaged. Spiritually meaningful. It's as if God said, "Let's create a fully immersive intimacy experience."

If sex is art, then women are the masterpiece.

And to top it all off? Let's use this cheeky but spot-on image: when your ear itches and you scratch it, which feels better—the ear or the finger?

Exactly.

In the same way, when a woman's body is aroused—her vulva, her vagina, her whole being—the pleasure is deep and consuming. Every inch is a canvas of erotic potential, from the tug of her hair to the curling of her toes. Her body was made to writhe, to gasp, to receive joy with abandon.

Not by accident. By design.

This isn't poetic fluff. It's neuroscience and theology holding hands. God made your body—**your body**—to be a source of delight. And He called it *very good*.

So if you've ever doubted whether your pleasure matters, whether your body was made for this kind of joy, let this be your answer:

Yes. It does. You were.

Because you were made to be **delighted in**.

All Things Are Permissible

So... what exactly counts as "Christian sex"?

What are married Christians actually *allowed* to do in bed?

If you've ever found yourself wondering—or worrying— you're not alone. And if you were raised on a steady diet of "don't," "never," or "God's watching," this might come as a joyful surprise:

There's a *lot* more freedom than you've probably been told.

The biblical framework for sex within marriage is actually pretty spacious. In fact, the guiding principle is this: **all things are permissible**—so long as they are **consensual**, **monogamous**, and **mutually enjoyable**.

That's it.

Within those sacred boundaries, the marriage bed isn't a battleground for guilt or a maze of outdated rules—it's a playground of connection, creativity, and delight. It's not a cage. It's an invitation.

Take Hebrews 13:4, for example: "Let marriage be held in honor among all, and let the marriage bed be undefiled." That word "undefiled" (in Greek, *amiantos*) doesn't mean "stoic and squeaky clean." It means uncorrupted—free from what would harm or degrade. It's not a warning against pleasure; it's protection for pleasure. It's about keeping sex safe, sacred, and sealed within covenant love.

Then there's 1 Corinthians 7:3–4—one of the most radically mutual statements in all of ancient literature. Paul writes that husbands and wives each have authority over the other's body. Not control. Not entitlement. **Mutuality.** This is about self-giving love, care, and responsive desire. No coercion. No manipulation. Just two people offering themselves to one another in trust and tenderness.

(*Side note: if someone's using that passage to pressure or guilt you into sex, that's not God's heart. That's emotional immaturity, and it's deeply damaging. If that's part of your story, please seek support. A great place to start is Leslie Vernick's* The Emotionally Destructive Marriage. *You're not alone, and you deserve safety.*)

Back to Paul—he goes on in 1 Corinthians 6:12 to say, "All things are lawful for me, but not all things are helpful." Translation: Freedom matters, but wisdom leads.

So the right question isn't, "Is this allowed?" It's:

- Is this loving?
- Is it safe for both of us?
- Is it something we both *want*?
- Does it strengthen our bond?

If the answer is yes, then friend—**go for it.**

Explore. Laugh. Discover what pleases each other. Make love with freedom and creativity, not fear and shame. God is not standing in the corner with a clipboard and a frown. He's clapping and cheering you on. He's the One who designed every nerve ending, every flutter of arousal, every longing for connection. This is His idea.

Just look at Song of Solomon. Chapter 5, verse 1? "Eat, friends, drink, and be drunk with love!" That's not metaphor. That's full-on celebration. Body and soul immersion. A God-ordained party for two.

Or go all the way back to Genesis 2:25: "The man and his wife were both naked and were not ashamed." No anxiety. No embarrassment. No hiding. Just two people, fully seen and fully safe, basking in each other's presence.

That's the original design. And it still holds.

So here's your simple summary: If it's between you and your husband, if it's consensual, faithful, and joyfully mutual—it's not only okay. It's *holy.*

And it's yours to enjoy.

It's None of Their Business

Jesus, Not Karen—Why Your Sex Life Is Between You, Your Spouse, and the Savior

Let's go ahead and say it loud for the ladies in the back:

Your marriage bed is no one's business but yours, your spouse's, and your Savior's.

Not your in-laws'.

Not your pastor's.

Not your small group's.

And definitely *not* Karen from Bible study.

Hebrews 13:4 makes this crystal clear: "Let the marriage bed be held in honor by all, and let it be undefiled." That means God sees it, celebrates it, and calls it sacred. Everyone else? They're called to respect it—not regulate it.

So whether your flavor is cozy, once-a-week missionary with snuggles and candlelight, or something a little more... *adventurous* (rope, heels, roleplay, secluded Airbnb, anyone?)—if it's consensual, monogamous, and mutually enjoyable, then not only is it permitted... it's *holy*.

Seriously. The marriage bed is a **playground of grace**, not a courtroom of shame.

And here's the bottom line: you answer to Jesus, not to judgmental people.

Romans 14:4 says it straight: "Who are you to judge someone else's servant?" In other words, you don't need anyone else's approval for the way you and your husband express intimacy. You don't need to justify your preferences or explain why you like what you like. If Jesus is smiling—and your spouse is too—you're right on track.

Let love lead. That's the real "rule."

1 Corinthians 16:14 reminds us to "do everything in love." Galatians 5 says there's *no law* against love, joy, peace, kindness—all those juicy fruits of the Spirit. So ask yourself:

- Is it loving?
- Is it safe?
- Is it consensual?
- Is it mutually enjoyable?

If yes—go for it. Really. There's **no biblical ban** on oral sex, anal play, dressing up, sensual massages, dirty talk, toys, or exploring your shared desires together. None.

And here's the freeing truth: your sex life doesn't have to be "clean"—it just has to be **yours**.

Have you *read* Song of Solomon? That book is a holy strip-tease. He praises her breasts and thighs and describes her body like a garden ripe for feasting. She invites him to taste her, explore her, enjoy her. There's fruit, milk, honey, moaning, pursuing—and God didn't censor a word of it. He *canonized* it.

So let's stop carrying shame that Jesus never handed us.

Colossians 2 warns us not to submit to legalistic "don't touch, don't taste" rules. We're not under law. We're under **love**. And love makes space for all kinds of expression, creativity, and fun.

If someone thinks your bedroom adventures are "ungodly"? Smile. Bless them. And don't invite them over.

Whether your style is slow, gentle, and tender—or playful, kinky, and covered in coconut oil—it's not theirs to judge. It's between you, your beloved, and your God.

So here's the truth, straight and holy:

Sex in marriage is sacred.

It's private.

It's personal.

It's playful.

And it's judged by no one but Jesus.

Whether you're moaning on a mountaintop, giggling through roleplay, lighting candles and reading Song of Solomon in the tub, or just showing up with love and intentionality—you are holy. You are free. You are unashamed.

Now go forth, lovers—and enjoy the freedom of the undefiled marriage bed.

Wrapping It Up

Let's take a breath and let this sink in:

You were created by an *erotic God*—a holy, passionate, deeply relational Creator who designed your body not only to function but to *flourish* in pleasure.

Your sexuality isn't a side note. It's a sacred part of your story. From the mind-blowing design of the female body to the wild freedom found within the covenant of marriage, God made this good. Really good.

We've explored the truth that sex isn't shameful—it's sacred. That your bedroom isn't a courtroom—it's a playground. That what happens between you and your husband—if it's loving, consensual, faithful, and mutual—is not just allowed... it's *blessed*.

And maybe, just maybe, it's time to stop wondering if your pleasure is okay and start celebrating the fact that it *absolutely* is.

So here's something to reflect on as you move forward:

- What have you believed about God and sex that might need to be unlearned?
- Where have shame, fear, or outside voices limited your freedom?
- What would it look like to invite Jesus into your sexuality—not to censor it, but to *celebrate* it?

Because when God made you, He wasn't blushing. He was beaming.

Now that we've laid a foundation for God's design and delight in your sexual self, let's explore how to *own it*. In the next chapter, we're diving into the art of seduction—how sexiness starts in your mind, why confidence is a turn-on, and how to cultivate both.

Spoiler alert: you're way more powerful than you think.

Chapter 4: The Art of Seduction

Laundry, Leggings, and That Lingerie Drawer

*E*mily *stared into her underwear drawer like it was a haunted house.*

Buried beneath a pile of stretched-out cotton briefs and three nursing bras from a baby who now used full sentences, there it was: the lacy red thing she bought on a "date night high" nine months ago. Tags still on. Confidence long gone.

She held it up with two fingers, like it might bite.

"Who even was I the day I bought this?" she muttered, tossing it onto the bed next to a stack of half-folded laundry and a Paw Patrol sippy cup. Her toddler had used her as a napkin that morning. Twice. Her hair was clean-ish, and she was wearing her "nice leggings," the ones without the thigh hole. She was technically winning. But sexy? She didn't even know what zip code that feeling lived in.

Her husband had been extra sweet lately—lingering hugs, playful glances, even folded the towels without being asked (a sure sign he was hoping for more than a high-five). And Emily wanted to want it. She missed feeling flirty, alive, connected. But every time she caught a glimpse of herself in the mirror— sports bra, top bun, toothpaste on her shirt—her desire slunk into a corner and played dead.

She sat on the edge of the bed, red lace in hand, and let out a long sigh. "Jesus, am I allowed to feel sexy when I feel like a human snack tray with adult acne?"

But then... a whisper. Not audible, but real:

Start with kindness.

So she looked in the mirror, softened her gaze, and said—awkwardly but sincerely—"Hey girl. Thanks for hanging in there."

And it wasn't a movie moment. There was no dramatic music or sudden transformation. But there was a spark—something real. A flicker of grace.

Maybe she didn't need to become someone else to feel sexy. Maybe she just needed to be a little more gentle with the someone she already was.

She didn't put the lace on that night. But she did text her husband:
"Hey... maybe this weekend. ;)"

And for the first time in a long time, she meant it.

Sexy and You Know It

Here's a fun fact that might shift how you think about seduction:

The number one driver of a **husband's** sexual desire? How *attractive he finds his wife.* (We know, no surprise there.) But, the number one driver of a **wife's** sexual desire? How *attractive she feels.*

Yep. Let that sink in. When a woman *feels* sexy, she's more likely to *want* sex. It's not about the mirror—it's about the *mindset.* The sexiest organ in your body? It's not your breasts or your booty. It's your brain.

Now, this isn't to say there aren't other important factors—like emotional connection, hormone levels, brakes and accelerators of desire (we'll get to those). But among all the things that either press the gas or slam the brakes on your desire, one of the biggest influences is *you*. Specifically, how you feel about you.

And if you're not feeling sexy? That's like pressing your foot down on the brake while someone's gently tapping the gas. It takes a lot more effort to get things moving.

When it comes to sexual intimacy, one quiet but powerful force shapes everything from desire to orgasm: **body image**. Not how your body *looks*—how you *perceive* it.

Studies consistently show that women who feel attractive—not necessarily those who match cultural beauty standards, but those who *believe* they're attractive—experience higher sexual desire, more engagement, deeper satisfaction, and a greater likelihood of orgasm. They're less distracted by appearance-based thoughts and more present with their husband. Presence leads to connection. Connection leads to pleasure.

This isn't just a fluffy self-esteem tip. It's neuroscience.

When a woman's body image is low, the brain goes into **"spectator mode."** That's when your mind is so busy monitoring how you look—"Is this angle okay?" "Do I look weird from here?" "Is my stomach jiggling?"—that it hijacks your ability to feel. Your brain checks out of sensation and into self-consciousness, which disrupts arousal and makes it harder (sometimes impossible) to enjoy the moment.

But when you *feel* good in your skin? Your brain lets go. Your body wakes up. Desire increases. You initiate more, communicate more, and receive more pleasure. And the ripple effect touches everything—your confidence, your relationship, and your overall joy.

Here's the best part: that shift doesn't require a different body. It starts with a different *perspective*.

This is more than a makeover. It's **sacred stewardship**. It's choosing to honor the body God gave you—not as a project to fix, but as a partner in pleasure. A temple. A vessel of joy and intimacy. A uniquely designed, holy space where connection happens and love is expressed.

You don't need to wait to hit a goal weight or look a certain way. You can start now. Feeling sexy is something you *cultivate*. It grows when you treat yourself with kindness, notice what feels good, dress in ways that make you smile, and lean into what stirs your confidence.

And here's the sexy bonus: when you feel good about you, you naturally become more flirty and playful. That energy is magnetic. It draws your husband in, which affirms you, which increases your desire—creating a snowball effect of intimacy and pleasure.

So if you're wondering where to begin in boosting desire and confidence, start here:

Get your mind right.

Because what happens between your ears has everything to do with what happens between your legs.

That Sexy Feeling

As discussed above, when it comes to sexual well-being, one of the most powerful game-changers isn't physical—it's perceptual. In other words, it's not about what your body *looks* like, but how you *feel* in it.

That internal sense of attractiveness—your felt sense of beauty—can radically impact your sexual desire, enjoyment, confidence, and connection with your spouse. And the best part? It has absolutely nothing to do with chasing some unattainable cultural beauty standard.

This is about reclaiming the truth that you are already worthy of love, pleasure, and presence—just as you are. It's about treating your body like a trusted friend, not a constant project.

To help you move from insecurity to empowerment, here are five powerful, research-backed pathways. These aren't surface-level fixes—they're soul-deep practices that reshape how you see and feel about yourself, from the inside out.

Mindset & Cognitive Restructuring

Speak Kindly to the Mirror

Most of us have an inner critic who's been narrating our body's flaws for years. And unfortunately, she's loud. "Your stomach is too soft." "Look at those thighs." "You should've lost the baby weight by now."

But here's the truth: self-compassion changes the game.

Speaking to yourself with the same kindness you'd offer a dear friend creates powerful shifts in your brain. It's not just "positive thinking"—it's rewiring. Replacing a thought like, "I hate my stomach," with, "My belly has carried life, held laughter, and deserves love," can begin to soften the shame and restore your sense of safety in your skin.

Try this:

- Start a daily **body gratitude journal**.

- Practice a 5-minute reflection each day, thanking your body for what it's done for you.
- Curate your social media feed to reflect diverse, real, beautiful bodies.

These small changes help shift your inner narrative from criticism to compassion—and that shift sets the stage for confidence.

Mindfulness & Embodiment

Feel More, Worry Less

A common roadblock to pleasure is something researchers call **"spectatoring."** That's when you're physically present but mentally watching yourself—analyzing, adjusting, and judging.

Mindfulness is the antidote. It brings you back into your body, where intimacy lives.

Try this:

- Take mindful walks. Feel your feet hit the ground. Breathe the air deeply.
- Enjoy a sensory bath. Light a candle. Use a body oil. Savor the warmth.
- Practice **mindful touch**—on your own or with your husband—where the goal isn't performance, but presence.

You can even create a playlist of music that makes you feel confident or powerful. Move your body to it. Dance without judgment. Let pleasure lead.

Self-Care & Personal Enjoyment

Live Like You Like Yourself

Confidence isn't just what you *think*—it's how you *live*.

Nourish yourself like someone you love. Wear clothes that make you feel radiant. Take breaks that restore you. Treat pleasure as something sacred, not selfish.

Try this:

- Keep a "**pleasure inventory**." Each day, jot down small joys: a warm cup of coffee, fresh sheets, the smell of your favorite lotion.

- Use affirmations rooted in truth: "I am worthy of love and desire." "My body is a gift."

This kind of care isn't superficial—it's spiritual. It tells your soul, "You're home here."

Expression & Exploration

Show Your Sexy Self

As your internal confidence grows, explore how you want to express it outwardly.

Start a "**Sexy Style**" Pinterest board. Pin outfits, textures, and vibes that feel powerful and playful—especially from women with body types like yours. Then experiment! Hit the thrift store. Try on that bold lipstick. Don the heels, the silk robe, or the cheeky lingerie—whatever makes you feel most *you*.

Want to make it fun?

- Invite your husband or a trusted friend to join you in discovering your look.

- Try the "**Alter Ego Experiment**"—create a playful, confident persona. Give her a name. Channel her energy when you want to feel powerful and sensual.

She's not a pretend version of you. She's a part of you you're finally allowing to come alive.

Communication & Intimacy

Let Yourself Be Seen

Sexy isn't something you keep to yourself. It's meant to be shared.

Try the "**I Appreciate...**" exchange with your husband. Sit face-to-face and name things you admire in each other—no critique, just celebration.

Or try the "**Admiration Album**" with a friend. Create a shared photo folder where you only post pictures that feel like *you*—not polished, not perfect, just radiant and real. Seeing yourself through loving eyes can undo years of shame.

And build **intimacy rituals** with your husband:

- Slow dancing in the kitchen.
- Shared showers.
- Eye-gazing while holding hands.
- Sensual touch with no performance pressure.

Let these become regular rhythms that restore safety, connection, and confidence.

Here's what we hope you'll hear most:

You don't have to become someone else to feel sexy. You just have to become more of yourself.

Your body isn't the problem. It's part of the solution. A vessel of delight. A partner in joy. A sacred space where the Spirit of God is pleased to dwell.

So speak kindly to your reflection.

Live like you like yourself.

And remember: You're already worthy of pleasure.

Let's start there.

Easier Said Than Done

Let's be honest: feeling sexy is rarely a straight line.

Sure, we can talk about affirmations, playlists, lingerie, and self-care—and those things *do* matter. But sometimes, when you try to lean into your sexy self, what bubbles up isn't confidence or desire. It's something a whole lot messier: shame, fear, anxiety, disgust... sometimes even grief.

And that doesn't mean you're broken.

It means you're **human**.

The truth is, many of us carry deep wounds around our bodies, our worth, and our sexuality. These aren't surface issues. They're rooted in our stories—moments when something painful happened or something important *didn't* happen. Moments that shaped how we see ourselves, how we feel in our skin, and how safe we feel giving and receiving pleasure.

But here's the good, and maybe surprising news:

When those hard feelings rise up, it's not a sign you're failing.

It's a sign you're healing.

Those uncomfortable emotions? They're not enemies. They're invitations. Your **Thrive-Drive**—that God-given force within you that moves you toward wholeness—is bringing these wounded parts to the surface so they can finally be seen, held, and healed.

So what do you do when the knot tightens in your stomach or the voice in your head whispers, "You're not enough"?

You *don't* push it down. You *don't* fake joy or slap on a smile. You don't distract it away.

Instead, you turn toward those feelings with **compassionate curiosity**.

You pause. You breathe. And you ask, "Where is this coming   from?"
You reach out to your people—your mentors, your Sage Circle, your iron-sharpening girlfriends—and you say, "Hey, this came up. Can you help me be curious?"

Maybe you talk through a memory. Maybe you weep. Maybe you just sit with someone who reminds you you're safe and loved. And maybe you find a good therapist, like a NICC-trained counselor from MyCounselor.Online®, to help you walk those feelings all the way through.

When you do that—when you follow those feelings back to the wounds they came from—you create space for **healing**.

And as those places begin to heal, something beautiful happens:

- Peace begins to settle in your body.

- Joy feels more accessible.

- Confidence feels less forced.

- Sexy starts to feel natural—like something rising from within, not something you're trying to manufacture.

Each brave step forward may stir up another part of you needing care. And each time you tend to that part with love, your **true self** emerges more fully. That grounded, radiant woman God designed—the one who knows she's worthy of delight—is rising.

And *that* is sexy.

The more healing you experience, the more those mindset shifts and sexy habits will *stick*. They'll drop from your head into your heart... and eventually settle into your body, where they belong.

Because the truth isn't just something you speak.

It's something you live.

And as you do, you become a woman who doesn't just look sexy...

You **feel** it.

You **believe** it.

You **embody** it.

And that, friend, is a holy kind of beautiful.

Wrapping It Up

Here's what we've uncovered in this chapter:

Feeling sexy isn't about looking a certain way. It's about learning to *see yourself* differently—to speak with kindness, move with mindfulness, live like you like yourself, and lean into relationships that reflect the truth about who you are. Confidence grows when you show up for your body not as an enemy to fix, but as a friend to enjoy.

It's not always easy. Sometimes, practicing these things will stir up shame or fear or old wounds you didn't know were still hanging around. But those feelings aren't the end of the story. They're invitations from your Thrive-Drive to heal—and healing is what makes the confidence last.

So here's your gentle next step:

Reflect on how you *feel* about your body, not just how you *think* about it.

Ask yourself: What helps me feel most like myself? What small practices help me reconnect with pleasure, presence, and joy?

And when hard emotions arise, don't run. Get curious. Let that curiosity lead you to healing, one brave conversation at a time.

In the next chapter, we're going to explore one of the most powerful (and overlooked) tools for understanding your sexual desire: your **nervous system**. Using polyvagal theory and the idea of body states, we'll unpack why some days you feel flirty and fabulous, and other days you just want to hide under a blanket—and how to work *with* your body instead of against it.

You don't have to guess what's going on inside you. Your body has a language. Let's learn how to listen.

Chapter 5: Green Means Go

The Target Tantrum & the Traffic Light Epiphany

*M*ia stood in the checkout line at Target, clutching a half-empty Starbucks and praying her toddler wouldn't lose it over the impulse-buy slime packs. *Again.*

He did.

"NOOOO! I need the green one!" he wailed, dramatically flinging himself onto the tile like a tiny protestor for justice.

Mia closed her eyes. She could feel it—the tightening in her chest, the burn in her cheeks, the rising internal scream. Her inner dialogue raced: Don't make a scene. Smile. Breathe. Jesus, take the whole cart.

The woman in front of her gave the classic "bless her heart" smirk. Mia wanted to throw the slime pack at her. Or cry. Or both.

By the time they got to the minivan, she felt like an exposed nerve. Her hands were shaking as she clicked her son into his car seat, and her husband's earlier flirty text pinged again: Can't wait for tonight ;-).

She stared at it. And suddenly felt...numb.

All the air left her lungs.

Tonight? After this day? After her kid went full WWE on aisle seven? After she'd already snapped at herself for feeling overwhelmed, then snapped again for not being the "calm mom"? She didn't feel sexy. She didn't even feel human.

As she drove home in silence, she heard a memory from her counselor's voice echo in her head: "You can't go from red to sexy. Safety first."

Red. Yellow. Green.

It hit her—her body wasn't broken. It was just in the red. Overloaded. Shutting down to survive. And maybe, just maybe, she didn't need to fake a sexy response. Maybe she needed to listen first.

That night, instead of pretending everything was fine, she curled up next to her husband and whispered, "I love that you're excited to connect. But my day's been a lot. Can we just snuggle tonight and talk? I want to be close—I'm just not there yet."

He paused. Then kissed her forehead.

"Of course, babe. Thanks for telling me."

And just like that, without even trying—something softened inside.

It wasn't sex.

But it was intimacy.

And that was a very green beginning.

Feeling Safe Is Key to Feeling Sexy

If you've ever wondered, *Why don't I feel more desire?* or, *Why does sex feel so hard for me sometimes?* We hope you know by this point in the book that you're not alone, and you're not broken.

What if the problem isn't a flaw in your femininity, but a signal from your nervous system?

Let's talk about that amazing, God-designed system inside your body that's quietly working 24/7 to keep you safe. It's called the autonomic nervous system, and it runs the show when it comes to how your body feels and responds to the world around you.

In NICC (Neuroscience Informed Christian Counseling®), we use a simple traffic light metaphor to describe how this system works—because let's be honest, biology terms can get a little nerdy fast. Think of your nervous system in three states:

- **Green = Safe and Connected (Ventral Vagal State)**
- **Yellow = Alert and Anxious (Sympathetic Activation)**
- **Red = Shut Down and Numb (Dorsal Vagal State)**

Let's break it down.

When you're in the **green zone**, your nervous system feels safe. You feel calm, connected, and present. This is the state where creativity blooms, playfulness awakens, and—drumroll please—*desire and confidence thrive*. In green, your body says, "All clear. It's safe to connect, to explore, to enjoy." Green is the sweet spot where sexual intimacy can be pleasurable, tender, playful, and deeply satisfying.

But when something feels off—maybe there's unresolved conflict, stress, a triggering memory, or even just too many to-do lists and not enough rest—your body may shift into **yellow**. This is your fight-or-flight mode. Think of it like your body's internal alarm system going off. You're not relaxed, you're scanning for threat. And here's the kicker: your brain doesn't always know the difference between a real threat (like a charging bear) and an emotional one (like a harsh comment from your spouse, or an old memory of rejection). The result? Your nervous system shifts into "not safe," and guess what shuts down? *Desire.* Because who's thinking about sex when you're just trying to survive?

Then there's the **red zone**—shutdown mode. This is the freeze response, where everything slows down or even numbs out. Emotionally, it can feel like burnout, depression, apathy, or deep disconnection. This is the nervous system's last resort when it senses danger but has no way to fight or flee. In red, sexy is not even on the radar—it's emotionally lights out.

But here's the beautiful, hope-filled truth: your body isn't stuck. Your nervous system is *meant* to move between these states. With the right support, safety, and connection, you can shift out of yellow or red and return to green. That's where healing happens. That's where sexual confidence rekindles. That's where desire begins to wake up—not because you're forcing it, but because your body finally feels safe enough to allow it.

God designed your nervous system this way on purpose. He wired you for both *protection* and *pleasure*. Both are sacred. And when you stop judging your low desire and start *listening* to what your body's telling you, the path to healing opens.

So the next time you find yourself feeling "off" in the intimacy department, pause and ask:

- Am I in green, yellow, or red?
- What's making me feel unsafe or disconnected?
- What could help me return to safety?

Because the goal isn't just to flip on desire like a light switch. The goal is to live in a body that feels safe enough to be open, curious, confident, and connected.

You're not defective.

You're **brilliantly designed**.

And with the right tools and support, you can begin to live—and love—from a place of green.

Learn to Listen

Sexual desire doesn't respond to pressure.

It doesn't blossom in shame.

And it certainly doesn't show up on command like a well-trained golden retriever.

Desire grows in the soil of *safety*—and that safety begins with a sacred practice called **attunement**.

Attunement is simply the holy habit of noticing what's going on inside you without judgment. It's tuning in to the signals of your body and nervous system with gentle, compassionate curiosity. Think of it like checking your internal weather report.

- Is it sunny and warm in there?
- Or stormy, tense, and overcast?
- Are you in green (safe and connected), yellow (anxious and alert), or red (shut down and withdrawn)?

When you begin to listen this way, you stop treating your body as a problem to fix and start honoring it as a messenger from God. Your nervous system isn't sabotaging your intimacy—it's trying to protect you. And the more fluently you learn to speak its language, the more empowered you'll be to return to safety—and from there, to pleasure and connection.

Sometimes, your body tenses up not because you're disinterested in your spouse, but because you don't feel emotionally safe in the moment. Sometimes, your numbness isn't about desire at all—it's about burnout. And sometimes, when you feel disconnected from your own sensuality, it's not because something's wrong with you. It's because you've been surviving, not thriving.

This kind of awareness is powerful. And it leads to a beautiful, redemptive question:

What do I need?

When you pause and ask your body this question—without shame—you open the door to healing. Maybe what you need is rest. Maybe you need laughter, or movement, or a really good cry. Maybe you need to talk to your husband or call your best friend. Maybe you need to be held—not sexually, but emotionally. These needs are not distractions from intimacy. They are the *pathway* to it.

We heal in the presence of safe others. Whether it's your spouse, a close friend, or a good counselor, letting someone "be with you" in your yellow or red can help your body return to green. This is what we call **co-regulation**—and it's not weakness. It's how God designed us. We were never meant to figure it all out alone.

When your nervous system feels safe, you don't have to force yourself to be sexy.

You already are.

You just become *available* to the goodness that's already in you.

In NICC, we describe this green zone as **true happiness**—a stable, embodied experience of peace, joy, and satisfaction in life, anchored in hope for the future. It's not a fleeting emotion; it's a deep nervous system state. It's what Scripture describes as **shalom**—wholeness, harmony, nothing missing, nothing broken.

And here's what's miraculous: when you learn to live from that place, intimacy becomes easier. You become more open to touch, to playfulness, to erotic curiosity—not because you're trying harder, but because you feel safe enough to *let go*.

So, how do you begin?

How to Practice Nervous System Attunement

Here are three simple steps to help you check in and care for your body in real-time:

1. Pause and Notice

A few times a day, stop and ask:

- What sensations am I feeling in my body?
- Is my breath shallow? Is my chest tight? Do I feel heavy, buzzy, or blank?
- If my nervous system were a color—green, yellow, or red—what would it be?

2. Name the State

Use these quick cues to identify where you are:

- **Green**: Calm, open, connected, playful
- **Yellow**: Anxious, edgy, overwhelmed, defensive
- **Red**: Numb, shut down, tired, hopeless

3. Get Curious (Not Critical)

Ask yourself gently:

- What might have pushed me into this state?
- Is there something in my story, my environment, or my day that triggered this?
- What do I need right now to feel just a little safer?

This is how healing begins. Not in grand, dramatic breakthroughs, but in small moments of noticing, naming, and nourishing.

When you stop performing and start *listening*—you unlock joy. You unlock intimacy. You unlock a version of yourself who feels sexy, whole, and beautifully alive.

You don't have to chase some external ideal.

You just have to come home to your body.

And your body is ready to welcome you back.

Compassionate Curiosity Is Sexy

One of the most powerful tools for healing—and unlocking desire—has nothing to do with trying harder, looking better, or checking more boxes.

It's about how you *see yourself.*

Specifically, how you respond to the messy, vulnerable parts of your inner world—the places that still feel anxious, ashamed, confused, or shut down. The secret to deep healing and authentic sexual confidence isn't in pushing those parts away. It's in learning to approach them with **compassionate curiosity**.

In NICC, we understand that your nervous system doesn't just carry stress. It carries stories. Emotional imprints from moments that shaped how you feel about yourself, your body, others—and even God. These stories live in what we call "parts"—little pockets of your heart that hold onto certain emotions and beliefs you felt in particular experiences.

Maybe there's a **scared part** that learned intimacy wasn't safe.
Or a **shamed part** that believes desire makes you "bad."
Or an **angry part** that's tired of always being the one to make things work.

These parts aren't mistakes. They're *protectors.* They showed up when life got hard—when things didn't go the way they should have—and they've been trying to help you survive ever since.

But here's the thing: **survival isn't the same as wholeness.** And when these parts stay stuck in old emotions like fear or shame, they can quietly sabotage your sexual confidence and connection—even when you want something different.

That's where compassionate curiosity comes in. Instead of judging these parts or trying to shut them down, you learn to listen:

- "What are you trying to tell me?"
- "Where did you first feel this way?"
- "What do you need in order to feel safe again?"

You don't have to go digging on your own. In fact, healing is meant to be **relational.** God wired our brains and bodies for co-regulation—which means we heal best *in the presence of safe people.* Whether it's a mentor, a trusted friend, or a NICC therapist, having someone sit with you in your story without trying to fix you is sacred work. It's what

Paul meant in Galatians 6:2 when he said, "Carry each other's burdens."

When someone witnesses your pain with kindness, your nervous system learns something new:

You're safe. You're not alone. You're worthy of love.

This kind of relational presence creates the ideal conditions for **memory reconsolidation**—a fancy way of saying your brain updates old emotional "truths" when new, safe, healing experiences show up to contradict them.

So instead of your anxious part driving the bus during intimacy, it begins to relax.

Instead of shame shutting down your desire, you feel more free to explore.

Instead of fear hijacking your body, you feel grounded, playful, and present.

This is how your nervous system rewires. This is how sexual desire and confidence are reborn—not from pressure or perfection, but from *presence.* From learning to know, love, and care for your whole self—just as God already does.

Because sexy isn't about having it all together.

Sexy is about being *whole*—fully alive, fully seen, and at peace with the you God created.

So the next time an old fear or feeling rises up, don't shove it down.

Turn toward it. Get curious. Invite Jesus in. Invite a safe friend in.

And know this: you are not broken. You are brave. You are healing.

And that, beloved, is *very* sexy.

From Disconnection to Intimacy

One of the most unexpected—and beautiful—gifts of understanding your nervous system is this: it doesn't just heal *you*. It can transform your *marriage*.

When you learn to recognize what's happening inside with compassionate curiosity, you stop blindly reacting to anxiety, shame, or shutdown. Instead of being swept away by your emotions, you begin to see them for what they are—important signals from your body asking for care.

And when you can name those signals and share them with your spouse, something sacred happens. You create a bridge—one made not of blame or defensiveness, but of honesty, empathy, and trust.

Without that self-awareness, though, it's easy to hurt the one you love most—completely unintentionally. Imagine this: your husband reaches for you one evening, hoping for connection. But your nervous system has slipped into yellow or red. You're not feeling safe. You instinctively pull away—not because you don't love him, but because your body has hit the brakes. The problem is, *he doesn't know that.* To him, it may feel like rejection. Disinterest. Disconnection. And suddenly, the two of you are islands, drifting.

But when you've learned to recognize your body's signals, you can pause and speak what's true. You can say, "Hey, I really want to connect with you, but I can feel my body tensing. I think there's some anxiety coming up for me—not because of anything you're doing wrong, but because something inside me needs a little care."

That kind of honesty is a game-changer.

It's not about putting up walls. It's about inviting your husband *in*—into your story, your experience, your healing process. It's what intimacy actually means: **In-to-me-see**. Letting someone see the real you, even when the real you is still learning how to feel safe.

When you offer that kind of vulnerable access, you're not just managing a moment—you're building connection. You're saying, "I trust you enough to show you what's real." And when your husband receives that with compassion instead of defensiveness, healing happens—for both of you.

Instead of withdrawing into confusion or hurt, he can step toward you with tenderness. He becomes a partner in your healing, not a pressure point. He gets to experience the joy of helping you feel safe, wanted, and loved—and in turn, you feel more open to connection, both emotionally and physically.

This is the shift from disconnection to intimacy.

From pressure to partnership.

From "What's wrong with me?" to "We're in this together."

You don't have to be perfectly healed to create this kind of connection.

You just need a willingness to be seen—and to see each other through the lens of grace.

As you grow in self-awareness, you create space for your marriage to deepen—not just sexually, but emotionally, spiritually, relationally. And that foundation? It's stronger than chemistry. It's richer than fantasy. It's *real love*—built on empathy, honesty, and the courage to show up, even when it's messy.

That's the kind of intimacy that grows desire.

That's the kind of trust that sustains passion.

And that's the kind of connection that keeps you coming back to each other—again and again.

You don't have to figure it all out overnight. You just have to take one brave step at a time. Look inward. Speak truth. Stay curious. Invite him in.

Because intimacy isn't about always feeling sexy.

It's about feeling safe enough to be fully seen—and deeply loved—in your most unsexy moments, too.

And from that safety, something stunning emerges: Desire. Delight. And a marriage that keeps getting better.

Green Means Grow

You made it. And not just through another chapter—but through a major mindset shift.

You've learned that low desire or sexual disconnection doesn't mean you're broken. It means your body and nervous system are trying to protect you. You now know how to recognize the signals of green (safe and connected), yellow (anxious or on alert), and red (shut down or overwhelmed)—and that those states don't define you. They simply guide you toward what you need.

You've discovered that listening to your body with compassionate curiosity is the first step toward healing, safety, and deeper intimacy—not just with yourself, but with your husband. And you've seen how being honest about your inner world, even when it feels messy, creates the very kind of emotional safety that desire needs to flourish.

You're learning to move out of survival and into connection. To shift from shutdown to presence. To let your husband in, not just to your body, but to your story—and to build a love that is anchored in truth and trust, not pressure or pretense.

So take a breath. Pause. Reflect:

- What nervous system state do you tend to live in?
- What helps you feel most safe, grounded, and open?
- What small step can you take to invite someone into your story?

You don't have to heal overnight. You just have to keep showing up—with curiosity, kindness, and courage.

And speaking of courage… in the next chapter, we're diving into something that doesn't come in a lacy box or show up in a mirror—but might just be the sexiest quality of all: **emotional maturity**.

Because, let's be honest: no matter how hot someone is, if they're a brat or a doormat, the sparkle fades fast. But true, grounded emotional strength? That's the kind of sexy that lasts a lifetime.

Let's go there—together.

Chapter 6: Brats and Doormats

When the Honeymoon Hid the Crazy

*L*ydia used to think she was a pretty easygoing person. Until she married Daniel.

It wasn't that he changed overnight—it was more like the spotlight of marriage exposed some things she hadn't quite noticed before. Like the fact that he loaded the dishwasher like a raccoon with a vendetta. Or that he "forgot" their anniversary dinner reservation because he got caught up watching a documentary about World War II tanks.

And then there was her. The woman who used to lovingly bring him coffee in bed started slamming cupboard doors like it was an Olympic sport. One Tuesday evening, she found herself dramatically whisper-shouting into the refrigerator, "I am not your mother!" while gripping a bottle of ranch like it owed her an apology.

She knew she wasn't being her best self. But wasn't he supposed to be helping her become more like Jesus or something? Instead, she felt more like a frustrated toddler in a grown-up's body. The kind that wants to throw her husband's socks out the window just to make a point.

But when she tried to talk to her small group about it, the advice was all over the place:

"Just let it go."

"Pick your battles."

"Have more sex."

(That last one was from Jen, who always looked like she had her life together and probably alphabetized her pantry.)

Lydia felt stuck between two extremes: blowing up or shutting down. Neither felt good. Neither felt sexy. And neither was getting her closer to the connection she craved.

Late one night, after yet another disagreement about who forgot to take out the trash, she sat on the bathroom floor in her favorite sweatshirt (which may or may not have marinara on it), and prayed something like:

"God... I don't want to be a brat. But I don't want to be a doormat either. Please teach me how to grow up... without losing my spark."

She didn't know it yet, but that prayer? It was the beginning of something holy. A turning point. Not just for her marriage— but for her.

Because sometimes, the path to real intimacy starts when you stop blaming, start growing, and realize that grown-up love— like grown-up sex—isn't about perfection. It's about maturity. And that, as it turns out, is incredibly attractive.

Low Tide

Somewhere between six and eighteen months into a steady, committed relationship—often not long after the wedding—the high tide of dopamine and adrenaline begins to roll back. The novelty that once made everything feel electric starts to settle, and in its place rises something deeper: a relationship mediated more by oxytocin—the bonding hormone—and less by the thrill of the chase. This is when the real work begins. And with it, the real us shows up.

Cue the brat. Or the doormat. Or, depending on the day, both.

You may have caught glimpses of your inner brat or doormat while dating, but let's be honest: we're all a little more polished when there's still a chance he could walk away. But once the deal is sealed and the "I do's" are said, the tide goes out... and what was hidden beneath starts to surface.

Let's talk about the brat first. She's that inner toddler who wants what she wants when she wants it—and if she doesn't get it, well, let the sulking, snapping, withholding, or passive-aggressive behavior begin. She's convinced the world (and definitely her husband) should revolve around her. And if it doesn't? Cue the tantrum.

Then there's the doormat. She avoids conflict like it's her job. She says "whatever you want" so often it could be her life motto. She might look peaceful and accommodating, even "godly" on the outside, but inside? She's aching. Conflicted. Unseen. Her voice is buried under years of people-pleasing and a chronic inability to say no without guilt.

And here's the kicker: neither of these personas is sexy. At least, not to a mature man.

Let's be real—grown men aren't attracted to emotional toddlers. Brat behavior might seem sassy or fun for a minute, and passive compliance might look like submission from a distance, but neither leads to lasting sexual connection. That's because neither is rooted in the maturity it takes to cultivate true intimacy.

And don't miss this—this isn't about being perfect. It's about being *grown*. You were made in the image of a wise, loving, powerful God. That means the journey toward sexual confidence and desire is also a journey toward emotional maturity. Because only grown women can own their sexual power. Only grown women can experience true pleasure. Children can't. They aren't meant to.

You weren't created to be a brat, or a doormat. You were created to be a woman—bold, whole, emotionally strong, and spiritually grounded. That's the kind of woman who builds great sex. That's the kind of woman who builds a great life.

Grow Up

Let's just say it—adulting is hard. Especially if the environment you grew up in didn't exactly roll out the red carpet for maturity. Maybe your parents coddled you, let you get your way too often, or avoided hard conversations altogether. Maybe they modeled brat behavior themselves—dishing out tantrums, manipulation, or passive-aggressive silence instead of mature, respectful engagement. Or maybe they over-accommodated, doing everything for you, shielding you from consequences, and never expecting you to grow up.

Whatever the reason, if your upbringing didn't consistently invite you into the reality of life and relationships—with both support and boundaries—you may still have some growing up to do. And hey, that's not a moral failure. It's just a developmental gap. But it *is* your responsibility to close it.

Because here's the truth: immaturity is a turn-off. Full stop.

If you married a man-child, you might feel the tension already. When you pout, he sulks. When you lash out, he shuts down. When you manipulate, he retreats—or retaliates. It becomes a pattern of two toddlers trying to run a household and wondering why intimacy feels so distant. Immaturity begets immaturity, and that cycle will take your marriage (and sex life) on a ride you do *not* want to be on.

And if your flavor of immaturity leans more toward the doormat? That's not working either. A healthy, emotionally grown man doesn't want to marry a ghost. He wants a peer. Someone with her own thoughts, feelings, desires, and voice. Someone who brings the full weight of her God-given identity to the table—and yes, even disagrees with him when it matters. He wants a teammate who can say "yes" *and* "no" with confidence. Not someone who melts into the wallpaper or chronically sacrifices herself in the name of "keeping the peace."

Growing up means knowing who you are, what you want, and what you need. It means showing up with confidence, emotional honesty, and boundaries. And guess what? That's incredibly sexy.

You can't access your sexual power if you don't own your personal power. You can't feel confident in the bedroom if you can't even pick where to eat for dinner without deferring, second-guessing, or apologizing. And you certainly can't cultivate deep intimacy if you're living out of emotional survival patterns that never got updated past age twelve.

It's time to mature into the woman God created you to be. Not perfect. Not polished. But real. Grounded. Adult.

Because true happiness—what NICC calls the embodied state of peace, joy, satisfaction, and hope—doesn't just happen. You don't find it at the end of a rainbow or stumble into it by marrying the right guy. You *mature* into it. Step by step, choice by choice, grace by grace.

Reality & Independence Are Sexy

Let's be honest—reality doesn't always come gift-wrapped in glitter and good vibes. Sometimes it shows up like a cold splash of water to the face. But here's the thing: facing reality—really facing it—is one of the most mature, magnetic, and yes, sexy things you can do.

Emotional maturity means you learn to hold realistic expectations. For yourself. For your husband. For life (including your sex life). You stop expecting others to meet needs they were never meant to carry. You quit blaming people for not reading your mind. You recognize your own limits and honor theirs too. This kind of maturity isn't rigid or cold—it's deeply respectful. It says, "You are fully human. And so am I."

It also means you set boundaries that protect your autonomy, your values, and your sense of self. You learn to use your "yes" and your "no" with clarity and grace. Not in a way that bulldozes others, but in a way that affirms your God-given agency. You are not a leaf in the wind—or a doormat on the porch. You are a grown woman, made in the image of God, with thoughts, feelings, desires, and dreams that matter.

And that's exactly what independence looks like. Not isolation. Not hard-hearted self-reliance. But the embodied confidence that says, "I can stand on my own two feet. I can speak up. I can make decisions. I am a whole person, capable of navigating life—not because I have it all together, but because I trust the Spirit of God within me and the maturity He's cultivating in me."

You weren't created to be half of a whole. In God's design, it takes two to become one; one plus one equals one, not one-half plus one-half. Marriage isn't about two incomplete people desperately clinging to each other for survival. It's about two whole, growing, emotionally mature adults choosing partnership from a place of freedom, not fear.

So yes—reality is sexy. Boundaries are sexy. Emotional independence is sexy. Because it means you're showing up fully present, fully adult, and fully capable of loving and being loved—not from neediness, but from strength.

And that, friend, is where the real magic begins.

The Power of One

Great sex doesn't spring from magic or marital luck—it blossoms between two emotionally mature adults who know who they are, take responsibility for themselves, and keep growing. But here's the secret: you don't have to wait on your spouse to grow up in order to get started. That's the power of one.

Every relationship is a system, like the intricate gears inside a vintage pocket watch. Each part affects the others. If one gear changes direction or speed, the entire mechanism has to adjust. It's relational physics: when one person matures, the whole relationship feels the shift. Things can't stay the same.

If you begin to grow—emotionally, spiritually, relationally—it will create a new kind of tension in your marriage. Not bad tension, but productive tension. It's the kind that invites change, asks for new patterns, and makes room for healthier connection. And yes, it often leads to better sex. Not just because you're "doing it better," but because you're becoming someone who brings more emotional presence, honesty, and joy to the bedroom—and the rest of life too.

Now, let's be real. Sometimes this growth reveals just how unhealthy or destructive a relationship truly is. And in some cases, it leads to separation—not because you failed, but because you finally got healthy enough to stop pretending things were okay when they weren't. That kind of honesty, while heartbreaking, is also redemptive. But more often than not, your courage to grow will invite your spouse into growth too. As you stop playing out old patterns—as you find your voice, set respectful boundaries, and start living with more confidence and maturity—your relationship begins to shift. The dance changes. And that new rhythm? It's often more vibrant, intimate, and life-giving than anything you've experienced before.

So don't sit around waiting for your spouse to change. Don't stay stuck in resentment or passive hope. Take radical responsibility for you. Lean into your own healing. Speak the truth in love. Grow into your God-given self. And watch what happens—not just in your heart, but in your marriage and your sex life too.

Because becoming whole is always sexy. And your wholeness has the power to shift everything.

Wrapping It Up

Brats throw tantrums. Doormats disappear. Neither has the strength—or the sexiness—of a grown woman fully alive in her identity.

This chapter called you to maturity—not because you're failing, but because you were made for more. When the honeymoon hormones fade and the real you begins to surface, that's not the end of intimacy. It's the beginning of something deeper. And more powerful.

You've learned that sexual confidence and great sex aren't about finding the right spouse or the perfect moment. They're about becoming the kind of person who can show up with courage, self-respect, and presence. A woman who knows her worth. A woman who uses her "yes" and "no" wisely. A woman who grows—not because she has to, but because she wants the full life Jesus promised.

So here's your invitation: Take ownership of your growth. Get curious about your brat or your doormat. Practice being the emotionally mature woman you were always meant to be. Not perfect. Not polished. Just real—and real sexy.

And as you do, get ready. Because now that you're stepping into personal maturity, it's time to build relational maturity too. Up next: we'll explore how communication and conflict—yep, even the messy kind—can become sacred tools for building intimacy and setting the stage for sex that's not just good, but deeply, beautifully connected.

Chapter 7: Sexy Talk

The Dishwasher Incident

Ellie stared at the open dishwasher like it had personally betrayed her. It wasn't the appliance's fault, of course—it was just sitting there, half-loaded with a weird mix of dirty mugs and a rogue salad spinner. But in her mind, it had become the battleground for every unresolved issue in her marriage.

"All I asked," she muttered, closing it with a little more force than necessary, "was for him to rinse the dishes. Rinse. Not just fling them in like an abstract art project."

It wasn't really about the dishes. She knew that. Deep down, beneath the irritation and internal snark, she felt the ache—the ache of not feeling heard, of feeling like a teammate running plays without a quarterback. But voicing that? Way harder than rolling her eyes and banging cabinet doors.

Later that evening, she caught her reflection in the microwave while microwaving peas (which felt symbolic somehow). She looked tired. Not just "long day at work" tired—but "I'm carrying emotions I don't know how to name" tired.

Her husband walked in, cheerful and totally unaware he was sitting on top of an emotional landmine.

"Hey babe. What's for dinner?"

She turned, spoon in hand, pausing at the edge of sarcasm. She took a breath. And for the first time that day, she didn't make it about the peas, or the dishwasher.

"I'm feeling kind of invisible today," she said, surprising even herself.

His face softened. "Tell me about it."

And just like that, the air shifted. Not because they solved everything. Not because he suddenly became the dishwasher whisperer. But because she peeled back the first layer—and he met her there.

It's Not About the Nail

There's this hilarious little video on YouTube called *It's Not About the Nail*. Maybe you've seen it. A man and woman are sitting on a couch, and she's describing this unshakable pressure she feels in her head. As the camera angle shifts, you see what he sees—there's literally a giant nail sticking out of her forehead. He, being the logical, fix-it kind of guy, gently suggests that, you know, maybe it has something to do with the nail. Her eyes flash. "It's not about the nail!" she snaps. "You always do this—just listen!" Chastened, he backs off and offers some sympathy instead. "That sounds… hard." She melts. Connection restored. Then she goes in for a kiss, *bonk!*—nail. Conflict reignited.

Funny? Absolutely. But also painfully real. Because in almost every marriage, there comes a point when the fight isn't about the thing we're fighting about. It's not about the dishes, or the sex, or the way he sighed too loudly at your story about your coworker. It's about something deeper—something under the surface. Something that sounds like: *Do I matter to you? Can I trust you? Are you with me in this?*

In every conflict, whether we're aware of it or not, we're making emotional bids for safety and connection. These are holy, human questions: *Will you be there for me? Will you respond with kindness? Are you truly with me—not just in the room, but in the hard things, the boring things, the things that make me feel small or scared?*

When we don't get a clear yes to those questions—when our bids for connection are ignored, dismissed, or met with criticism—we panic. Sometimes that panic comes out in the form of nagging or nitpicking, blaming or yelling. Other times, it looks like shutting down, withdrawing, going cold. Either way, it's the same dance. The cycle. The loop of fear, disconnection, and hurt that keeps us stuck.

And here's the thing: that cycle doesn't just hurt your communication—it hijacks your intimacy. Unresolved conflict is a real desire killer. Bitterness is not an aphrodisiac. You can't feel sexually safe with someone you emotionally don't trust. You can't crave closeness with someone your nervous system has learned to brace against.

So when the sex is off—or gone altogether—it might not be about the sex at all. It might be about all the unspoken, unresolved, unprocessed hurt that's piled up between you like emotional laundry no one wants to fold. And for your husband? It might feel like his own bid for connection (through sex) is constantly rejected, and now he's wondering, *Do I even matter to her?*

But here's the good news: when you can see the deeper dance underneath the surface issues, you can stop playing the same old steps. You can learn to pause, get curious, and speak to the heart of the matter—not just the symptoms. That's where healing begins. That's when intimacy—emotional *and* physical—starts to grow again.

Because, sister, it's not about the nail. And it's not just about the sex either. It's about learning to listen beneath the surface, to your own heart and his, and creating the kind of connection where love—and libido—can flourish again.

Let's Talk About It

No one emerges from the womb with emotional intelligence and conflict resolution baked into their brain. If you've got solid relational skills today, it's because you learned them somewhere—probably through modeling, mentoring, or (let's be honest) trial and error. And if you don't have them yet? There's no shame in that. You simply haven't had the opportunity to learn them yet.

Maybe your parents didn't know how to model healthy emotional expression. Maybe no one ever showed you how to name your feelings, sit with them, and communicate them with clarity and compassion. Or maybe what you learned was to either explode or implode—yell or disappear. That's not a character flaw. It's a training gap. And it's absolutely one you can close.

Let's get one myth out of the way first: emotional intelligence is not the same thing as emotionality. Emotionality is when your feelings take the wheel and drive off a cliff. It's unprocessed, unfiltered emotion—emotional puking. It may feel cathartic in the moment, but it rarely leads to understanding, healing, or connection.

Emotional intelligence, on the other hand, is the ability to recognize what you're feeling, understand where it's coming from, regulate it, and express it in a way that invites others closer instead of pushing them away. It's the wisdom to ask: *What am I feeling, why am I feeling it, and what do I need to do with it?*

Now for the good news—and the not-so-good news.

Good news: you can absolutely learn emotional intelligence and conflict resolution skills, even if you didn't get them growing up. Bad news: you can't learn them in a vacuum. Just reading about them—no matter how brilliant the book or how many podcast episodes you binge—won't build the muscles you need for real-time intimacy. It's like reading a book on how to throw a baseball and expecting to be ready for the major leagues. You've got to practice. With real people. In real life.

That's why relational learning is so important. You grow these skills not just from knowledge, but from experience—safe, supportive, guided experience. This might look like learning from a mentor couple who's a few steps ahead and willing to show you the ropes. Or working with a NICC-trained marriage counselor who doesn't just tell you what to do but models it and helps you practice it. Most of all, it looks like experimenting with your husband—on purpose, and when the pressure is low.

Think of it like playing catch. You don't want to be learning how to throw during the World Series. You want to be in the backyard, tossing the ball back and forth, building trust and skill. Practice when things are calm so that when the heat rises, you've got the tools ready.

These skills are learnable. You're not behind. You're not broken. You're just growing. And the more you practice, the more confident you'll become—not just as a communicator, but as a partner, a lover, and a whole, emotionally intelligent woman.

Emotional Communication 101

Effective communication in marriage—especially about tender or triggering topics—starts with one crucial skill: emotional attunement. You can't communicate what you don't understand. And you certainly can't do it well when your nervous system is in the red or yellow.

Let's rewind. Remember those polyvagal zones we talked about? Green means calm and connected. Yellow is fight or flight. Red is shutdown. When it comes to healthy communication, especially in moments of tension, you *must* be in green. Trying to navigate a sensitive conversation while your nervous system is in yellow or red is like trying to steer a car while blindfolded. It's not just ineffective—it's dangerous.

Before you ever open your mouth to "talk it out," take a deep breath and check in with your body. Where are you? Are you grounded and present—or simmering, spinning, or checked out? If you're not in green, pause. Seriously. Hit the brakes.

Take some time with Jesus. Let Him hold the big feelings for a minute. Journal. Go for a walk. Call your Iron Sharpening friend. Book a therapy session. Give yourself permission to *do the work* before you try to fix the conflict. Why? Because when your system is dysregulated, you can't hear clearly—either your spouse's heart or your own.

This kind of inner work includes identifying what wounded parts of you might be activated. Is this about now, or is this poking an old bruise from your story? Maybe your husband's tone reminded you of how your dad talked to you when you felt small. Or maybe your body's reaction is bigger than the moment, because the moment tapped into something that never got fully healed. That's not weakness—that's a clue.

Start by naming what you're feeling. Go beyond "mad" or "upset." Try: "I'm feeling overwhelmed, anxious, embarrassed, rejected." And then ask: *What are these feelings trying to tell me?* What meaning am I assigning to his actions?

Here's a powerful phrase to anchor you: "The story in my head is..." It's humble, it's open, and it reminds both of you that you're working with interpretation—not fact. Ask yourself: *Why would a reasonable, rational, decent human being act this way?* Offering alternative explanations opens the door to dialogue instead of accusation.

And if your emotional intensity is above a 5 on a scale of 1 to 10? That's a solid sign there's an old wound involved. Be curious. Where did this come from? What part of you needs care before you move forward?

Then, and only then, invite the conversation. Don't demand it on your schedule. Find a time that works for both of you. Be curious about his internal world. Ask open questions. Gently explore what might be happening under the surface for him too. Lead with love. As Stephen Covey said, "Seek first to understand, then to be understood."

When it's your turn to share, keep it grounded and clear. Use this format:

- **Facts:** "When ABC happened..."
- **Feelings:** "I felt PDQ..."
- **Interpretation:** "And the story in my head was XYZ..."

Stick to what actually happened, how it made you feel, and what meaning you gave it. Then invite him to reflect back what he heard—not to parrot it, but so you feel truly seen. Model this for him while he shares, and you'll create a safe space for emotional honesty.

Will you hit bumps? Of course. But that's not failure—that's growth. When things get sticky, bring in reinforcements. That's what wise couples do. Find a mentor couple. Talk to a NICC-trained counselor. You don't have to figure this out alone.

This is the path to deeper emotional intimacy—and yes, to better sex too. Because when you can talk about the hard stuff with tenderness, trust grows. And where there's trust, desire blooms.

Let's Talk About Sex

Sex, money, and kids—these are the Big Three topics that spark the most tension in marriages. If you and your husband have ever ended up in a teary standoff or an icy silent treatment over one (or all) of them, you're not alone. These conversations are hard because they're deeply personal and often tied to vulnerability, identity, and deeply held beliefs.

And among the Big Three, sex is often the most vulnerable to talk about. Why? Because it touches the core of who we are—our desires, insecurities, hopes, and fears. Sex isn't just physical—it's emotional, relational, even spiritual. So talking about it requires more than vocabulary—it requires maturity, emotional attunement, and relational safety. It demands the full toolkit of good communication and conflict resolution skills.

But here's the thing: if you want a vibrant, growing, deeply satisfying sex life, these conversations are not optional. They're foundational.

You need to be able to talk about your likes and dislikes, your turn-ons and turn-offs, your accelerators and brakes. And not just once. These conversations need to happen before, during, and after sex. They aren't critiques—they're opportunities. Opportunities to deepen understanding, build trust, and discover what brings you joy and connection.

That might sound intimidating, but it's actually empowering. Your ability to talk openly about sex is a core skill in becoming a sexually confident woman. And like any skill, it gets easier with practice.

Yes, it will feel awkward at first. You'll stumble over your words. You might giggle. You might feel embarrassed. That's okay. Awkwardness is not a sign of failure—it's a sign that you're doing something new and brave. Keep going.

Over time, as these conversations become more natural, you'll notice something powerful: your sexual enjoyment will grow. Your sense of freedom and playfulness will increase. Your connection with your husband will deepen. And you'll find yourself less afraid and more curious, more able to learn and share, explore and adapt.

This kind of communication is what allows couples to overcome obstacles together, try new things, and evolve their sexual relationship over time. It's what turns sex from a task into an adventure—one where both partners feel seen, valued, and fully alive.

So take a deep breath. Dare to speak up. Your voice is a gift, and using it well is one of the most powerful ways you can honor your body, your marriage, and the God who made both.

Wrapping It Up

Communication isn't just a life skill—it's a love skill. And in marriage, it's a superpower. What you say, how you say it, and even what you don't say has the power to shape your connection, heal old wounds, and build something beautiful and strong between you and your husband.

In this chapter, we uncovered a hard but freeing truth: the fight is usually not about the fight. It's not about the laundry or the sex or the tone in that text. It's about whether we feel seen, safe, and supported. And when we can name that longing, when we attune to our own emotional world and invite our partner into it, everything changes.

You've learned that emotional communication starts with self-awareness. You can't share what you don't understand. That's why staying in the green zone—where your body feels safe and regulated—is key to meaningful dialogue. And from that place of groundedness, you can listen better, speak clearer, and show up with compassion and confidence.

You've also learned that talking about sex—yes, even the awkward, messy, and vulnerable parts—isn't just necessary. It's transformational. It creates the kind of relational soil where desire can take root, where intimacy can deepen, and where delight can grow.

So here's your next step: practice. Not perfection—just practice. Start small. Use the tools. Name your emotions. Share your story. Be curious about your husband's. And when you get stuck, get help. That's not failure—that's wisdom.

Because here's what's coming: when communication thrives, connection does too. And when connection deepens, so does sexual confidence, desire, and fulfillment.

In the next chapter, we're going to explore how a strong, healthy sex life doesn't just feel good—it actually helps secure your marriage. Couples who connect well between the sheets tend to stick together through life's storms. So if you're ready to take your connection from strong to unshakeable, keep reading.

Let's talk about how to divorce-proof your marriage—starting in the most unexpected, yet powerful place: your bedroom.

Chapter 8: Divorce-Proofing Your Marriage

Molly and the Magic Tupperware Lid

Molly wasn't mad, not really. Not in a capital-M melt-down kind of way. But as she stared at the mountain of mismatched Tupperware avalanche-ing out of her kitchen cabinet for the third time that week, she was... spiritually irritated.

"I swear these lids multiply like rabbits," she muttered, crouching down to wrestle a rogue container. *"And not one of them has a match. Like the ark, but without the coordination."*

Her husband, Jake, was upstairs, blissfully unaware of the domestic Tupperware war raging below. He'd offered earlier—cheerfully, she might add—to "handle dinner" which had apparently translated to grilling three burger patties and leaving every seasoning bottle, cutting board, and greasy pan in his wake like some kind of culinary crime scene.

It wasn't about the lids. Not really.

Molly knew that. She'd been around the marriage block long enough to recognize when she was spiraling. But still—was it so hard to rinse a dish? Or fold the laundry without being asked? Or...initiate something more than a forehead kiss at bedtime?

That last thought hit harder than she expected.

She sighed, leaning her head against the fridge. Maybe she wasn't mad about the containers. Maybe she missed feeling connected. Desired. Teammates instead of task managers. Lovers instead of logistics coordinators.

They still loved each other. That wasn't in question. But lately, love looked a lot like survival. And sexy? Ha. Sexy had left the chat.

The door creaked, and Jake appeared, sheepish, holding out a half-melted chocolate bar.

"Found this in the freezer. Thought you could use a peace offering?"

Molly snorted despite herself. "Only if it comes with a dishwasher coupon."

They both laughed. Then he hesitated, his voice quieter. "You okay?"

She paused. Maybe she was. And maybe she wasn't. But something inside whispered: this was a moment. A door cracking open.

"Can we talk?" she asked. "Not just about the dishes.

About...us?"

He nodded. "Yeah. I'd like that."

And just like that, amidst chocolate and chaos and crusty casserole pans, something shifted. Connection stirred. Hope flickered.

It wasn't perfect. But it was real. And maybe—just maybe—that was the first step toward something beautiful.

A Marital Barometer

Okay, deep breath—because what we're about to say might ruffle a few feathers. Ready?

Your sex life is a barometer for the health of your marriage.

Now hang with us. We're not saying it's the only barometer or even always the most important one, but it is a highly revealing one. Sex—or the lack of it—is never just about the act itself. It reflects what's happening beneath the surface: the quality of your connection, the maturity of your emotional intimacy, your patterns of communication, your willingness to show up as whole people. In short, sex reflects *the state of the union.*

And here's a bold truth: couples who have a genuinely healthy, vibrant, mutually satisfying sex life—where both husband and wife look forward to it and enjoy it—*rarely* get divorced.

We're not just talking about frequency. You can have high-frequency sex that's disconnected, selfish, or even toxic. That's not the goal. We're talking about the kind of sex that flows from emotional safety, mature love, playful affection, and mutual delight. That kind of sex—the kind that nourishes rather than drains—is a powerful glue for connection. It binds you together in ways that help weather storms.

We know someone out there might misquote this and make it sound like we're saying sex is the only thing that matters. It's not. But it *does* matter. And it deserves your attention—not as something to be weaponized or avoided, but as a vital and sacred expression of your covenant.

So if things in the bedroom feel strained, silent, or just "meh," it's not a reason to panic. It's a reason to get curious—with compassion, not condemnation. What's beneath the surface? What's not being said? Where might healing be needed?

Here's the beautiful truth: you can't cultivate a thriving sex life without maturing—and that same maturity will ripple out to bless every area of your marriage. Emotional honesty, self-awareness, mutual respect, vulnerability, laughter, freedom, forgiveness—these are the ingredients of both a great marriage *and* great sex. That's embodied spirituality. That's integration. That's healing.

And that's very good news.

Selfishness is NOT Sexy

Sin has warped a lot in this world—especially the things closest to God's heart. And you'd better believe sex is one of those sacred things that the enemy loves to target. After all, sexuality is a reflection of God's desire for deep, covenantal intimacy. Of course it would have a bullseye on it.

One of the biggest distortions? Selfishness.

From the man who manipulates or pressures a woman into sex—whether they're dating or married—to the massive global systems that exploit the vulnerable for profit, selfishness has desecrated something meant to be holy. Pornography, coercion, emotional pressure, spiritual guilt-tripping—it all grieves the heart of God.

Even within marriage, selfishness can wear a disguise. Sometimes it comes dressed in Christian language, using Scripture like a club. Take 1 Corinthians 7:3–4, for example. It's one of the most radical statements of mutuality in ancient literature—an invitation to self-giving love, not a mandate for duty sex. When someone weaponizes that passage to shame, pressure, or demand sex, it's not biblical obedience—it's emotional immaturity. And it deeply wounds.

Sex is never about entitlement. It's about offering. It's about loving each other well.

If you've been pressured, manipulated, or spiritually bullied into sex—please hear this: that's not God's heart. It's not your fault. And you deserve safety, healing, and support. (Leslie Vernick's *The Emotionally Destructive Marriage* is a beautiful starting place for help.)

But selfishness doesn't only live in demanding sex. It also shows up in *withholding*—especially when it's paired with apathy or avoidance. If you've concluded, "I'm just not into sex—it doesn't really matter to me," and you've stopped exploring why that might be... friend, that's worth a second look.

We're not talking about shame. We're talking about stewardship.

God made you a sexual being. And ignoring that part of yourself—refusing to get curious, refusing to grow—doesn't just impact your spouse. It impacts you. It blocks joy, it hinders connection, and it stunts your growth into the vibrant woman God created you to be.

Paul's vision in 1 Corinthians 7:3–5 is a mutual one. It's not about power—it's about partnership. It's not about demanding—it's about delight. Each spouse offering their body not as a burden, but as a gift. Sex isn't meant to be one-sided. It's a sacred dance of giving and receiving, of knowing and being known.

And here's the truth: neither pressure nor neglect makes for satisfying intimacy.

A husband demanding sex "because he needs it" is not loving like Jesus. Ephesians 5:25 is clear: "Husbands, love your wives, just as Christ loved the church and gave himself up for her." Jesus doesn't coerce. He woos. He gives. He sacrifices.

And a wife who refuses to explore her own barriers—who emotionally checks out without seeking healing—is also not walking in love. Yes, there may be trauma. Yes, there may be grief. But healing is available. Help exists. And love chooses to grow.

That's what NICC teaches us. So often, withdrawal isn't about selfishness—it's about pain. But staying stuck in that pain without seeking help? That's where selfishness starts to sneak in.

Because love leans in. Love gets curious. Love says, "This matters—not just for us, but for me."

God's design isn't transactional—it's transformational. It's not "you owe me" or "leave me alone." It's "we're in this together." And that, friend, is where true intimacy—and real healing—begin.

So whether you've found yourself demanding or detaching, hear this: Jesus is inviting you to more.

More presence. More honesty. More healing. More connection.

Because in His kingdom, no one gets used. And no one gets ignored.

"Do not merely look out for your own interests," Paul writes in Philippians 2:4, "but take an interest in others, too."

Yes—even (and especially) in bed.

What's Good for Your Sex Life...

Here's the beautiful truth: what's good for your sex life is good for your *whole* life.

We're not compartmentalized creatures. You're not just a brain with a body or a spirit with a sex drive. You're an integrated, embodied, wonderfully complex image-bearer of God. Which means that growth in one area of your life inevitably brings goodness to the others. Especially when that growth includes healing, maturing, and deepening your capacity for connection.

That's why your sex life is such a revealing barometer of your overall well-being—not because it's the most important thing (it's not), but because it reflects so many things at once. It's tied to your nervous system, your spiritual security, your emotional intelligence, your relational maturity, and your personal wholeness. When those things are growing, sex often becomes one of the places where the fruit shows up first—and the tastiest.

And that, friend, is the heartbeat of this whole book.

Sexual confidence, desire, and fulfillment don't come from learning just a few techniques, positions, or anatomy terms (though yes, those matter, and yes, we're absolutely getting there!). They come from healing and maturing the *roots* of who you are. When you cultivate strength and health in the core areas of connection, independence, reality, emotional maturity, and spiritual integration, sex becomes a natural overflow. Not forced. Not fake. Just delicious, soul-deep fruit.

This is what we call embodied spirituality.

It's a sacred, whole-person journey—and it changes everything. Not just in the bedroom, but in the kitchen, the car ride, the grocery line, the prayer time, the parenting, the conflict, the laughter, the ordinary Tuesday afternoon. A better sex life isn't an isolated goal. It's the cherry on top of true happiness.

So yes, it's worth the effort. All of it.

And if you're looking for a way to get your husband interested in the growth journey? Start here: "I'd really like to improve our sex life." You'll have his attention. Even if he doesn't yet know that journey involves character development, relational maturity, and maybe a few counseling sessions—he's probably more likely to show up when the words "sex life" are part of the invitation.

And you know what? That's okay.

Because once the journey begins, the impact will touch every corner of your lives. And the joy that awaits on the other side? It's not just a hotter marriage. It's a holier one. A whole one.

And a whole lot of fun.

Wrapping It Up

You've just explored one of the most powerful truths in the whole journey of intimacy: your sex life is a reflection of your *whole* life. And when it's healthy, mutual, and connected—it becomes one of the strongest glue points in your marriage. Not because it's about performance or perfection, but because it reveals the level of safety, trust, and emotional maturity you've built together.

We talked about how selfishness, whether expressed as pressure or avoidance, distorts God's design for sex. Real love—the kind that mirrors Christ's—doesn't demand and it doesn't detach. It shows up with humility, curiosity, and courage. It says, "I want to understand you," and, "I'm willing to grow for you." That kind of love is magnetic. It makes intimacy irresistible, sustainable, and sacred.

You also discovered that the path to a vibrant sex life isn't separate from your spiritual walk—it *is* your spiritual walk. Because what's good for your sex life (like healing, maturing, and showing up as your true self) just so happens to be good for your *whole* life.

So take a moment. Reflect. What's one small step you can take today to invest in this sacred connection between you and your spouse? Maybe it's a conversation. Maybe it's a prayer. Maybe it's a counseling session or simply choosing to be honest about what you need. Whatever it is, know this: you're moving toward something beautiful. Something deeply worth it.

Now, as we move into the next chapter, we're going to explore something that takes a lot of the pressure off: *desire looks different for everyone.* If you've ever wondered why you don't always feel like initiating, or why arousal sometimes shows up late to the party—you're not alone. Let's unpack the different kinds of desire, and how receptive desire (the kind that comes after things get going) is just as holy and powerful as the spontaneous kind.

Because desire isn't just a spark—it's a spectrum. And understanding yours can change everything. Let's dive in.

Chapter 9: Secret Desires

The Yoga Pants Revelation

*K*elsey was halfway through folding the Mount Everest of laundry on her living room couch when her husband, Ben, strolled in holding a cup of coffee and gave her that look. The one that said, "Hey girl..." paired with a mischievous eyebrow wiggle that should've come with a warning label.*

She squinted at him over a pair of mismatched socks. "Seriously? I haven't showered. I smell like Goldfish crackers and Febreze."

He just grinned and shrugged, like that was part of the appeal. She blinked. "Is he... aroused? Right now? Like this?"

It wasn't that Kelsey didn't love her husband. She did. Deeply. It wasn't even that she didn't enjoy sex—once things got going. It was the getting there that always felt like climbing out of a fog in hiking boots tied together with yarn.

Because most of the time, her body didn't exactly scream sexy! It whispered nap. Or Netflix. Or Is that baby powder in my hair or dry shampoo?

She sat back, letting the warm laundry pile into her lap, and tried to summon the spontaneous, sexy confidence she imagined "those women" had—you know, the ones who initiated intimacy like a rom-com heroine and had perfectly timed lingerie to match. But what she felt was more like, "If you touch me before I finish this basket, I might cry."

Still, when Ben came around the couch and gave her a slow, sweet kiss on the forehead, something inside her softened. Not arousal exactly, but... curiosity. She let her head rest against his chest and sighed.

Maybe she didn't feel "in the mood." But maybe, just maybe, the mood could come find her.

Initiating and Receptive Desire

When most people think about sexual desire, they picture one thing: a sudden wave of horniness that hits like a craving for chocolate and sends you hunting for your spouse instead of the pantry. That's what we call **spontaneous initiating desire**—and yes, it's real. It's common. But it's not the only kind of desire.

There's another form of sexual desire that's just as normal, just as valid, and far more common among women (and many men) than most of us realize. It's called **receptive desire**, and it's beautifully nuanced. Receptive desire isn't about starting from a place of arousal. It's about starting from a place of openness. A willingness to lean in, to say yes to connection, even if the sparks aren't flying yet—and trusting that the sparks often follow once the fire gets going.

Research tells us that around **85% of couples** experience this pattern, where one partner tends to be more of the initiator and the other more responsive. For many women, this means not feeling "in the mood" at the drop of a hat, but still desiring closeness and being open to connecting—knowing that once things get going, arousal can build and pleasure can follow.

This doesn't make you broken. It makes you normal.

Now, if your body doesn't warm up even after you've mentally said yes, that's not a moral or marital failure. It's a signal—an invitation to check in with your whole self. Are there brakes being pressed? Stress? Exhaustion? Conflict in the relationship? Anxiety, grief, hormonal shifts, sensory overwhelm, chronic pain, or trauma history? These can all act as internal red lights that override your yes. That's not rejection—it's a request for compassion, curiosity, and care.

And here's something else that might surprise you: **men can experience receptive desire too**. Yep, even though culture paints male desire as an always-on light switch, the reality is more human than that. Men can feel disconnected, stressed, or hormonally off. They may not feel that automatic spark—but with loving initiation, safe connection, and time, their bodies often respond. Or not—and that's okay, too.

Receptive desire grows stronger in environments of trust, emotional connection, and low pressure. It thrives when both partners understand that **sex isn't just about orgasms—it's about shared experience**. That's why couples in midlife or later—when hormone shifts affect both sexes—often find great value in redefining what intimacy looks like. Not every encounter has to end in fireworks. Sometimes, the beauty is in just being close.

So if you're not feeling spontaneous sparks, don't panic. You're not less sexual, and your marriage isn't doomed. You just might be a receptive desirer—and that's not a defect. It's a different rhythm. One that still leads to pleasure, connection, and yes, very real desire.

Let Me Count the Reasons...

If you've ever wondered why you sometimes want to be close to your husband even when you're not feeling especially turned on—you're not alone. And more importantly, you're not broken. The reality is, sexual desire doesn't look the same for everyone. And it certainly doesn't always start with fireworks and a rush of hormones.

Most men—though not all—tend to experience desire in a way that's spontaneous. They feel physically aroused, and that sensation motivates them to pursue sexual release. If the encounter doesn't lead to climax, it often doesn't feel satisfying. That's one pattern, and it's valid.

But it's not the only one.

For many women, desire functions very differently. Instead of being sparked by arousal, it often grows **after** sexual engagement begins. You might not feel "in the mood" initially, but as you lean in—emotionally, relationally, or physically—your body warms up, and desire follows. This is what researchers call **responsive or receptive desire**, and it's beautifully normal.

Dr. Rosemary Basson, a Canadian researcher, introduced a model of female sexual desire that changed the way we understand women's experiences. Her research highlights what so many women have always known deep down: sexual desire is often born from connection—not the other way around.

And here's what's stunningly freeing: women choose to engage sexually for many valid reasons—not just because they're physically aroused. Some long to feel emotionally close. Others want to feel desired or express love. Some seek stress relief, comfort, or simply the delight of being touched by someone who knows them deeply. These motivations aren't secondary or selfish. They're human. They're relational. They're deeply spiritual.

From a biblical perspective, this reflects the richness of God's design. Genesis 2:24 speaks of two becoming one—not just in body, but in life and love. And 1 Corinthians 7:3-5 paints a picture of mutuality, where spouses give of themselves not out of obligation, but out of care. That means coming to sex because you want to connect, give, receive, be known, or rest in your partner's arms is holy. It's not lesser. It's love.

And while orgasm is a beautiful part of God's design (hello, divine creativity!), it's not the only measure of a satisfying experience. Many women describe feeling fulfilled and deeply bonded with their spouse through skin-to-skin contact, laughter, eye contact, or simply lying together in peaceful presence. That counts.

So if your reason for sex today is "I just want to be close," or "I want to share something intimate," or "I miss you"—go ahead and count that. If your reason tomorrow is "I'm turned on and need you now," that's good too. You are allowed to show up with all the reasons, all the rhythms, and all the nuances that make up your sexual story.

Sexual desire doesn't have to look like a firework. Sometimes it's a warm ember that grows as you tend it with kindness, openness, and intention.

And every time you choose to connect—not from pressure, but from presence—you are stepping into something sacred. Something that nourishes not just your body, but your soul and your marriage.

A Poke in the Eye

Let's be honest: have you ever found yourself longing for a good, satisfying poke in the eye?

No?

Exactly.

We don't crave what doesn't feel good. In fact, we do everything we can to avoid it. And while that might sound obvious, it holds the key to understanding something deeper: if you find yourself avoiding sex—or feeling indifferent toward it—there's a good chance it's because it hasn't consistently felt good to you, physically or emotionally.

Now, this doesn't mean every sexual experience you've had was awful. In fact, many women live in this strange in-between space where sex is both appealing and off-putting. Maybe you avoid it like the plague...until you finally give in and actually enjoy it. That mix of resistance and reward can feel confusing, even frustrating—but it's also completely normal when you understand how desire works.

In NICC, we talk about the "dual control model" of sexual desire, which simply means this: your sex drive has **accelerators** (things that turn you on) and **brakes** (things that turn you off). And here's the twist—both can be activated at the same time. You might have a strong accelerator like physical closeness, a loving partner, or good past experiences. But if the brakes are jammed—think stress, past trauma, body shame, exhaustion, relational conflict, or physical pain—your system stalls. Or worse, it shuts down completely.

And this brings us to something really important: **the pleasure principle**. It's a simple truth from neuroscience that says we are drawn to what feels good and avoid what doesn't. If sex regularly leaves you feeling disappointed, disconnected, or in pain—why would you desire it?

This is especially relevant for women when it comes to orgasm and sexual satisfaction. If you're not experiencing pleasure—or if you're experiencing pain—your body is going to protect you by turning off desire. Not out of stubbornness or brokenness, but out of wisdom. It's your body saying, "This doesn't feel safe or worth it."

Now, can sex still be enjoyable even if it doesn't always end in orgasm? Absolutely. Quickie sex can be playful, connecting, and meaningful—like grabbing McDonald's fries in a pinch. But if **every** sexual encounter is a rushed, one-sided trip through the drive-thru with little pleasure on your end, your desire will eventually starve. That's not selfish. That's biological. And spiritual. Your lack of desire is not a failure. It's a signal—one worth listening to.

So what do we do with that signal?

We get curious. We start exploring what's blocking the pleasure, what brakes are stuck, what wounds still need healing. And then we learn how to unleash our capacity for wild, unabashed, holy pleasure. Yes, the toe-curling, breath-catching, full-body joy kind of sex God designed you to enjoy.

Because here's the secret: when sex feels safe, connected, and truly pleasurable, desire follows. You'll start thinking about it more. Wanting it more. Initiating more. Enjoying more. Not because you "should," but because you **get to**—and it feels amazing.

So if you've been wondering why you're not feeling it lately, don't beat yourself up. Get curious. Tune in. And let's troubleshoot the brakes—so the accelerators can do their beautiful, God-designed thing.

Wrapping It Up

Desire isn't one-size-fits-all. You've learned that there's more than one way to feel drawn toward intimacy—and that both **initiating** and **receptive** desires are beautifully valid. You've seen how a woman's sexual motivation often includes a whole bouquet of reasons—emotional closeness, feeling loved, stress relief, connection—not just arousal alone. And you've discovered that wanting sex doesn't always start with being "in the mood." Sometimes, the mood comes **after** the moment begins.

You've also learned a vital truth: we don't long for what doesn't feel good. So if you've been avoiding sex, struggling with desire, or feeling confused about your own body's response, it's not a sign of failure. It's a sign to get curious. Your brain is simply trying to protect you from something that hasn't consistently felt safe, good, or rewarding.

And that means there's hope. Real, tangible, holy hope.

Because once you understand how your desire works, you can stop feeling ashamed—and start getting intentional. You can explore what **lights you up**, what shuts you down, and what your body is really trying to tell you.

That's where we're headed next.

In the next chapter, we'll dive deep into the **arousal accelerators and brakes**—those internal switches and signals that shape your sexual experience. We'll help you identify what turns you on, what turns you off, and how to craft sexy, sacred contexts where confidence, desire, and pleasure can actually thrive.

So take a breath. Celebrate the progress you've made. And get ready to uncover the keys to turning desire from a mystery into a masterpiece.

Let's go explore what makes your sexy engine run—and what's been stalling it out. You're about to gain some powerful tools.

And friend? You've got this.

Chapter 10: Accelerators and Brakes

The Spark That Never Sparks

*L*auren stared at the ceiling fan, its slow, hypnotic spin matching the energy level in her body: barely moving. Her husband's hand gently brushed her hip under the covers, the universal sign for "I'm interested." And she was... kind of. Maybe. Okay, not really. But also, not not interested?

She sighed quietly and turned to him with a soft kiss. "I love you," she whispered, which was code in their marriage for please don't take this personally, but I am completely unmotivated to take off my flannel pants right now.

And it wasn't him. She knew it wasn't him. He still had that crooked grin that made her stomach flutter back in college. He still prayed with their daughter before bed in that voice that made her heart squeeze. But tonight, like most nights lately, her brain was in twelve different places—none of them sexy.

Earlier that day, she'd burned dinner (again), cried over a passive-aggressive PTA email, and used a baby wipe to clean a mystery smear off the fridge. Her body didn't feel like a temple—it felt like a garbage disposal. And every time she tried to want sex, her brain shouted, "Do you even remember how to be sexy? You haven't shaved your legs since March."

Still, she missed the closeness. She missed feeling... alive. Wanted. Engaged in her own body. She wanted to want it. But lately, desire felt like chasing fog.

What was wrong with her?

As she lay there, her husband pulled her in gently, kissed her temple, and didn't push. She was grateful—and also frustrated. She wanted the spark to just show up. Light her up. Sweep her away.

But maybe, just maybe... she didn't need to wait for it. Maybe the spark wasn't a mystery. Maybe it was something she could learn.

She snuggled a little closer. Maybe tomorrow, she'd start getting curious.

Understanding Your Pedals

Picture your sexual desire like a car. Most people assume the key to better intimacy is pressing the gas—more passion, more spontaneity, more lacy lingerie. But the truth, according to science (and let's be honest, experience), is a little more nuanced. Your sexual "drive" isn't just about pushing the accelerator—it's about understanding both the gas *and* the brakes.

Enter the **Dual Control Model**, a groundbreaking framework developed by researchers Eric Janssen and John Bancroft. It explains why desire sometimes feels like a smooth ride, and other times like you're stuck in park with the emergency brake on.

Your brain is constantly scanning for cues—some that say "let's go!" and others that scream "not a chance!" These cues come from your environment, your emotions, your relationship, even your past experiences. The way your body responds isn't random—it's deeply wired.

Meet Your Two Pedals:

- **The Accelerator (Go!):** This is all the stuff that turns you on—flirty texts, emotional connection, candlelight, that *look* your husband gives you when you're both vibing. Feeling desired, safe, and relaxed? Your accelerator says, "Let's do this."

- **The Brake (Whoa There!):** This is what shuts things down. Stress, body shame, unresolved conflict, dirty dishes in the sink, feeling pressured or disconnected—these stomp the brakes hard. And the stronger the brakes, the harder it is to get going, no matter how hard you're pressing the gas.

Why This Matters

A lot of women enter marriage expecting their desire to work like a man's—or like it does in rom-coms. Instant arousal, passionate kisses, and falling into bed. But for most women, desire is not a light switch—it's a dimmer, shaped by everything happening in and around them.

And friend, if your desire doesn't show up spontaneously or loudly? You're not broken. You're gloriously complex. You are *fearfully and wonderfully made* (Psalm 139:14), with a sexual rhythm that honors your whole self—body, mind, and spirit.

Discovering Your Unique Mix

Step One: Get Curious (Not Critical)

Begin by gently paying attention. Keep a simple journal or notes app. Reflect on days when desire feels easier, and days when it doesn't. Ask yourself:

- What was going on emotionally?

- How was my stress level?

- Did I feel connected—to God, my husband, myself?

- Was I tired, anxious, or preoccupied?

These are clues to your brakes.

Step Two: Explore Your Accelerators

Think about:

- When do I feel most alive or desirable?

- What words, touches, or settings make me feel safe and sexy?

- How does emotional or spiritual connection influence my desire?

For many women, the biggest turn-on isn't a sexy playlist—it's feeling seen and valued.

Step Three: Invite Jesus In

Yes, even here. Especially here. Your sexuality isn't separate from your spirituality—it's a part of it. Jesus isn't blushing about your body or your pleasure. He's your Healer and your Creator. Let Him speak truth over any shame, silence, or struggle.

How Sensitive Are Your Brakes and Accelerator?

Every woman's sexual desire system is as unique as her fingerprint. Some of us are wired with a turbo-charged accelerator and just a light tap on the brakes. Others have highly sensitive brakes and a slower-to-rev accelerator. Neither is wrong. You're not broken—you're built uniquely by a wise and creative God. But understanding how you're wired helps you navigate your sexual desire more wisely and with much more grace.

Let's find out how your system is tuned. Grab a pen, your journal, or the Notes app on your phone, and take a few moments to check in.

Brake Sensitivity Check: How Strong Are Your Brakes?

Instructions:
Rate each of the following from 0 to 4.

(0 = Not at all like me | 4 = Exactly like me)

1. Sometimes I have so many worries that I'm unable to get aroused.

2. Unless things are "just right," it's difficult for me to become sexually aroused.

3. If I'm uncertain how my husband feels about me, it's harder for me to get aroused.

4. If I worry about taking too long to become aroused or reach orgasm, it interferes with my arousal.

5. I sometimes feel so shy or self-conscious during sex that I can't become fully aroused.

Add up your total score:

- **0–7**: Low brake sensitivity – Your brakes aren't overly reactive. That means desire can flow more freely even in less-than-perfect conditions.

- **8–14**: Medium brake sensitivity – Your context matters. Stress, conflict, or emotional disconnection might hit the brakes more often.

- **15–20**: High brake sensitivity – Your system is finely tuned, and your desire may be especially responsive to stress, safety, and emotional factors.

If your score leans high, this isn't a flaw—it's an invitation. It likely means your nervous system is highly responsive and alert to your environment, and that's something Jesus cares deeply about. These brakes may also be pointing to past hurts or unhealed wounds that He wants to gently touch and redeem.

Accelerator Sensitivity Check: How Strong Is Your "Go" Pedal?

Instructions:
Rate each of the following from 0 to 4.

(0 = Not at all like me | 4 = Exactly like me)

1. Seeing my husband being competent or confident (like solving a problem or being a good dad) can make me feel sexually aroused.

2. When I fantasize about sex or think about my husband, I become aroused quickly.

3. The idea of someone overhearing us having sex doesn't bother me—it doesn't interrupt my arousal.

4. Certain smells—his cologne, his skin after a shower—can be strong turn-ons.

5. When I'm bored, I often think about sex or fantasize.

Add up your total score:

- **0–7**: Lower accelerator sensitivity – Your desire likely builds more slowly and may depend more on emotional safety and context.

- **8–14**: Mid-range sensitivity – You're flexible and can be turned on with the right mix of internal and external cues.

- **15–20**: High accelerator sensitivity – Desire comes easily when you encounter certain triggers or settings.

Whatever your score, you're right where you're meant to be. Desire isn't a race—it's a journey. What matters is understanding your personal rhythm so you can respond to it with wisdom and care.

Now What?

Understanding your brakes and accelerators is a powerful first step. When you can name what helps you feel open—and what makes you shut down—you can start crafting a sexual environment that works *with* your body and brain, instead of against them.

This is where the real beauty begins: when you and your spouse can lovingly co-create a sexual space that honors your unique wiring, desires, and needs. Want to take it even deeper? Start a **Desire Map Journal** together. Note what settings, emotions, conversations, or touches feel like green lights, and gently name the red lights too. If you're working through this with a counselor or mentor couple, bring your journal with you—it's a goldmine of insight for building Omazing® intimacy.

No matter what your numbers are, you are gloriously normal, profoundly loved, and wonderfully designed.

The Power of Context

Here's something most of us never got taught in youth group or premarital class: when it comes to sexual desire, context is everything. Not just what's happening in the bedroom—but what's happening in your heart, your head, your body, and your life. Your sexual desire doesn't exist in a vacuum; it's deeply shaped by your surroundings, your relationship, your stress levels, your sense of connection, your hormones, your sleep (or lack thereof)—literally *everything.*

This is why one night, you can feel playful and open... and the next, completely shut down. It's not because you're broken or inconsistent—it's because you're exquisitely responsive. God wired your body and brain to pay attention to your environment so that sex would be more than mechanical—it would be meaningful.

So let's get curious. Below are some key areas of context that shape your desire. As you read, try reflecting on how each one shows up in your own life.

Mental and Physical Wellbeing

If your body isn't on board, your desire probably won't be either. When you're exhausted, overwhelmed, or dealing with chronic pain, your system will prioritize survival over pleasure.

- **Sleep & stress**: If you're running on fumes, your libido will likely be in hibernation mode.

- **Body image**: Feeling uncomfortable in your skin makes vulnerability harder. Ask yourself: *When do I feel most at home in my body?*

- **Mental health**: Depression, anxiety, or emotional disconnection can quiet desire. Your nervous system needs to feel safe to let arousal rise.

- **Performance pressure**: If you're anxious about doing sex "right" or feeling guilty about taking too long, your brakes are probably slamming down. Presence is key—but presence is impossible under pressure.

Husband Characteristics

Yes, your man plays a role—but not just in the ways culture tells us.

- **Attentiveness and kindness** often go farther than abs and cologne.

- **Scent** is surprisingly powerful—some smells might draw you in, others might shut you down.

- **Emotional state**: When he's distant, distracted, or angry, desire usually dips. When he's grounded, warm, or laughing with the kids? Yep—accelerator hit.

Relationship Dynamics

Your emotional connection is the soil in which desire either flourishes or fades.

- **Trust & safety**: Vulnerability is impossible without them.

- **Respect & mutuality**: If the power dynamics feel off, so will the desire.

- **Feeling desired**: Knowing you're wanted, chosen, pursued? That unlocks the gates to arousal.

- **Sexual frequency**: When it feels like pressure, desire withers. When it feels like play, desire often multiplies.

Physical Setting

Sometimes the location makes all the difference.

- **Privacy**: Knowing you won't be interrupted = essential for many women.

- **Distance intimacy**: Some women feel aroused by flirty texts or calls. Others find it awkward. Know your lane.

- **Watching your husband shine**—in worship, parenting, leadership—can turn up the heat unexpectedly. Don't ignore those moments. Lean into them.

Life Circumstances

What's happening outside the bedroom walks right in with you.

- **Stress from work, finances, or parenting** impacts your nervous system—and your brakes.
- **Holidays, anniversaries, or big moments** can create connection—or pressure. Give yourself permission to feel what you feel.

Playfulness and Fantasy

Play is not just for kids. It's essential for adult connection too.

- **Imagination**: Giving yourself permission to mentally wander into sexy or romantic spaces is part of healthy desire.
- **Exploring what touches feel good** (and which ones don't) helps you reclaim agency.
- **Oral sex, intercourse, and other acts** aren't obligations—they're invitations. You get to choose what feels nourishing.

A Gentle Invitation

Now that you've walked through these context clues, take a moment to reflect. What have you noticed about the settings where desire thrives for you? What consistently shuts it down? Can you name any patterns?

Try journaling what you discover. You might even share it with your spouse—or with a counselor or mentor who can help you shape those contexts more intentionally. Sometimes the smallest shifts (like turning off your phone early or carving out unrushed time) create the biggest difference.

Context isn't just background noise. It's the stage. And when you learn to set that stage with care and wisdom, your desire begins to feel less confusing... and a whole lot more inviting.

Wrapping It Up

You're not broken. You're beautifully complex. And your desire is not a button to push—it's a rhythm to understand.

In this chapter, we explored how your sexual desire is shaped by both accelerators and brakes. We unpacked how emotional connection, physical health, relational safety, spiritual intimacy, and even scent and space can either light your fire or hit the brakes. The Dual Control Model helped us see what so many of us were never told: your body is responding to *context,* not just chemistry.

You also learned to explore your unique wiring through self-assessments and compassionate curiosity—not shame. And we highlighted how cultivating desire isn't about forcing yourself to feel something, but about creating space where desire is more likely to rise. Intentionally tending to your mind, body, and spirit opens the door to the kind of intimacy that's not just hot—it's holy.

So take a moment to reflect:

What are your top accelerators?

What are your most sensitive brakes?

And what's one small shift you could make this week to honor your design?

Because when you honor your design, you honor your Creator.

And speaking of honoring your design...

In the next chapter, we'll look at one of the biggest, most heartbreaking brakes of all: unwanted pain during sex. It's far more common than you might think, and you are not alone. If that's your story—or someone you love—you won't want to miss what's coming next.

We're going there. With tenderness, truth, and hope.

Chapter 11: (Unwanted) Pain is NOT Sexy

She had a Plan. Her Vagina Had Other Plans.

A bby had lit the candle. The candle. The one she bought after that "Fun & Flirty Wives" workshop at church where everyone blushed during the Q&A. She'd shaved her legs, put on the silky thing that made her feel slightly like a rotisserie chicken (but in a cute way), and even queued up the worship playlist with the saxophone bridge—because she was a woman of God and vibes.

Tonight was the night.

She and Evan hadn't connected in over three weeks. Between her period, that stomach bug from their toddler, and a mild existential crisis over the dishwasher, sex had slipped way down the list. But tonight? The stars had aligned. The kids were asleep. The house was clean(ish). She was determined.

Until... well... things started, and then promptly stopped.

Not because of a lack of enthusiasm on Evan's part. No, he was definitely present. And sweet. And totally on board. But when it came time for actual intimacy, Abby's body slammed on the brakes.

The pain wasn't new. It had shown up before, but she'd always chalked it up to dryness or stress or that one time she tried the keto diet. But tonight it was worse. Sharp. Immediate. Like her body was saying, "Access denied."

"Are you okay?" Evan asked, gently pulling back, his eyes laced with concern and that helpless look that made her want to scream and sob and apologize all at once.

She offered a tight-lipped smile. "Yeah... I just... I don't know what's wrong with me."

She did know. Kind of. Sort of. This had been happening more. And every time it did, she felt a little more broken. A little more scared that something was really wrong. And a lot more pressure to just suck it up, fake it, and get it over with next time.

But tonight, she didn't.

She wrapped herself in a blanket, let Evan hold her, and whispered, "I think I need help with this."

And for the first time in a long time, she didn't feel like a failure. She felt brave.

Don't Play Through the Pain

Let's start by clearing something up: some women love a playful spank or a bit of consensual pain in the bedroom—and if that's you, fantastic. And if it's not? Also fantastic. As we've said before: if it's *consensual* (no pressure, no manipulation), *monogamous* (just you and your husband), and *mutually enjoyable*, then it's fair game. Jesus isn't shocked by your creativity. He's smiling. So, no shame here. (We'll unpack this more in the "Kinky?" chapter.)

But that's *not* what we're talking about in this chapter.

We're talking about unwanted pain—the kind you don't consent to, don't enjoy, and definitely don't want creeping into your sex life. That kind of pain is *not* normal. And no matter how many well-meaning voices have told you otherwise, that myth needs to die a swift and merciful death.

Painful sex is actually *common*—but it's not *normal*. And here's the good news: it's treatable. Often very treatable. But here's the not-so-good news: if you try to push through it, it only gets worse.

Why? Because your brain is taking notes. And it's super good at pairing experiences. If you consistently endure pain during sex—whether out of obligation, guilt, or hope that it'll magically disappear—your brain starts linking sex and suffering together. It's like forming a Pavlovian reflex: cue the husband's flirty smile, and suddenly your body's screaming "Abort mission!"

This is what we call an aversion. And once it's in place, it sticks around—even if the original cause of pain eventually goes away.

We've walked with many women who, early in marriage, endured painful sex out of love or duty. Later—after healing from childbirth or hormone shifts—they found themselves still dreading sex. The pain was gone, but the dread remained. Their bodies had learned to brace, avoid, shut down.

The beauty? Aversion isn't permanent. But it does take intention to heal. Better still? You can *prevent* it by choosing today to stop doing anything that causes pain.

That doesn't mean stopping sex altogether. You can still explore pleasure, enjoy intimacy, and stay connected while you address what's causing the pain. There are so many other ways to experience sexual delight that don't involve pushing through discomfort.

And you don't have to figure this out alone. A well-trained Christian sex therapist—especially one who understands both body *and* soul—can help unwind what's going on and walk with you toward healing.

Friend, your body deserves compassion. Your story matters. And pleasure isn't something you have to earn—it's a gift God designed for you to enjoy.

Let's stop reinforcing the pain. Let's start building trust with your body again. Because pain is not your portion—and sexy doesn't have to hurt.

Workarounds

Let's say it again for the ladies in the back: stop doing anything that causes unwanted pain. Seriously. Full stop.

And—lean in close here—we want you to keep having sex.

Sounds contradictory? It's actually a beautiful, life-giving invitation. Because "sex" isn't limited to one specific act. If your definition of sex is just penis-in-vagina intercourse, friend, your sex life is due for a major upgrade.

Sex is anything that builds sexual arousal, pleasure, and intimacy between you and your husband. And that leaves a *lot* of room for creativity and joy.

The most common type of painful sex is pain during intercourse—clinically categorized as dyspareunia. But here's the good news: you can build a rich, satisfying, non-intercourse sex life. In fact, you *should* have one. Not only is it fun, but it's also incredibly practical. Throughout your lifespan—during pregnancy, illness, postpartum recovery, your period, surgery, stress, aging, or just a Tuesday night when penetration doesn't feel appealing—intercourse might not be possible or desirable. That doesn't mean intimacy is off the table. Far from it.

Mutual pleasure can look like clitoral stimulation (by hand, mouth, vibrator, or other creative means), sensual massage, extended foreplay, skin-to-skin cuddling, breast stimulation, mutual masturbation, or exploring full-body arousal in ways that feel exciting and safe. And guess what? Most female orgasms *already* come from clitoral stimulation—not intercourse. So if intercourse is uncomfortable for now, you're not missing the main event—you're just exploring a different route to the fireworks show.

Let's talk about the miracle of your design for a second. Every inch of your skin can be a source of sensual pleasure. And here's a sneak peek from the upcoming orgasm chapter: orgasms come from your brain. Yep. Your beautiful, God-designed brain. That's why veterans with spinal injuries who've lost all sensation below the waist *can still learn to orgasm.* That's how incredible God made your body. That's how deep and rich your capacity for sexual pleasure really is.

So please—don't stop having sex. Instead, expand your definition. Explore new ways to experience connection and delight. Teach your body that sex doesn't have to hurt. Let pleasure rewire the pathways that pain may have carved.

Sex can still be sacred. It can still be hot. And it can absolutely be pain-free.

Let your journey toward healing be filled with curiosity, compassion, and yes—plenty of laughter and toe-curling goodness along the way.

Trust Your Doctor...Usually

One of the most important things we do as sex therapists when addressing sexual pain is collaborate with other professionals—especially those in the medical world. Pain during sex isn't always "just in your head" (though emotional pain is absolutely real and valid too). There can be physiological reasons for your pain that need to be ruled out or treated medically.

That's where pelvic floor physical therapists, OB-GYNs, endocrinologists, and primary care doctors can be incredibly helpful. A skilled pelvic floor therapist, for example, can work wonders—especially if childbirth or injury disrupted the delicate balance of muscles and tissues in your pelvic region. These amazing folks specialize in strengthening, stretching, and retraining those muscles to work in harmony again. Many women find real relief with their help.

But—*and this is important*—as much as we appreciate the medical community, let's also be real: not every medical provider gets it. And when they don't, it can do real damage.

Case in point: we've heard too many stories of well-meaning (or utterly clueless) providers recommending numbing cream as a solution to vaginal pain. *Numbing cream.* For your genitals. As if turning off your ability to feel pleasure is a brilliant solution. Spoiler alert: it's not. It's a fast track to becoming a glorified human sex toy, stripped of sensation and agency—basically a very sad and passive participant in your own sex life.

We're not being dramatic. That's exactly what it can feel like. And it makes us want to find that doctor, walk into their office, and kindly—but firmly—shake some sense into them.

Why would a provider suggest something like that? It's not because they're cruel. It's because most doctors are *not* trained in sex therapy. Their training focuses on anatomy, physiology, and pain management—which is great for treating infections, torn ligaments, and broken bones. But sex is more than skin and nerves. It's interpersonal. It's emotional. It's spiritual. It involves your story, your wiring, your past experiences, your beliefs, your body image, and your relational dynamics.

So when a provider offers a solution that doesn't feel right to you—trust your gut. Push back kindly. Ask for alternatives. Seek a second opinion. And above all, remember this: their expertise is *valuable*, but it's also *limited.*

Good medical care can lay the foundation—helping your body heal physically and clearing the roadblocks that stand in the way of arousal and pleasure. But medical care alone won't heal the psychological and emotional scars, rebuild your sexual confidence, reawaken desire, or create a vibrant, pleasure-filled sex life. That's where good sex therapy comes in.

So yes, trust your doctor... *usually.* Be grateful for their help. Use their wisdom. But also know when to smile, nod, and go find someone who actually gets what intimacy is really about.

That's where the real healing—and the real fun—begins.

Home Remedies

If you've started exploring non-intercourse sexual connection—and you're genuinely enjoying it, maybe even regularly reaching orgasm and looking forward to those experiences—then first of all, *yay you!* That's already a huge win. And second, you may be ready to gently experiment with a few home remedies that could help ease the pain that's gotten in the way of intercourse. No doctor or sex therapist required—yet.

But here's the golden rule: if it hurts, *stop.* We only want you moving forward if you're already having pleasurable, pain-free sexual experiences in other ways. Got it? Good. Let's talk next steps.

Step 1: Lube Like It's Your Job

If we could shout this from every rooftop, we would: **use more lube.** No, seriously. Use *lots* more lube. The number one cause of pain during sex is dryness. And no, your natural lubrication is not a reliable indicator of your arousal level. That's a myth. Some women get wet when they're not turned on at all, and some women can be wildly turned on and still feel like the Sahara. Hormones, stress, hydration, medication—there's a whole soup of factors at play.

So don't overthink it. Just grab a good water-based or silicone-based lube—brands like *Wet* or *KY* work well. If you're more the crunchy-mama type, olive or coconut oil can be solid options too (just don't use them with latex condoms). Apply lube generously on the vulva (the outer lips and clitoris), and on anything that's going in—fingers, toys, or your husband.

Sometimes, that alone solves the problem. But if it doesn't, don't worry—there's more you can try.

Step 2: Relax... Really

Your body remembers pain, and if sex has been painful in the past, your pelvic muscles may brace for impact anytime intimacy starts—even if things are physically healed. This can become a self-fulfilling prophecy, where tension creates pain, which creates fear, which creates more tension, and round and round we go.

So, what do we do? We help your body feel safe again.

Start by taking a warm bath. Breathe deeply. Create a slow, sensual environment where there's *zero* pressure to have intercourse. Reassure yourself: "We can still have fun, orgasm, and feel connected without penetration." Give your nervous system time to relearn that sex can feel good again.

Kegel exercises can also help. These involve intentionally tightening and relaxing the pelvic floor muscles—kind of like stopping your pee midstream. Biofeedback devices or apps (yes, some even come with video games you control with your pelvic muscles!) can help you learn if you're doing it right.

If penetration still isn't possible—even with a finger—you may be dealing with vaginismus, a condition where the muscles involuntarily tighten, making penetration painful or impossible. This is *so common* and very treatable.

Look into vaginal dilators—gentle, graduated silicone tools that help your body slowly get used to the sensation of penetration without pain. Start with the smallest one, pair it with tons of lube, deep breathing, and calming self-talk. Over time, you can work up to the next size, eventually matching (or slightly exceeding) your husband's size.

When you're ready, you can even use one as a "warm-up" before sexual connection. Think of it like stretching before a workout. Once you're relaxed and comfortable, add in generous foreplay, emotional connection, and boatloads of lube, and try this: let him gently enter, but no thrusting yet.

Just pause, hold each other, smile. Maybe make it playful—see who can hold the longest eye contact without giggling. Then pull out and finish playfully without intercourse.

Do this a few times, creating a new experience of pain-free penetration. Let your body relearn safety. And when that's in place, you can slowly introduce movement—again, only if it feels good.

When to Get Help

If the pain persists, or if these suggestions don't feel doable based on your symptoms or emotional response, *don't worry*. That's exactly what good sex therapists are for. We know how to troubleshoot what you're facing and craft a custom plan that's compassionate, effective, and doable.

You don't have to settle for pain. And you definitely don't have to do this alone. Relief is possible. Sexy is possible. And your healing journey is already underway.

Emotional Pain is Real Pain

Let's be really clear here—emotional pain counts. Like, *really* counts. And when it comes to sex, emotional pain can be just as powerful, and just as disruptive, as physical pain.

In fact, our brains don't do a great job of separating the two. Whether your body was injured, your heart was broken, or your sense of safety was shattered, your brain processes all of that as threat. And when those threats get paired with sexual experiences or cues—whether it was explicit content, pressure you didn't know how to say no to, childhood molestation, sexual assault, or even consensual sex that still felt emotionally overwhelming—your nervous system goes on high alert.

Even if today's situation is safe. Even if you *want* to want sex. Your body may still respond as if it's not safe. That's not dysfunction. That's protection.

And it makes sense.

Your brain is wired to guard you. It logs painful experiences—especially ones linked to fear, shame, or confusion—and forms neural pathways to avoid similar pain in the future. That's part of what we call aversion: your body starts saying *no* even when your mind is saying *yes please*. It's not betrayal. It's a trauma-informed survival strategy.

The problem is, if that protective response isn't addressed, it can keep you stuck in a loop. Every time your husband reaches for you or intimacy is initiated, your body might brace, shut down, or emotionally disappear. Even if he's gentle. Even if you love him. Even if you *really* wish it felt different.

Here's the hopeful part: emotional pain can be healed. And when it is, desire and safety and even pleasure can return—not in a forced way, but in a genuine, embodied way that feels like *freedom*.

Good sex therapy (like the kind rooted in Neuroscience Informed Christian Counseling®) gently uncovers those hidden memories, the unhealed wounds that may be driving the aversion. With compassion and expertise, it helps you and your husband rebuild a new foundation—one grounded in safety, tenderness, trust, and joy. One baby step at a time, you can create new, positive experiences that overwrite the old fear-based scripts. That's the miracle of memory reconsolidation—it rewrites your internal narrative.

So if emotional pain is the source of your sexual struggle, you're not broken. You're not crazy. You're not alone. You've just been hurt. And healing is real. Jesus sees your pain, and He doesn't shame you for it. He wants to meet you there—right in that place of ache—and write a redemptive chapter you didn't think was possible.

The enemy doesn't get the last word. Your story isn't over. There is hope, and it's holy.

Wrapping It Up

Let's just say it plainly: unwanted pain is not part of God's good design for your sex life. It's not normal. It's not something to push through. And it's definitely not something to ignore.

Pain—whether physical or emotional—can shut down desire and hijack the body's beautiful, God-given wiring for pleasure. Playing through the pain, even with the best intentions, often backfires. It reinforces aversions and teaches your nervous system that sex equals suffering. But here's the good news: pain is treatable. And healing is absolutely possible.

This chapter invited you to listen to your body, honor your pain, and say a holy *no more*. It also gave you permission to keep enjoying intimacy while you heal, discovering new forms of pleasure that don't trigger hurt. Whether your path includes medical support, sex therapy, or both, you don't have to walk it alone—and you don't have to put your sex life on hold while you do.

We also named the reality of emotional wounds. If your body feels like it's fighting against you, it might be protecting you from something unresolved. And if that's the case, healing those inner places matters just as much as physical recovery. You're a whole person—body, mind, and spirit—and God cares about all of you.

So what's next?

We're about to get into a topic that might make you squirm...or breathe a sigh of relief. Because now that we've talked about pain, we're ready to talk about *pleasure*. Specifically, learning how to explore your body in a way that builds sexual confidence and understanding. Yes, friend—we're going there. It's time to talk about the M word (you know the one).

Don't worry—we'll guide you with grace, honesty, and just enough humor to make it feel doable. Because you deserve to feel sexy, safe, and deeply connected—to God, to your husband, and yes, to yourself.

Let's go.

Chapter 12: Just Me, Myself,...and Jesus

"The Drawer"

Rae didn't mean to have a meltdown over a sock drawer. But there she was—kneeling in her bedroom, mismatched socks and tangled bras scattered like confetti, holding a tiny pink bullet vibrator in one hand and a pair of fuzzy Snoopy socks in the other. Classic.

She'd forgotten it was in there. The little thing had been a bachelorette gift from her best friend, tucked away nearly a decade ago in an "I'm-not-that-kind-of-girl" panic. Rae hadn't touched it since. Not because she wasn't curious—oh, she was—but because every time she thought about trying it, she heard the voices from youth group: Your body isn't your own. Lust is the devil's playground. Wait on the Lord. Also, your grandma is watching.

But today, something was different. She'd spent the morning listening to a podcast on sexuality and theology, which left her feeling confused, a little mad, and surprisingly hopeful. Could it really be true that God wasn't grossed out by her body? That pleasure wasn't a trap but a gift? That curiosity wasn't rebellion?

She sat back on her heels, staring at the ceiling like it might offer answers. "Jesus," she whispered, feeling somewhere between *a confession and a dare, "if You're cool with this, You're gonna have to help me believe it."*

Rae wasn't sure what she expected—lightning? A guilt trip? A spontaneous Bible verse in the sky? But all she felt was a strange calm. Like maybe, just maybe, she wasn't disappointing God by finally being honest with herself.

She didn't do anything dramatic that day. She folded the Snoopy socks, gently placed the vibrator back in the drawer, and smiled for the first time in a long time. The drawer was still messy, but something in her heart felt a little more sorted.

Maybe God wasn't afraid of her questions.

Maybe He was inviting her to explore.

Maybe this chapter of her life was going to be... a lot more interesting than she thought.

I Touched Myself... and I Liked It

If you've got toddlers, then you already know—kids don't need a single tutorial to figure out how to touch themselves. It's like it's hardwired. One minute you're sipping coffee in the church lobby, and the next you're trying to subtly redirect your precious angel who's gone hands-deep in their pants with a grin on their face. Nothing like a spontaneous anatomy lesson in the house of the Lord.

Now, depending on what kind of Christian community you grew up in, you probably heard one of two messages about that moment. Either: "That's normal curiosity, just something we explore privately, no big deal," or... "Don't do that, it's dirty, shameful, sinful, and also, God and your grandma are watching and they're both deeply disappointed." If you got the first message—good for you, friend. You're one of the rare ones who was handed a healthy, biblically grounded framework for your body and sexuality. But if you got the second, well, welcome to the club most of us didn't want to join.

Let's flip the script for a second. Imagine you buy your child a toy you know they'll absolutely love. You leave it for them to find and watch them discover it with delight. Now picture this: the moment they start playing with it, you burst into the room, scowling and scolding them for touching it. What kind of parent would that be? And yet, that's the lens so many of us have been taught to see God through when it comes to our own bodies and pleasure.

But here's the thing—God designed your body, including your genitals. He wired them to feel good when touched. And He didn't put a single verse in the Bible that says, "Don't touch." So maybe, just maybe, if we feel shame or fear around this topic, it's not Jesus talking—it's someone else's voice we picked up along the way.

A Theology of Masturbation

Okay, deep breath—because this is the part where things might feel a little tender or controversial. But let's start here: I, Josh, have a degree in Biblical Languages. I spent three years digging deep into Greek and two into Hebrew because I believe the Bible isn't just a sacred book—it's God's Word to us, our compass for life and godliness. The doctrine of the sufficiency of Scripture tells us that the Bible contains everything we need to know to live in right relationship with God. So when we talk about big, intimate topics like masturbation, we want to go there biblically, not just culturally. And yes, we're diving into theology... while talking about touching ourselves. Welcome to a truly unique Bible study.

So—what does the Bible actually say about masturbation? Not much, as it turns out. In fact, not anything. It doesn't reference it at all. You might've heard someone quote the story of Onan from Genesis 38. He did, in fact, "spill his seed," and God did strike him dead. But slow down—he wasn't masturbating; that was coitus interruptus, and his sin had nothing to do with self-pleasure. He was deliberately disobeying a family and cultural duty to give his deceased brother's widow children. Not even close to the same thing.

Still, this passage gets trotted out regularly to shame people into silence about masturbation. But here's what's critical to understand: If masturbation were inherently sinful, the Bible would say so. Scripture does not hesitate to call out sexual sin—adultery, lust, abuse, idolatrous sex practices. But it's completely silent on masturbation. According to 2 Timothy 3:16-17 and 2 Peter 1:3, Scripture gives us everything we need for "life and godliness." If God didn't include it, it's not central to the issue of sin. That silence isn't permission to do whatever we want—but it is a caution against calling sinful what God never did.

Now let's talk about something many of us have experienced: shame that feels spiritual. Even if the Bible doesn't condemn masturbation, many women feel deep guilt around it. Why? Because shame was taught to us—sometimes in subtle ways, sometimes outright. And your brain remembers those messages. That guilt isn't necessarily the Holy Spirit convicting you—it might be your inner wiring repeating what you learned from a fearful youth group leader or a deeply embarrassed parent. That doesn't make it biblical. That makes it programming. And Jesus came to rewrite that script (Matthew 11:28–30).

Let's reframe the conversation. What if, instead of asking "Is this bad?" we asked, "Is this wise?" Masturbation is not inherently selfish or sinful. In fact, it can be an intentional, wise act of stewardship. In some situations, masturbation has served as a healthy outlet: for married couples navigating long-distance seasons, for women recovering from sexual trauma, or for those wanting to understand their own sexual responsiveness in a safe, private space. It can help you avoid harmful substitutes like pornography or inappropriate emotional entanglements. In the context of honoring your marriage, body, and conscience—it can be a gift.

Now, a warning: just because something isn't inherently sinful doesn't mean it's always beneficial. Boundaries are important. Pornography? Out of bounds. Absolutely not— it warps your brain, exploits others, and robs your soul. And compulsive masturbation that becomes an escape from stress, intimacy, or spiritual growth? That's bondage, not freedom.

Romans 14 helps us hold this tension. Paul tells us that in disputable matters—where Scripture is silent—we're called to live by faith, not fear. "Whatever does not proceed from faith is sin" (Romans 14:23). That means masturbation isn't universally right or wrong—it depends on your heart, your context, and your conscience.

Now, here's something most Christian women haven't heard enough: sexual self-awareness can actually strengthen your marriage. For many women raised with purity culture, who were told to shut down desire until their wedding day, connecting with their own bodies feels foreign or even scary. But gentle self-exploration—apart from shame, porn, or guilt—can help you discover what brings you pleasure, what helps you feel safe, and how your body responds. This is part of what sex therapists call "sensate focus"—and it's a beautiful way to bring more confidence and clarity into your sexual relationship with your husband.

Bottom line? Your body is not your enemy. Your pleasure is not a sin. And your sexuality is not a source of shame—it's a reflection of God's design, meant to be explored with wisdom, joy, and freedom.

So if you've ever asked, "Is it okay that I touched myself... and liked it?" Here's your answer:

You are not dirty.

You are not alone.

You are not outside of God's love.

Jesus isn't trying to catch you in sin. He's trying to call you into wholeness. Your body is a temple. And yes, God is okay with temples experiencing joy. That includes you.

Where to Start

Let's begin with a deep breath... and a sacred reminder: exploring your own body isn't a betrayal of your faith—it can actually be an act of worship. Yes, worship. That might sound strange, especially if you grew up in a church culture where the body felt more like a battleground than a blessing. But hear this, friend: the God who knit you together didn't stop at making you functional. He designed you with the capacity for delight.

Learning to experience sexual pleasure—including orgasm—isn't a departure from holiness. It's part of stewarding the good gift of your body. If you've never explored this part of yourself before, or you're not sure where to start, you are not alone. You're not behind. And you're not weird.

You're simply stepping into something new—and we're right here with you.

Step One: Creating a Sacred Context

Before you ever think about touching your clitoris, start by creating space. And not just physical space—though yes, you'll want privacy, comfort, and at least 30 uninterrupted minutes. But also emotional and spiritual space. Light a candle. Take a warm bath. Put on soft music. Pray. Breathe. Journal. Let this moment be one of intention, not impulse.

You're not "getting it over with." You're honoring your body with presence and care. The atmosphere you create matters—it signals to your nervous system that this is safe, sacred ground, not something rushed or hidden.

Step Two: Getting to Know Your Body

Begin with non-sexual touch. Slowly run your hands over your arms, your scalp, your legs. Linger at your neck and shoulders. What feels soft? Warm? Electric? For your first few sessions, stay here. This is about building trust between you and your body—showing your nervous system that touch can be both safe and pleasurable.

When that feels natural, let your hands explore your breasts, belly, and inner thighs. Let curiosity—not performance—be your guide. You're not trying to "achieve" anything. You're learning the language of sensation.

Step Three: Meeting Your Clitoris

Here's the headline: your clitoris is not a mistake. It's a divine design feature. It has one purpose: to bring pleasure. With over 10,000 nerve endings, it's more sensitive than any other part of your body—and it connects to a whole internal network of erectile tissue. In short, it's kind of amazing.

But take your time. Start with indirect attention. Breathe into your pelvic area. Rock your hips gently. Even just thinking about your clitoris or placing your hand over your pubic mound can help you become more attuned to what you feel. If grief or shame bubbles up here, that's okay. That's normal. And Jesus is with you in it.

Step Four: Indirect Stimulation

When you're ready (which might take days or even weeks—there's no rush), try these gentle warm-up movements:

- **Tug your labia:** Gently stretch the outer lips from side to side. This moves the skin around the clitoris and brings increased blood flow.

- **Palm pressure:** Cup your hand over your mons pubis (the soft mound above your vulva) and press upward gently.

- **Thumb press:** Place your thumbs on either side of your vulva and rock your hips into the pressure.

These movements are not meant to make you climax. They're meant to awaken awareness and curiosity without overwhelming your senses.

Step Five: Direct Clitoral Stimulation

Only when you're already feeling some pleasure—tingling, warmth, or subtle arousal—try moving to direct touch:

- Use one or two fingers to circle the clitoral hood (the skin that covers the glans).

- Try light back-and-forth strokes across the tip.

- Vary your speed and pressure, listening to how your body responds.

If your muscles tense, that's totally normal. If your brain starts to overthink, gently guide your attention back to sensation. This isn't a science experiment or a performance review. It's a sacred invitation.

Step Six: Using a Vibrator

Adding a vibrator can be incredibly helpful—especially if your fingers get tired, or you need consistent stimulation. Using a vibrator isn't "cheating" or unspiritual. It's a tool—like using a crockpot instead of cooking everything by hand.

Here's what to keep in mind:

- **Start small:** A simple bullet vibrator is great for beginners.

- **Use lube:** A water-based lubricant enhances comfort and pleasure.

- **Start slow:** Place the vibrator on your clitoral hood—not directly on the tip—and allow your body to warm up gradually.

Vibrators can help you learn what feels good, build confidence, and even break through shame-related tension.

Step Seven: Letting Orgasm Come (Literally)

Orgasm isn't something you force—it's something your body surrenders into when it feels safe, excited, and relaxed. You may feel tension building, muscles clenching, breath shortening. Let it come. Breathe into it. And if it doesn't happen? That's okay, too.

Pleasure is a win. Orgasm is not a test of worth. You're building trust with your body, and that takes time. Some women reach orgasm quickly. Others need practice. And others benefit from working with a NICC-trained therapist to address deeper emotional or spiritual blocks.

Wherever you are—there is no shame.

You are not performing.

You are not sinning.

You are learning to inhabit your body the way God designed you to—with dignity, delight, and joy.

Wrapping It Up

You've just taken a brave step—one that may have challenged long-held beliefs, stirred up old shame, or invited a new kind of curiosity. That's no small thing. In this chapter, we named a sacred truth: your body is not your enemy. It is not dirty. It's not something to hide or be afraid of. It is a masterpiece—crafted by a God who delights in delight.

We explored what Scripture *doesn't* say about masturbation and what Christian theology *does* affirm about your body and your freedom in Christ. We unpacked false guilt, reclaimed sexual self-exploration as a tool for healing and connection, and gave you a permission slip to learn how your body responds to pleasure—without shame, without fear, and with Jesus present in the process.

Now, we invite you to take this knowledge and actually *experience* it. Not as a checklist or a performance, but as an unfolding journey. Reflect: What did this chapter stir in you? What voices from your past still need to be replaced with the voice of truth and love? What does it feel like to imagine God smiling—not scowling—over your discovery of sexual joy?

Because friend, we're just getting started.

Up next, we're diving into your brain—your primary sex organ. We'll explore how your imagination and mental engagement shape everything from arousal to orgasm, and why sexual fantasy (yes, even that) can be a powerful, holy, and healing tool when used with wisdom. If that makes your eyebrows raise... perfect. We're going there together.

Let's turn the page.

Chapter 13: Imagine That

The Daydream That Got Away

Mallory was trying to pray. Really, she was.

She had her worship playlist on, her coffee in hand, her Bible open to Psalm something-or-other... but all she could think about was the way her husband looked this morning when he walked out of the shower in just that towel. The same towel he never actually hangs up. And the way his voice went all gravelly when he said, "See you tonight." Lord have mercy.

She shook her head and tried to refocus. "Be still and know..." she whispered, closing her eyes.

But instead of spiritual serenity, her brain delivered a mental movie reel that started with him kissing her neck and ended somewhere much steamier.

Her eyes popped open.

"Oh my gosh," she muttered, taking a gulp of coffee like it could baptize her from the inside out. "I'm basically trying to worship and fantasize at the same time. Jesus, are You even okay with this?"

The guilt crept in. That old tape—Don't think like that, don't feel like that, that's not holy... But underneath it all was a quiet question she couldn't shake: What if this part of me isn't bad?

What if my imagination is something God actually wants to redeem and use—for intimacy, for joy... even for arousal?

Mallory wasn't trying to become some sex-goddess prayer warrior. She just wanted to stop feeling like she had to shove her desire in a closet.

And maybe—just maybe—Jesus wasn't asking her to.

Try This at Home

Did you know that Jesus designed your imagination? Yep—your vivid, playful, sometimes awkward, occasionally steamy imagination. And He wired it so that when you think about sexy, connecting things, your body doesn't just sit quietly by. It perks up. Literally. That's not a bug in the system—it's one of God's brilliant features.

Here's the theological truth: You were never meant to be disjointed. God created you as an embodied soul—a full, whole person where your thoughts, feelings, body, and spirit all work together in harmony. That means your sexual experiences aren't just physical. They're emotional. They're spiritual. And they're deeply shaped by what happens between your ears.

Enter: your imagination.

Modern neuroscience confirms what the psalmists and prophets already understood—your brain has a powerful influence over your body. When you imagine a warm embrace from your husband, his breath on your neck, the way he looks at you when he wants you—your body can respond as if it's actually happening. Your heart rate rises. Your breath slows. Your pelvic floor muscles might even subtly activate. Why? Because the brain doesn't fully differentiate between lived experience and vividly imagined experience.

And guess what? That's sacred.

Using your imagination to build sexual anticipation with your husband isn't just "okay." It's a holy practice. It's pre-loading your nervous system for joy. It's choosing to dwell on what is good, lovely, and... well, hot (Philippians 4:8, slightly paraphrased).

If desire sometimes feels far away—which, let's be honest, happens for just about all of us at some point—your imagi-nation can serve as a bridge back to your own arousal. You don't have to sit and wait for the elusive "mood" to descend. You can gently pursue it. You can stoke the embers. You can imagine connection, closeness, and pleasure—and let those mental rehearsals awaken your body.

Try it sometime: picture a sweet or steamy scene with your husband. Imagine his touch, your laughter, the chemistry between you. Let yourself feel it in your body. Breathe it in. Let the corners of your mouth lift. Maybe even let out a sigh. Jesus isn't scandalized by that. He's the One who knit that erotic imagination into your brain.

And if you find your imagination feels rusty, blocked, or hi-jacked by shame, you're not alone. Many of us carry sto-ries—traumas, religious messages, awkward encounters—that have clouded this area. That doesn't mean you're bro-ken. It just means healing is needed. And healing is abso-lutely possible, especially with the help of a compassionate Christian therapist trained in sexual wholeness.

So yes, friend. You're allowed to fantasize. You're allowed to rehearse goodness in your mind and let your body follow. It's not dirty—it's devotional. You are fearfully, wonder-fully, and imaginatively made.

Taking Thoughts Captive (and Using Them on Purpose)

Let's pause for a quick Scripture break—2 Corinthians 10:5 says we're to *"take every thought captive to obey Christ."* If you grew up hearing that verse in youth group, it might've been used to shut down any "impure" thoughts like a holy buzzer on a game show. But that's not the full picture.

Taking thoughts captive doesn't mean slamming the door on your imagination. It means opening it to the *right things*—aligning your inner world with God's good design.

It's not about fear—it's about stewardship. Not every thought deserves free rent in your mind, especially ones that drag you toward shame, secrecy, or comparison. But thoughts that fan the flame of covenant love? That stir up desire for your spouse? That help you picture connection, confidence, or courageous intimacy?

Those are exactly the kind of thoughts you're meant to *keep*—to nurture, even.

By choosing to use your imagination in a way that enriches your marriage and honors God's design, you're not flirting with sin. You're practicing obedience. You're "taking captive" your thought life—not to shut it down, but to aim it toward life-giving, marriage-deepening joy.

Mental Practice

Talking about sexual fantasy might feel a little edgy, but it is actually packed with holy potential. Now, if you grew up in a Christian environment where "thought life" was strictly policed, even the idea of imagining something sexual might feel like tiptoeing through spiritual landmines. But take a breath—this is safe ground. You were created by a God who delights in your wholeness, not a God who flinches at your wiring.

Your imagination is not a problem to control—it's a gift to cultivate.

As long as your fantasies honor God's design for sex—that is, within a loving, monogamous marriage—you've been given tremendous freedom to explore. That means your mental playground is not off-limits. It's sacred territory. You're allowed to be curious. You're allowed to imagine good, thrilling, joy-filled things. Not only is it okay—it's wise.

Why? Because your imagination is like a rehearsal room for real life. It's where you get to safely explore different desires, try on new emotional tones, practice how you want to show up sexually—all without the pressure of performance or judgment. Whether you're engaging in solo touch, preparing your heart for connection, or just tuning into your inner world, fantasy is one of the most helpful tools you've got.

Here's where science meets Spirit: your brain is constantly shaping itself based on what you practice. This is the gift of neuroplasticity. When you imagine yourself confidently initiating sex, boldly wearing something spicy, or expressing pleasure without shame, you're not just pretending. You're literally building new neural pathways that make those experiences easier and more natural in real life.

So what does that look like? Try imagining:

- Yourself slipping into that little outfit you've stashed at the back of the drawer.

- A new position that's felt intimidating but intriguing.

- The bold initiation you've wanted to try—walking up to your husband, pulling him close, and letting him know with a look what you have in mind.

Picture it. Really let yourself feel it—what you're wearing, how he reacts, the warmth in your body, the courage in your chest. You're not being silly or sinful. You're partnering with the Holy Spirit to renew your mind and awaken your body to God's beautiful design.

And if shame tries to knock on the door? Remind it of this truth: Jesus is not scandalized by your imagination. He's the One who designed it to reflect the creativity, intimacy, and joy of His love. You are safe to imagine. You are safe to desire. You are safe to grow.

So dream boldly. Imagine freely. And keep using that beautiful mind of yours to cultivate a sex life full of confidence, connection, and pleasure.

More Leads to More

Yes, yes, yes—let's clear the air and speak some holy truth over your beautiful, God-designed sexuality.

Here's something you might not have heard in Sunday school (but definitely should have): when it comes to female desire, more leads to more. That's right—sexual desire grows not by ignoring it, but by engaging with it. Your desire isn't a fragile spark that needs to be coddled or stuffed away—it's a fire that grows stronger the more you tend to it.

This isn't selfish. It's not indulgent. It's how Jesus wired your brain and body.

Unlike the male sexual system, which typically needs a pause after orgasm (known as the refractory period), women don't have that built-in "time out." In fact, the female sexual system is incredibly resilient and responsive. The more positive sexual experiences you have—whether alone or with your husband—the more your body says, "Let's do that again." Your brain registers pleasure as a good thing worth repeating, which strengthens the desire pathways and makes it easier to get in the mood next time.

So let's paint a scene: you're curled up with a soft blanket and your favorite playlist, letting your imagination wander into a steamy, romantic vision of you and your husband. Maybe you're exploring your body, discovering what feels good, letting your arousal build. Maybe you even reach orgasm. That's not a betrayal of your husband. It's a gift to your whole marriage. You're nourishing your libido, resetting your stress levels, and creating a deeper emotional and physical openness.

You're priming your brain to associate sex with joy, safety, and connection.

And if in that moment you're feeling a little playful— maybe you snap a sexy photo, send a flirty text, or drop a teasing comment for later? Friend, that's not taking something away from your husband. That's inviting him into the glow of a desire you've been building. That's foreplay that starts hours—or even days—before the bedroom. That's holy flirtation.

So let's bust the myth that says if you enjoy sex "too much," you'll somehow lose control or go off the deep end. That's fear-based legalism, not gospel truth. You are not a danger to yourself or your marriage because you're tuning into your sexuality. You're stewarding one of God's most glorious gifts.

You can't over-sex yourself. You're not going to run out of desire by using it. You're feeding the system God designed to grow through joy, connection, and repetition. And when you do it with love and intentionality, it becomes something truly sacred.

So go ahead—fantasize about your husband, explore your body, pursue pleasure, and invite him in on the adventure. You're building momentum, confidence, and anticipation. And that's not just sexy—it's sanctified.

Wrapping It Up

You made it, friend—and what a chapter it's been! We've unpacked the beauty and power of your imagination as a God-given tool for desire, arousal, and holy exploration. We've named the truth: Jesus isn't shocked by your sexual thoughts. He designed your brain and body to work together in this beautifully integrated dance of intimacy. Your mind isn't the enemy—it's a playground where desire can be safely awakened, confidence can be rehearsed, and connection can be cultivated.

You've learned that fantasizing about your spouse is not just okay—it's sacred, sexy, and smart. You've seen how using your imagination can actually retrain your brain, making confidence and pleasure more accessible. And you've heard it loud and clear: the more you engage desire, the more it grows.

So take a breath. Reflect on what feels new, freeing, or even a little scary. Where did your imagination spark today? Where did shame try to creep in? Take those reflections to Jesus—He already knows, and He delights in walking with you through every part of your story, including this one.

And now, as we turn the page, it's time to talk about the grand finale of sexual pleasure—the one that gets all the headlines and giggles and myths. Yep, we're going there. In the next chapter, we're diving into orgasms: what they are, how they work, and how you can experience toe-curling, back-arching, soul-satisfying climax—solo and with your spouse.

Get ready. It's going to be fun.

Chapter 14: Oh, Oh, Oh, Omazing® !

Baking Soufflés and Chasing Fireworks

*L*ila stood in the bathroom, clutching a towel around her still-damp body and staring at herself in the mirror like she was hoping for a pep talk. Instead, her reflection just blinked back at her, looking slightly tired and 30% more confused than when she got into the shower.*

She had googled "how to know if you've had an orgasm" more times than she'd like to admit—usually late at night, quietly, while her husband snored beside her. And now here she was, half-wrapped in terry cloth and half-wrapped in self-doubt, trying to figure out if that thing she felt last Tuesday during "one of their better attempts" counted.

"I mean... I think something happened? Maybe? Possibly?" she muttered to herself. "There was definitely a moment... kind of... where I stopped thinking about the laundry."

She sighed. Not exactly toe-curling ecstasy.

It wasn't that her husband didn't care. Sam was kind and patient, and he genuinely wanted her to enjoy sex. But Lila often felt like she was trying to bake a soufflé with no recipe. One wrong move, and poof—the whole thing collapsed. And how do you even explain what's not happening when you're not sure what it's supposed to feel like?

She grabbed her phone and scrolled to a text from her best friend: "Don't stress. You're not broken. You're learning. Be kind to yourself." Ugh. Why was it easier to believe that for everyone else but not for herself?

Still, something in her chest softened. She wasn't alone. And maybe—just maybe—she could stop trying to force fireworks and start getting curious. What if it wasn't about performing, but about exploring? About being present instead of perfect?

Lila smiled at herself, just a little. She didn't have all the answers yet, but for the first time in a long time, she wasn't dreading the questions. She was kind of... intrigued.

Maybe this journey to pleasure was less like solving a puzzle and more like learning to dance—with herself, with her husband, and with the God who created it all.

The Big Sneeze

She could feel it building. Everything in her body tensed. Her breath shortened. Her toes curled. Her back arched. And then in one climactic, full-body release she let it out— "Ah, ah, ah... CHEWWW!"

Yep. A sneeze.

Not what you were expecting? That's exactly the point.

Because orgasms, like sneezes, are a reflex. They're not something you "make" happen by trying harder. They're something your body does when the right elements come together—intensity builds, your body crosses a threshold, and *boom*, you release.

If you've ever wondered, "Wait... have I even had one?"—you are *so* not alone. That question is more common than you think. And no, you're not broken. You're just beginning a journey of learning how your body, mind, and heart experience pleasure. Let's break it down.

So, What *Is* an Orgasm?

An orgasm is your body's involuntary response to prolonged sexual arousal and pleasure. It's not a test. It's not a goal. It's not even a gold star that proves you "did it right." It's a natural, whole-body reflex—kind of like laughing at something funny or crying at a heartfelt moment. It just *happens*.

But only when your body feels emotionally safe, physically relaxed, and sensually attuned.

In other words: you don't *work* for an orgasm. You *allow* it.

What Does It Feel Like?

Everyone's experience is a little different—but here are some common sensations:

- **Breath and heart rate increase**—sometimes you hold your breath without meaning to.
- **Muscle tension builds**—especially in your pelvic floor, legs, and core.
- **Then, rhythmic contractions**—typically every 0.8 seconds—move through the pelvic muscles.
- **You may feel waves of warmth or tingling**, followed by a deep release.
- **Emotionally**, you might feel giddy, peaceful, tender, teary, or just deeply relaxed.

Neuroscience tells us the brain lights up during orgasm with a cocktail of chemicals:

- **Dopamine**, the feel-good hormone
- **Oxytocin**, the bonding hormone
- **Endorphins**, which reduce pain and increase pleasure

This is not random. This is *design.* Jesus made your body to enjoy and benefit from pleasure. That's worth saying again—Jesus made your orgasm. Not the enemy. Not Cosmo. Not some self-help guru. Jesus.

"But I'm Not Sure If I've Ever Had One…"

That's okay. It doesn't mean anything's wrong with you. Orgasms don't always look like they do in the movies.

Maybe you haven't had one yet because:

- You've been focused on your spouse's pleasure more than your own.
- You were raised to think sex was for him—not for both of you.
- You're distracted or disconnected during intimacy.
- You haven't had the time or space to explore what feels good to you.

And here's the truth: orgasms vary. Some are tidal waves. Some are ripples. Some come fast. Some come slow. All of them are valid. And the more you practice noticing and enjoying the sensations in your body without pressure, the more easily they come.

Your orgasm is not a performance metric. It's a sacred signal from your body that you are safe, aroused, and fully alive in the moment.

So if you're still learning—or wondering where to even begin—just know: you're in the right place. You were fearfully and wonderfully made. And the journey toward Omazing® pleasure is holy ground.

The Clit Truth

Here's a little-known truth they definitely didn't teach in youth group: most women do *not* orgasm from intercourse alone.

And guess what? It's not a flaw in your body or your faith. It's just biology.

Research consistently shows that **70 to 90 percent of women require direct clitoral stimulation** to climax. That means intentional touch—rubbing, circling, pressure, or vibration—focused on the clitoris itself. Even women who *do* climax during intercourse? Most of the time, it's still the clitoris doing the heavy lifting—just getting stimulated indirectly because of how their pelvic nerves and anatomy are uniquely wired. Basically, intercourse may be part of the story, but it's almost always the clitoris that writes the big finale.

So, what does that mean for you?

It Means You Need to Befriend Your Clitoris

Let's break this down with some holy awe: God gave you a clitoris with one purpose and one purpose only—**pleasure**.

That's it. It's not for peeing. Not for birthing. Not even for cycling hormones. Its one sacred assignment is to bring delight. This tiny powerhouse holds over **10,000 nerve endings**—twice as many as the entire penis—and connects to a vast internal network of pleasure tissue. It's not a mistake. It's a miracle. And it's yours.

If you've been focusing only on intercourse and wondering why you're not getting the fireworks while your husband's show seems to start and end with ease, it might be time to reframe your definition of sex. Think of intercourse not as *the* main event, but as one *part* of a much bigger, more satisfying buffet. When you center sexual connection on shared pleasure—and honor the clitoris as a key player—everything starts to click. And *feel* a whole lot better. And honestly, it works better for both of you if you come first!

A Spiritual Reframe

Let's be clear: this isn't about being selfish or demanding. It's about stepping into the full beauty of mutual pleasure and connection that God *designed* for marriage.

The **Song of Songs** isn't a shy book—it's an intimate, poetic celebration of lovers enjoying one another with abandon, reverence, and joy. It's full of tender touches, longing glances, passionate delight—and zero shame.

When David wrote, "I praise you because I am fearfully and wonderfully made" (Psalm 139:14), that included your sexual wiring. Your capacity for pleasure isn't a loophole in God's plan—it's part of His intentional craftsmanship.

So, what do you do with that?

You explore. You laugh. You invite your husband into the journey with curiosity and grace. You turn down the volume on shame and crank up the volume on compassion, truth, and joy. And you remember: Jesus doesn't cringe at your pleasure. He created it.

So go ahead—get to know your clitoris. She's not the enemy of holiness; she's a friend of connection. She's a sacred little reminder that your delight matters deeply to the One who designed you.

Better With Practice

If you've ever felt like sex is more confusing than your Instant Pot settings—welcome. You're in good company.

Here's the truth most women don't hear often enough: **sexual enjoyment isn't just something that magically happens—it's something you learn**. Arousal, desire, and orgasm aren't lightning bolts from heaven. They're more like a warm oven. They take time, attention, and practice to heat up. And once you know how to work with your wiring, things start to sizzle.

That's why, for so many women, **sex gets better over time**. Not because their bodies change dramatically, but because they become more familiar with their rhythms, cues, and needs. They learn how to engage their imagination, how to communicate with their husbands, and how to lead their own arousal—mentally, emotionally, and physically.

And here's a liberating truth: **you don't need to wait for someone else to figure you out**. In fact, no one can. Not even your sweet, well-meaning husband. Especially not the overconfident ones who think they've got you "all figured out" (bless them). Women's sexual response isn't a lock-and-key system—it's a living, breathing dance that changes from day to day.

What felt incredible last week might fall flat tonight. What lit you up during your last cycle may not hit the same way this one. Hormones, stress, emotional connection, fatigue—it all plays a role. And that's okay. There's no formula because you're not a machine. You're a masterpiece.

So what's the key? **Learning to attune to your body in the moment.** Practicing arousal—not just physically, but mentally and spiritually. Paying attention to what your body is saying. Letting it lead. And then leading your husband in turn.

This is the heart of Omazing® sex. Not performance. Not perfection. **Presence**. That brave, curious willingness to listen, to explore, and to grow. Practice doesn't make perfect—but it *does* make pleasure more possible, more often, and more connected.

So keep showing up. Keep getting to know yourself. And remember: every time you practice tuning into your body, you're stepping closer to the kind of intimate, life-giving pleasure God created you for.

Orgasms Matter!

Let's clear something up right away: **you absolutely can enjoy sex without having an orgasm every time**. But if orgasms are rare or nonexistent for you, over time, that lack of fulfillment will likely start to chip away at your sexual desire—and eventually, your sex life.

Why? Because your brain, body, and nervous system are designed to crave what feels good and avoid what doesn't. If your sexual encounters consistently end without that delicious payoff, your system may quietly decide that sex isn't worth the effort. That's not brokenness—that's biology. God designed your pleasure to matter.

Now, let's take some pressure off your husband's shoulders. **It's not his job to "give" you an orgasm.** He's not the Orgasm Fairy. But it *is* his job to be a caring, invested teammate in your pleasure. Think of orgasm as a team sport—you both play a role. And your role? Learning how your own body works and advocating for what helps you thrive.

This isn't selfish. It's not indulgent. It's good stewardship—of your body, your sexuality, and your marriage. Pursuing orgasm is part of honoring the full experience God designed you to enjoy. So please, speak up. Lean in. Chase down your pleasure with holy boldness.

And trust us—**what's good for you is *very* good for your husband**. Nothing is more arousing to most men than watching their wife thoroughly enjoy herself. A highly aroused woman is intoxicating to a man. The entire pornography industry is (tragically) built on that reality. But you don't need fake scripts or filters. You have a God-designed body, an imagination, and the freedom to fully show up in your pleasure. That's better than any video— and it's real.

As you learn to build arousal in your body, to savor sensation, and to enjoy yourself with freedom, **you're going to blow his mind**. And not just because of what it does for him—but because of how it draws you both into deeper connection, confidence, and joy.

So go after your pleasure, friend. It's not just allowed—it's *essential*.

Wake the Neighbors

When sexual arousal gets intense—and especially when orgasm hits—it's totally natural to vocalize. Moaning, gasping, calling out your husband's name... even a good old-fashioned shout. And guess what? That's not only okay— it's **amazing**. Your husband isn't turned off by your pleasure—he's *wildly* turned on by it.

In fact, hearing and seeing you enjoy yourself is one of the most powerful accelerators for male arousal. Your expressions of pleasure are like fuel to the fire. The more uninhibited you are, the more connected he feels, and the more arousal builds for you both. Sexual expressiveness isn't about putting on a performance—it's about allowing your-self to be fully present and fully alive in your body.

Now, let's be real: if you're used to staying quiet or you've internalized messages that sex should be modest and si-lent, this might feel *super awkward* at first. That's normal. Most women feel a little silly the first time they try moan-ing or letting loose vocally. But don't let that initial discom-fort keep you from the freedom and intensity that lies on the other side of inhibition.

Worried about thin walls or curious kids? No problem. **Get creative.** Grab a sound machine. Crank up the playlist. Put a pillow under the door or pick a time when you've got the house to yourselves. You don't need to shout from the roof-tops (unless you want to!), but do whatever you need to cre-ate a space where you feel safe enough to let go.

As you give yourself permission to express your pleasure, your body will respond. You'll find that orgasms come more easily, arousal builds more quickly, and connection deepens. Because when you're not busy holding back, your whole self gets to show up.

So go ahead—wake the neighbors. Or at least make them wonder what's got you so radiant and relaxed the next day.

Self-Exploration & Fantasy: Your Orgasm Gym

If orgasms had a gym membership, self-exploration and fantasy would be the personal trainers. That's why we cov-ered them in the chapters leading up to this one—because these aren't side topics or optional extras. They're the core workouts that build your orgasmic strength and sexual confidence.

Like with any muscle, practice leads to progress. The more you engage your imagination and your body in safe, pleasure-centered ways, the more those neural pathways get reinforced. Your brain starts to say, "Oh, this is good. This is safe. Let's do more of that." Over time, arousal builds faster, orgasms come more easily, and desire flows more freely.

This isn't about trying harder or striving to "achieve" something. It's about tuning into your body, awakening your God-designed pleasure potential, and learning what feels good to *you*. There's no magic pill. No five-minute fix. Just steady, playful practice that leads to breakthrough. The more you explore—without shame, without pressure—the more confident you become. And confident women? They radiate sexiness, inside and out.

So get in the gym, friend. Explore your body. Feed your imagination. Let it be fun, sacred, and full of discovery. You're not just working out—you're working toward Omazing®.

Sexy Toys: Not a Crutch—Just a Great Tool

Imagine someone with blurry vision saying, "I don't want to wear glasses—that would mean I'm weak." Or someone cooking over an open flame every night insisting that air fryers are cheating. Sounds a little ridiculous, right?

And yet... when it comes to vibrators and other sex toys, some people still carry that mindset. "It's a crutch." "It's not natural." "It's just for people who can't do it the 'real' way." Friend, that's nonsense.

Using a vibrator isn't lazy. It's not a shortcut. It's just a tool—like eyeglasses, like a blender, like indoor plumbing. It enhances what's already good and can make things more enjoyable, efficient, and customized to your needs. And you get to decide what works best for *you*.

Let's say it clearly: there is *zero* shame in using toys as part of your sexual experience. Whether you're exploring solo or spicing things up with your husband, toys can help awaken pleasure, increase orgasmic potential, and build sexual confidence. That's not a detour from intimacy—that's leaning into it.

Sure, some men might initially feel unsure. There's a myth floating around that if a woman enjoys a toy, it must mean her man isn't "enough." That's a lie. In truth, most husbands quickly become fans once they see their wife radiating pleasure and joy. One playful, buzzy welcome later, and they're asking, "Where can we get another one?"

As always, keep the core values in mind: Consensual. Monogamous. Mutually fun. If what you're exploring meets those criteria, it's on the table—vibrators, dildos, remote controls, you name it. Don't want to use toys? Totally fine. Curious and ready to try? Go for it. Your bedroom is not a courtroom. It's a playground for delight.

And if your curiosity leans a little kinky—say, handcuffs or a playful spanking—we'll get into all of that in the "Kinky?" chapter. Promise.

Bottom line? Use the tools that serve your desire, deepen your connection, and bring pleasure. That's not cheating—it's creative, courageous intimacy.

Squirting

Let's talk about female squirting during orgasm—something that's often shrouded in mystery, misunderstood, or even met with shame. So first things first: yes, it's real, and no, it's not "just pee." While there's some overlap with the urethra (the same pathway urine travels), what many women experience as squirting or "gushing" is actually fluid released from the Skene's glands—sometimes called the "female prostate." During intense arousal or orgasm, especially with G-spot stimulation (which is often accessed during oral sex with fingers involved), some women expel this fluid involuntarily. It's a normal, healthy response for some—though not all—women.

Here's the freeing truth: squirting doesn't mean something's wrong, dirty, or even that you're "too much." It means your body is responding in a way God designed. Remember, God made pleasure—not just for procreation, but for bonding, delight, and joy in marriage (Song of Songs is a whole book about that!). And neuroscience tells us that when we feel safe, connected, and relaxed, our bodies are more likely to respond with deeper pleasure and release. So whether you've experienced squirting or not, know this: you're not broken either way. There's no "right" way to orgasm. If this is part of your story, it's nothing to hide, be embarrassed about, or to envy. It's one of the many beautiful varieties God designed bodies to respond to love, connection, and delight with.

Help Is Available

If you're trying all the things—practicing, exploring, fantasizing, using your voice, and still finding that orgasm feels just out of reach—don't panic. And definitely don't give up. You're not broken. You're not failing. You're just hitting a roadblock, and that's normal.

Good news: help is absolutely available. A skilled sex therapist, especially one trained in Neuroscience Informed Christian Counseling®, can walk with you to uncover what might be getting in the way. It could be physical tension, emotional blocks, past trauma, subconscious associations, or something else entirely. But whatever it is, it's figure-out-able.

You don't have to stay stuck in frustration or confusion. Whether it's your first orgasm or your first in a long time, whether you're looking to deepen intimacy or heal through difficulty, a trusted Christian sex therapist can help you develop a customized plan to get you where you want to go. They've walked this road with many women before you—and they'll help you get to your Omazing® destination with compassion, grace, and practical tools.

You deserve support. And it's okay to ask for it.

Wrapping It Up: From "Maybe Someday" to Omazing® Today

Friend, you've just taken a deep dive into one of the most beautiful—and misunderstood—aspects of female sexuality: the orgasm. And here's what we hope is sinking in loud and clear:

Orgasms are not performance goals. They are God-designed, body-blessing, spirit-cheering gifts of pleasure. They're not proof of your worth or your holiness. They're just good. Really good. And worth pursuing—not out of pressure, but out of joy.

You've learned that:

- Orgasms are reflexes, not checklists. You don't force them—you cultivate space for them to unfold.

- The clitoris is the VIP of female pleasure, and it deserves your attention.

- Practice—through touch, imagination, self-exploration, and communication—is what builds arousal and confidence.

- Pleasure is holy. Your desire matters. And your delight is not selfish—it's sacred.

- Toys, sounds, movement, imagination, laughter, and curiosity all belong in the bedroom (and beyond!).

- Help is available. And it's okay to ask for it.

So here's your invitation: reflect on what most resonated in this chapter. What feels new? What feels exciting? What feels a little intimidating? Then ask Jesus to walk with you into more freedom, more confidence, and yes—more Omazing® orgasms.

Next up, we're zooming in on a topic that can bring both giggles and blushes: oral sex. What does it mean to give and receive joyfully, without shame or pressure? How do we make it fun, safe, holy, and hot?

Let's go there. With love. With honesty. With freedom.

Chapter 15: Tongues of Fire

"Fruit of the Spirit...?"

*E*rin was pretty sure Song of Songs was never read out loud in her youth group. And definitely not the "his fruit was sweet to my taste" part.

She sat cross-legged on her unmade bed, laundry in semi-folded piles around her, laptop open to a Google search she immediately regretted: Christian wife oral sex help. The browser pinged back with a mix of medical articles, sketchy advice columns, and one particularly enthusiastic blog that made her feel like she needed to both light a candle and repent.

She sighed, flopped back, and stared at the ceiling. "Lord," she muttered, "You turned water into wine. Could You maybe turn this awkward panic into something remotely sexy?"

It wasn't that Erin didn't want to try. She adored James—her good-hearted, kind-eyed husband of seven years. He'd never pressured her, never made her feel less-than. But the whole idea of oral sex? It lived in this murky soup of Christian modesty, middle school shame, and mental checklists about cleanliness, technique, and oh-my-gosh-what-do-I-do-with-my-hands.

She'd joked with her best friend at Bible study last week: "You think 'tongues of fire' was about the Holy Spirit or foreplay?" They'd laughed until someone walked by and gave them a Look.

But now, curled in her worn sweatshirt and mismatched socks, the question didn't feel so funny. It felt real. Could this—this vulnerable, foreign, slightly terrifying thing—actually be holy? Could it be good? Could it be something she might enjoy, not just endure?

A tiny hope flickered. Maybe it didn't have to be perfect. Maybe it could be playful. Even sacred.

She sat up, tossed a baby sock onto the "clean-ish" pile, and reached for her journal. "God," she wrote, "help me be brave enough to explore something good."

Blow Jobs in the Bible

Let's just name it—most of us didn't grow up hearing sermons about oral sex in Sunday school. But tucked right into the pages of God's inspired love poetry, you'll find something that might just surprise you: oral sex. Yes, really.

The Song of Songs is more than just romantic—it's richly sensual. It doesn't shy away from desire; it celebrates it. In Song of Songs 2:3, the bride says, *"I sat down under his shadow with great delight, and his fruit was sweet to my taste."* That's not just a picnic under a fig tree, friend. This vivid metaphor has long been understood by biblical scholars as a poetic nod to a wife pleasuring her husband orally. The imagery is lush, evocative, and undeniably intimate.

And it's not just the man being adored. Flip to Song of Songs 4:16 and you'll find the bride boldly inviting her beloved: *"Awake, north wind, and come, south wind! Blow on my garden, that its fragrance may spread everywhere. Let my beloved come into his garden and taste its choice fruits."* Her "garden"? It's her body. Her "fragrance" and "choice fruits"? A poetic invitation to oral delight. And in the very next breath, her husband responds: *"I have come into my garden... I have eaten my honeycomb and my honey, I have drunk my wine and my milk"* (5:1). That's not duty. That's delight.

This back-and-forth of desire is not crass—it's sacred. God didn't skip over the sensual when inspiring Scripture. He included it. These verses give us a picture of mutual pleasure, free from shame and full of love. When oral sex happens in a context that's consensual, monogamous, and mutually enjoyable, it's not only okay—it's celebrated.

So, if shame or hesitation has you wondering whether oral sex is "Christian enough," let this be a gentle nudge: you're not stepping outside God's will by wanting to explore this kind of connection. You're walking right into the garden He designed for you and your spouse to enjoy together.

You're not dirty. You're not weird. You're beautifully made for delight. And the same God who designed your body designed it with this kind of intimacy in mind. Let's celebrate that.

The Joy of Giving

Let's start with this liberating truth: God designed sex to be good—really good—for both of you. That includes oral sex. And that means giving it isn't about pressure, performance, or pretending to be someone you're not. It's about presence—being fully there, body and soul, in a moment of shared delight with your husband.

For many women, oral sex can feel like a tightrope walk between two extremes. On one side, there's the cultural pressure to perform like you're in a steamy scene from a movie. On the other, there's the quiet whisper from past church messages that even *talking* about this kind of intimacy might be too much. But here's the good news: you don't have to choose between shame and performance. There's a beautiful, sacred middle way—and it's paved with joy.

This chapter isn't a rulebook—it's more like a treasure map. We're inviting you to explore curiosity, connection, and confidence as you grow in giving (and receiving) oral pleasure in your marriage. It's not just about technique (though we'll absolutely give you some practical tips). It's about intimacy. Real, soul-deep intimacy—emotional, spiritual, and yes, physical.

Because giving pleasure isn't just a skill. It's a language. A love language that speaks through touch and taste, through eye contact and laughter, through trust and vulnerability. You're not just using your mouth—you're bringing your whole self to the moment. And that's what makes it Omazing®.

From a neuroscience perspective, pleasure isn't just physical—it's profoundly relational. Your brain lights up with bonding hormones (like oxytocin and dopamine) when you feel emotionally safe and connected. When oral sex happens in a setting of trust, kindness, and mutual joy, it actually deepens that sense of safety and connection. It's not about performing a task—it's about enjoying a gift. Together.

And biblically? You're in solid, sacred company. The Song of Songs is overflowing with unashamed erotic joy. It doesn't tiptoe around passion—it revels in it. Proverbs 5:18-19 celebrates a husband's delight in his wife's body, and we can confidently infer that the invitation to be delighted in goes both ways. God didn't blush when He designed the mechanics of oral pleasure. He called it good.

So as we move into the how-to's and holy whys, let this be your anchor: this is not about becoming a different person.

It's about becoming more *you*—a woman fully alive, connected, confident, and free to love and be loved with joy.

Ready to take the next step? Let's keep going.

The Foundation: Building Trust, Safety, and Sacred Space

Before we dive into techniques or tantalizing tips, we need to start with something more foundational: trust.

You could be a certified oral sex ninja (if there were such a title), but without emotional safety and mutual respect, it's like trying to play a love song on a piano that's completely out of tune. True pleasure—the deep, connected kind that leaves you both feeling seen, secure, and satisfied—doesn't start with your hands or your mouth. It begins in your nervous system, in the quiet knowing that you're safe, wanted, and welcomed. That's the real secret to Omazing® intimacy.

This section is about laying that foundation. Because while hot is great, holy is better—and they're not mutually exclusive. We're talking about the kind of intimacy that strengthens your marriage, ignites your desire, and nourishes your souls.

The Language of Desire: Starting the Conversation

How you talk about oral sex matters just as much as how you do it. These conversations set the emotional temperature for your experiences together. If the vibe is curious, kind, and connected, you're already halfway to a great time.

Think of it like setting a table for a sacred meal. It's not, "Can you do this for me?" but, "How would it feel to explore this together?" That one little shift transforms the conversation from a favor to an invitation—a mutual journey.

Try leading with affirmation: "I love how close I feel when we're being playful like that. I've been thinking about how oral sex could be something really special for us—what are your thoughts?" This kind of tone opens doors, not defenses.

And when he shares—especially if he's nervous or uncertain—don't rush to correct or convince. Just listen. Holding space for his honesty, even if it doesn't match your expectations, builds the kind of trust that leads to deeper, more fulfilling experiences later on.

Enthusiastic Consent: A Continuous "Yes"

God never designed sex to be an obligation. The most satisfying intimacy comes from enthusiastic, ongoing consent—a living, breathing "yes" that can shift and evolve moment to moment.

This doesn't mean pausing every five seconds for a verbal check-in (though there's nothing wrong with that!). It means cultivating a dynamic of attuned presence. Little phrases like "Do you like that?" or "Is this still good for you?" aren't interruptions—they're extensions of your care.

This kind of mindful communication doesn't kill the mood; it deepens it. It tells your husband, "I see you. I care how this feels for you." That awareness is powerful—and wildly sexy.

Consent also means being willing to stop if something isn't working. No pouting, no pressure. That level of mutual respect creates safety, and safety is the bedrock of pleasure.

Reading the Signs: The Power of Non-Verbal Communication

You don't need a master's degree in body language—just some mindful attention. His body will tell you a lot if you're watching for it.

Positive signs? Rhythmic movement, moans, pelvic engagement, that hungry-leaning-in vibe. Signs of discomfort? Sudden stillness, tension, pulling away, or quietness that feels disconnected.

And then there's eye contact. Whew. That's not just hot—it's holy. When you look up at him while you're giving pleasure, it can create this electric moment of connection that goes way beyond technique. He sees your desire. You see his delight. That bridge between your eyes? Pure gold.

And don't be afraid to express your enjoyment. Your sounds—soft sighs, playful giggles, or humming around him—can reassure your husband that you're not just going through the motions. You're savoring the moment.

Setting the Scene: Creating a Sanctuary for Pleasure

Crafting a sensual atmosphere isn't about being impressive—it's about being intentional. A thoughtful environment communicates, "You're safe. You're special. This matters."

Here are a few simple ways to elevate the vibe:

- **Lighting:** Go for a warm, gentle glow. Candles, fairy lights, or even a dimmed bedside lamp can create a cozy, romantic feel.

- **Scent:** Use subtle essential oils or a favorite perfume. Scents like sandalwood, jasmine, or lavender can set a relaxing, sensual tone.

- **Sound:** Curate a playlist with slow, sultry songs or soft instrumental tracks. Music can help your brain shift from to-do lists to desire.

- **Texture:** Think cozy robes, soft blankets, or silky sheets. Sensuality starts long before genitals are involved—it's a full-body experience.

You're not trying to recreate a movie scene. You're creating a sacred space—one that allows you both to feel safe, centered, and free to explore with joy.

Hygiene Best Practices: Before and After

Let's talk about hygiene—not because we're afraid of germs, but because we're big fans of honor.

Thoughtful, intentional hygiene isn't just about fresh breath or avoiding awkward odors (although, let's be honest, that's a nice bonus). It's about creating a context of care. When you take time to tend to your body, you're saying to your spouse, "You matter. This moment matters." It's not about shame or pressure—it's about love that shows up prepared.

Think of it like setting the table for a special dinner. You don't use chipped plates or a crusty fork. You set the mood, light a candle, and make it beautiful. Not because the meal isn't delicious on its own, but because presentation adds to the experience. The same is true here.

Before: A Little Prep Goes a Long Way

A quick rinse or shower before oral intimacy is one of the simplest ways to make both partners feel confident, relaxed, and ready. It's not just hygienic—it's genuinely sexy. That moment of preparation can become a shared ritual, a playful part of your foreplay. You're not just getting clean; you're getting close.

Use warm water and a gentle, unscented soap to cleanse your genital area. Skip the perfumed sprays, douches, or harsh scrubs. They can irritate your skin and mess with your body's natural balance. You don't need to smell like a cupcake. You just need to be clean and present.

And hey, if you want to level it up, consider showering together. It's a sensual way to ease into the moment, with touch, teasing, and shared intention.

The "No Brushing" Rule: Protecting Your Mouth Matters

Okay, here's a fun fact that might blow your mind: brushing your teeth right before or right after oral sex? Not the best idea.

Your gums are lined with tiny blood vessels and serve as part of your body's immune defense system. Brushing or flossing—even gently—creates tiny micro-tears in that tissue. During oral sex, those little openings can make it easier for bacteria or viruses to enter your bloodstream. It's not something to panic about—but it is something to be wise about.

So instead of brushing beforehand, rinse your mouth with water or use an alcohol-based mouthwash. If you're concerned about breath, sugar-free gum or a mint can freshen things up without damaging that protective barrier.

This small shift protects your health without sacrificing intimacy. And it makes the whole experience more relaxed and guilt-free.

After: Rinse, Don't Scrub

Once the fun is done, keep it simple. For the giver, rinse your mouth with water or a gentle mouthwash—but avoid brushing for at least 30 minutes to allow your gum tissue time to recover. Your mouth knows how to bounce back—just give it the grace to do so.

For the receiver, a quick rinse with warm water and a mild soap is plenty. No need for scented wipes or complex routines. Just basic, kind, respectful care.

Why does all this matter? Because when you and your spouse both feel clean, respected, and confident in your bodies, it frees up emotional space. No distractions. No awkwardness. Just presence, playfulness, and the ability to fully enjoy each other.

Clean isn't just about hygiene—it's about love expressed through care.

Understanding His Body

If you want to give great oral sex, it helps to know what you're working with—not just the landscape of your husband's body, but the emotional terrain that shapes his experience of pleasure. This section is your guided tour: not just in how to touch, but why your touch matters so deeply.

God designed your husband's body to respond to pleasure. That's not an accident—it's a gift. But pleasure, especially in the context of marriage, is never just physical. It's personal. It's relational. And it's sacred. Which is why we're not just going to skim the surface with technique—we're diving into the heart of it all.

The Anatomy of Pleasure: A Guided Tour

The penis isn't a one-size-fits-all pleasure button. It's a symphony of sensitive areas, each with its own preferences. Think of it like a musical instrument. You're not pounding out a drum solo—you're playing a love song, one note at a time. The more you understand the "keys," the more confidently and creatively you'll play.

Here's a gentle breakdown:

- **Glans (Tip)**

  The head of the penis is highly concentrated with nerve endings and often the most sensitive area. Soft kisses, tongue swirls around the corona (the ridge), and light suction can send powerful signals of pleasure. Think finesse, not force.

- **Frenulum**

  That little V-shaped band underneath the head? It's a secret weapon of pleasure. Gently flicking, tracing, or focusing suction here can be incredibly stimulating. It's often key to climax.

- **Shaft**

  While not as sensitive as the tip, the shaft still loves rhythmic, consistent touch. Your hand, your mouth, or both together can create a seamless sensation that builds arousal steadily. Play with pressure, speed, and pattern.

- **Scrotum & Testicles**

  These are tender—literally. Gentle cupping, light licking, or even just warm hands can make this area feel safe and honored. The trick here is attentiveness. Every man's preferences vary, and they can even change moment to moment.

- **Perineum**

This is the space between the scrotum and the anus. It's connected to the same internal nerve system as the prostate, and gentle pressure here (using a thumb, palm, or heel of the hand) can deepen arousal in a subtle, powerful way.

Knowing these areas gives you options. You're not following a formula—you're in a fluid dance, responding to his body's feedback, discovering what delights him in real time.

The Science of Arousal: What's Happening Inside

While you're doing your thing on the outside, something beautiful is happening on the inside. It starts in his brain—when he sees you, hears you, feels your closeness, his limbic system lights up. That's the emotional center of the brain, and it sends out dopamine (which fuels desire) and testosterone (which helps ready his body for physical intimacy).

These brain signals activate the parasympathetic nervous system—the "rest and receive" mode. It's his body's way of saying, "I'm safe. I'm wanted." Blood flow increases, and his body responds with an erection. But this isn't just a physiological reflex—it's an emotional green light. His body is saying yes to connection.

You're not just stimulating arousal—you're helping him feel emotionally grounded, valued, and known.

The Psychology of Pleasure: Why Your Joy Matters

Here's the part that often gets overlooked: how your husband experiences oral sex has just as much to do with your presence as your technique.

When you show up with joy, curiosity, and delight—not dread or duty—something sacred happens. He doesn't just feel good physically. He feels seen. Chosen. Celebrated.

Many men carry silent insecurities about their bodies or fear they're "too much." When you approach him with enthusiasm, it's healing. It's intimate. It tells him, "You're safe with me. You're wanted here."

Your eye contact? Magnetic. Your voice? Powerful. Your pleasure? Contagious. A relaxed, confident wife sends her husband the clearest message of all: this is good. You are good.

When oral sex becomes a moment of shared joy—not a favor, not a performance, but a real experience of delight—it transforms everything. The more you enjoy giving, the more he enjoys receiving. And the beauty? That feedback loop heightens your own pleasure and confidence, too.

The Beginner's Guide

Let's just go ahead and name it: trying something new in the bedroom can feel both thrilling and terrifying. Especially if oral sex has long lived in the "taboo" column or come with unspoken pressure. Maybe you're wondering, *Am I doing this right? Is it even okay to enjoy this? What if I look ridiculous?*

Take a deep breath, friend. This is your safe, shame-free space to learn and explore. No judgment. No performance pressure. Just loving guidance and grace.

This chapter isn't about achieving a gold-medal routine or mimicking what you've seen in media (which, let's be honest, often leaves out real connection anyway). This is about helping you build confidence, practice techniques that actually work, and enjoy the process with your whole heart—and your whole body.

Positions for Comfort and Connection

Let's start here: *comfort is sexy*. If you're straining your neck, cramping your hips, or worried about falling off the bed, it's going to be hard to stay present.

The right position supports not just physical ease but emotional safety. It helps you relax, feel in control, and stay connected.

Here are a few beginner-friendly setups to experiment with:

- **Him on His Back**

  The classic. He lies down while you kneel, sit, or lie between his legs. This offers great visibility and control. If he props his knees or rests his feet on your shoulders, you get better access and he gets extra stimulation.

- **Edge of the Bed**

  He lies with his hips at the edge, while you kneel on a pillow or soft rug. It's great for long sessions with minimal strain on your body.

- **Side-Lying**

  Both of you on your sides (spooning or facing opposite directions). It's cozy, gentle, and takes pressure off your arms and neck.

- **69 Position**

  A more advanced move where you both give and receive at the same time. It's intense and deeply intimate, but can be tricky at first—start slow and communicate often.

Play with positioning. Adjust as needed. Feeling comfortable isn't cheating—it's wisdom.

The Warm-Up: The Art of Anticipation

God designed our brains to *love* anticipation—it's part of how He wired sexual arousal. So don't rush to the main event. Build tension. Create delight.

- **Start Slow and Away**

  Begin by kissing his chest, belly, thighs. Linger. This builds arousal like a slow-burning fire, rather than a quick spark.

- **Over-the-Pants Teasing**

  Yes, it's a real thing. Let your lips, breath, and tongue flirt through fabric. The added texture adds mystery and heat.

- **Use Your Breath**

  Hover your mouth over him and let your breath dance on his skin. Warm air, cool moments—it's delicious anticipation.

These small moments send his brain this message: *I'm wanted. I'm safe. I'm loved.*

Hands Matter: The Secret Superpower

Here's the truth: oral sex isn't just about your mouth. Your hands are co-stars in this scene.

- **Add Rhythm**

  Use your hand to stroke the shaft while your mouth focuses on the tip—or alternate using your hand and mouth to give yourself a breather while keeping pleasure going.

- **Touch Beyond the Obvious**

  Gently cradle his testicles, run your hands along his thighs, press into his hips. Every touch adds layers of intimacy.

- **Perineum Magic**

  That soft spot between the testicles and the anus? Apply firm, steady pressure with your fingers or palm—it can create deep, almost full-body pleasure.

Think of your hands as guides, grounding you in connection and keeping you both relaxed and responsive.

Foundational Techniques: Your Oral Toolkit

Ready to put it all together? Here's a gentle guide to some beginner-friendly techniques. No rush. No pressure. Just curiosity and connection.

- **Start Soft**

  Begin with slow, tender movements. This is a warm-up, not a sprint.

- **Protect Your Teeth**

  Form a soft "O" with your lips and tuck them over your teeth slightly. This cushions him and keeps things comfortable.

- **Lollipop Lick**

  Use the flat of your tongue to slowly slide along the shaft, top to base. Steady and simple is often super effective.

- **Swirl the Head**

Focus on the glans (tip). Circle it slowly with your tongue, especially around the corona (the ridge). It's a sweet spot.

- **Frenulum Flick**

  This little underside groove is extra sensitive. Try light, quick flicks or focused suction here. Pay attention to his reactions—he'll let you know what he loves.

Above all? Don't forget to breathe, smile, and *enjoy* him. This isn't about checking boxes—it's about sharing something sacred. Every sigh, every look, every new discovery is a way to say, *I see you, I choose you, I love this with you.*

Advancing Your Skills

Once you've found your groove with the basics, oral sex can become a creative and deeply connected playground—a space of delight, discovery, and intimacy that grows with time and trust. This next stage isn't about pressure to perform or impress. It's about layering in nuance, curiosity, and confidence.

Think of it like learning to play an instrument. You already know the melody—now you're adding harmony and rhythm, not because you *have* to, but because you *get* to. These are not "must-dos" but "might-enjoys." Every technique is an invitation, not an obligation.

Mastering Rhythm and Pace: Conducting Arousal

Arousal, like music, thrives on dynamics. Fast and loud is exciting—for a bit. But if there's no variation, it becomes noise. The real magic? It happens in the build.

- **Mix It Up**

Vary your pace and pressure. Move between slow, teasing licks and firm, rhythmic strokes. Alternate hand and mouth patterns. Each shift creates novelty, and novelty intensifies pleasure.

- **Follow His Lead**

   His breathing, his moans, the tension in his thighs— all of it tells you something. If he's getting close, you get to decide: back off to stretch the moment or lean in to finish strong.

- **The Build-Up Curve**

   Start soft. Slow. Let tension grow gradually. The closer he gets to climax, the more consistent your movements should become. That steady rhythm near the end? It's like riding a wave all the way in.

Temperature Play: A Sensory Surprise

Want to surprise his senses in the best way? Try introducing safe temperature play.

- **Cool Contrast**

   Take a sip of a cold drink, or let an ice cube melt slightly in your mouth. Then—go in. The temperature contrast between cool lips and his warm skin? Fireworks.

- **Warm Tease**

   Hover your lips and blow softly across his skin before touching it. It's subtle, sensual, and heightens anticipation.

Important note: No candles, no wax, and no extremes. Stick to safe, body-friendly temperatures that spark pleasure, not pain.

Teeth—Used Wisely and Gently

Okay, this one sounds daring—but hear us out.

Some men enjoy the contrast of a little texture—a barely-there scrape of teeth followed by a soothing sweep of the tongue. It's not biting (please don't bite), and it's not for everyone, but for the curious and communicative, it can add a surprising twist.

- **How to Try It**

  Lightly draw your front teeth along the shaft, then immediately follow with your tongue. Think "curious kitten," not "chewing toy."

- **Ask Before You Explore**

  Try, "I read about a technique that adds just a little texture using teeth—would you be open to experimenting with that sometime?" That conversation, by itself, builds connection.

Deep Throating: Optional, Not Required

Let's get this out of the way: deep throating is *not* the gold standard of oral sex. It's just one option. If it interests you, great. If not, you're still an amazing lover.

- **Focus on Relaxation**

  Success isn't about "pushing through." It's about staying relaxed and breathing deeply through your nose. The calmer you are, the more control you'll have.

- **Use Empowering Positions**

  You should be in charge of depth and speed. Try kneeling while he lies down, so you can adjust at your own pace. Avoid standing/thrusting setups, especially when starting out.

- **Take Your Time**

  This is a learned skill, not an all-or-nothing move. Explore it gently, if and when it feels right. Your comfort and curiosity are more important than any technique.

Every one of these ideas is a tool you can pick up—or leave on the table. The real "advance" in advanced oral sex? It's not about daring moves. It's about deeper presence. Sharper attunement. Greater joy.

You're not just becoming more skillful—you're becoming more connected.

Overcoming Common Hurdles

Even with growing confidence and the best of intentions, it's totally normal to run into a few speed bumps on the road to Omazing® oral intimacy. Things like jaw fatigue, gag reflexes, awkward positioning, or that all-too-familiar inner critic whispering, *"Am I doing this right?"*—these aren't signs that you're failing. They're just signs that you're human.

The good news? Every one of these common challenges has a workaround. This section is here to help you face those moments with compassion, curiosity, and grace. You're not broken, you're learning. And this kind of learning? It's sacred work.

Managing the Gag Reflex: Finding Comfort and Control

Let's start with a common concern: the gag reflex.

This reflex is part of your body's natural defense system—
an automatic way to protect your airway. But when it kicks
in at the wrong time (say, when you're trying to lovingly
connect with your husband's body), it can feel frustrating
and even discouraging.

Here's the hope: with gentle practice and a few clever hacks,
you can train your body to feel more relaxed and in control.

Quick Fixes (In-the-Moment Tools):

- **Thumb Squeeze:** Make a fist with your left hand and
  tuck your thumb inside. Squeeze. It sounds odd, but
  this acupressure technique can distract your nervous system just enough to help minimize the gag reflex.

- **Salt on the Tongue:** Place a tiny pinch of salt on the
  tip of your tongue. The sudden sensory input can redirect your brain's attention and soften the reflex.

- **Throat-Numbing Spray:** A quick spritz of over-the-
  counter throat spray (used for sore throats) can dull
  the area just enough to reduce sensitivity. Use spar-
  ingly—numbness isn't the goal, relaxation is.

Desensitization Techniques (Long-Term Help):

- **Toothbrush Training:** Use a soft toothbrush to gently brush the back of your tongue, gradually working
  your way further as your comfort grows. Daily practice for just 10–15 seconds can retrain your reflex
  over time.

Mind-Body Grounding Tools:

- **Deep Nasal Breathing:** Breathe in through your nose,
  slow and steady. This calms your nervous system
  and helps your throat stay relaxed.

- **Humming:** Yep, hum. It keeps your throat muscles engaged in a controlled way and offers pleasant vibrations for your partner, too. Win-win.

Preventing Jaw Fatigue: Giving Without Strain

If your jaw has ever felt sore after oral sex, you are definitely not alone. Great intimacy shouldn't come at the cost of physical discomfort. These practical tips will help you build stamina and reduce strain:

- **Alternate Mouth and Hands:** Let your hands take over periodically while your mouth rests. You're not taking a break—you're being smart. This combo is often even more pleasurable for your husband than continuous oral alone.

- **Vary Your Movements:** Shift between kissing, licking, stroking, and suction. Variety keeps both your body and his sensations engaged.

- **Pause and Reposition:** It's okay to stop, stretch your jaw, or adjust your posture. Keep one hand on him while you reposition so the connection doesn't break.

- **Choose Supportive Positions:** Don't twist yourself into a pretzel. Find angles that allow your neck and jaw to stay relaxed. Remember: your comfort enhances your pleasure—and his.

- **Strengthen Outside the Bedroom:** Try simple jaw exercises like opening wide and holding, side-to-side movement, or slow circular chewing motions. It's like yoga for your mouth.

Navigating Performance Anxiety: From Pressure to Presence

Let's talk about the internal stuff—the head games that whisper, *"You're not doing enough. He's bored. You're bad at this."* Lies. Every last one.

Here's what's true: great oral sex is not about performance. It's about presence.

- **Practice Mindfulness:** Focus on what you feel, hear, and see. Let his breath, your hands, and the connection between you anchor you in the moment. If your mind drifts into worry, gently bring it back to what you're enjoying together.

- **Open the Dialogue:** You're allowed to say, "Hey, I'm still figuring this out—can you tell me what feels amazing to you?" Vulnerability turns anxiety into intimacy.

- **Redefine Success:** The win isn't an orgasm. It's connection. It's closeness. It's a shared moment that says, "We're safe, we're loved, we're in this together." That, right there, is sacred.

You're learning. You're growing. And every hurdle you clear is a step closer to joyful, confident, connected intimacy. You're doing beautifully.

The Climax and Beyond

Oral sex doesn't end with climax—it flows into something just as essential: aftercare. That warm, grounding exhale that follows the passionate inhale. It's the part where nervous systems settle, where emotional connection deepens, and where both partners feel seen, safe, and soothed.

And yes, it's also where some really practical questions show up—like *what do I do with the semen?* and *how do we wrap this up without it getting weird?*

Let's walk through what to expect, how to talk about it, and how to finish well—because good sex isn't just about the buildup. It's about the landing.

The Ejaculation Conversation: Spit, Swallow, or Somewhere Else?

Let's be real—this is one of the most stressy parts for many women, especially if oral sex is new territory. And that's exactly why you don't want to wait until your husband is about to finish to figure it out.

Trying to have this conversation mid-climax is like asking your waiter for a new entree after you've already eaten most of the dish. It's messy, confusing, and rarely satisfying.

Have the talk outside the bedroom—maybe over coffee or during a walk. Approach it with curiosity, not pressure. You could say, "Hey, I've been thinking about oral sex and want to feel confident about what we both enjoy. Can we talk through what we're comfortable with when it comes to finishing?"

Your main options are:

1. He ejaculates in your mouth (and you either swallow or spit).

2. He ejaculates outside your mouth (on your body, his body, a towel, etc.).

Whatever you choose should be mutual, respectful, and based on clear communication. Once you've made a plan, agree on a signal he can give when he's getting close. This gives you a heads-up and helps transition smoothly—no surprises, no panic.

If the plan is to finish outside your mouth, simply shift to your hand while keeping the rhythm steady. This helps him stay in the moment and feel cared for.

You're not expected to be a mind-reader. What matters is showing up with grace, intention, and a willingness to love each other well.

To Swallow or Not to Swallow? Facts Over Fear

Let's bust some myths, shall we?

Swallowing semen is a **personal** choice—not a spiritual badge, not a sign of sexual prowess, and definitely not a moral issue. It's about comfort, not character.

Here's what's true:

- **Allergies are rare.** A small number of people are allergic to seminal fluid (a condition called seminal plasma hypersensitivity). If anything feels off, talk to your healthcare provider.

- **Taste is natural.** It varies person to person—slightly salty, sometimes bitter or sweet. Some say diet affects taste (like pineapple or avoiding red meat), but there's no strong science on that. Explore if you want, but don't feel pressure.

- **Nutritional claims are overblown.** Semen isn't a magical health shot. It contains trace nutrients, but nothing life-altering. Also, some early studies suggest hormonal mood effects—but again, not a reason to base your decision.

Here's the bottom line: **your comfort is the standard.** If you're okay with swallowing, go for it. If not, spitting or choosing an alternative location is just as valid. This is about mutual honor, not obligation.

Aftercare: The Sacred Wrap-Up

Aftercare is where the emotional magic settles in. Skipping it can leave even great sex feeling a little… unfinished. But when you slow down and linger with kindness, aftercare becomes the sacred seal on your experience.

Physical Care:

- **For Him:** Encourage him to urinate after sex—it's good hygiene and helps prevent infections. A quick rinse with mild soap and warm water is also helpful.

- **For You:** Rinse your mouth with water or a gentle, alcohol-based mouthwash (and skip brushing for 30 minutes post-oral to protect your gums). Washing your face, if needed, is perfectly normal.

Emotional Care:

- This is where intimacy blossoms. Snuggle up. Kiss. Whisper something kind like, "That felt really special," or "I loved getting to love you like that."

These tender, tiny moments are where nervous systems sync, hearts rest, and love roots deeper. They say, "You're not just a body I touched—you're my beloved."

Oral sex, when practiced with care, laughter, and presence, doesn't just end in climax. It ends in closeness. And that's what makes it Omazing®.

The Joy of Receiving

Stepping into a new chapter of sexual intimacy is sacred ground. When you and your husband explore oral sex— with curiosity, love, and mutual consent—it becomes more than just a physical act. It's an embodied act of worship, a holy adventure that calls you both into vulnerability, trust, and deeper union.

This section is about receiving. And for many women, that's the scariest part.

Being the focus of your husband's affection. Letting go of the to-do list in your head. Resting into your own pleasure instead of worrying about his. It can stir up all sorts of feelings—excitement, nervousness, self-consciousness, guilt. If that's where you are right now, please know this: you are not broken. You are not alone. And you are not the only one navigating these emotions.

In fact, you're in excellent company.

So many Christian women were raised with silence (or suspicion) around female pleasure. You may have never been told—much less shown—that your sexual enjoyment matters deeply to God. That your body was fearfully and wonderfully made (Psalm 139:14) not just for function, but for delight. That receiving pleasure isn't selfish or indulgent— it's an act of trust, a gift of intimacy, and a reflection of mutual joy in marriage.

Let's say this clearly: **receiving oral sex isn't just okay—it's good**. It's not indulgent. It's not dirty. It's not a loophole. It's part of the abundant, relational, richly pleasurable design God baked into marriage. Song of Songs is full of invitations and celebrations of physical delight, mutual giving, and unashamed receiving.

This isn't a list of techniques your husband "should" be doing. And it's certainly not a measuring stick for your sex life. This is a soft, soul-deep invitation to explore what it means to be truly known and cherished—body and spirit. To receive without guilt. To express without shame. And to discover that pleasure is not the enemy of holiness—it's often the very place where the sacred sneaks in.

When you allow yourself to be tenderly received by your husband—to surrender your striving and lean into joy—you're not just having sex. You're participating in a love story. One God Himself authored. One that's still unfolding, still blossoming, still growing in holy goodness.

So, sister, take a deep breath. You don't have to arrive. You just have to begin.

And we'll be with you every step of the way.

The Foundation of Intimacy

Before we explore the *how* of receiving oral sex, we need to talk about the *where*. Not your location—your emotional space. Because intimacy, especially the kind that welcomes new forms of pleasure, doesn't flourish under pressure or perfectionism. It flourishes in safety. In warmth. In trust.

And that kind of emotional safety isn't a happy accident. It's intentionally built—one honest conversation, one brave question, one gentle touch at a time. That's what this section is about: creating a safe harbor where sexual exploration becomes not just possible, but joyful.

You're a Team: From Performance to Partnership

Let's reframe this right out of the gate: this isn't a test. This isn't about him "doing it right" while you secretly grade his technique in your head. It's not about you trying to prove you're "cool" with it while secretly battling anxiety. It's about both of you—two unique, messy, marvelous people—navigating something tender and new, together.

The Gottman Institute talks about facing challenges as a team. And that's what this is. Not a problem, not a failure—

just unfamiliar ground. You're not alone in the awkwardness. New things are always a little clumsy at first. But when you treat it as *"us against the unfamiliar"* rather than *"you better get this right,"* everything softens.

This mindset invites laughter, removes pressure, and opens the door to real connection. He's not there to perform. You're not there to react a certain way. When the goal is shared discovery, every moment becomes a win—whether it ends in orgasm or simply in deeper closeness.

You don't need to be an expert. He doesn't either. You're just two beloved image-bearers, showing up with curiosity and grace. That mindset? It builds emotional intimacy far beyond the bedroom.

Golden Rules for Talking About Sex (Outside the Bedroom)

Want to know the best time to talk about sex?

When you're *not* having it.

These low-pressure conversations—over coffee, on a walk, cuddled on the couch—make space for clarity and connection without the heat of the moment clouding the message.

Here are four golden rules to guide those talks:

1. **Name Your Intentions**

   Let him know your why. When your husband understands that your heart is for deeper intimacy, not critique, his walls come down. Try: "I've been thinking about how we could grow even closer... and I'd love to explore something with you."

2. **Start Softly**

Gentle starts lead to connected endings. A soft tone, kind words, and maybe even holding hands set the stage for openness. This says, "We're in this together."

3. **Use "I" Language**

Instead of "You never..." or "You always...," try, "I've been feeling curious..." or "I think I'd feel really close to you if..." It keeps the conversation grounded in your experience, not his performance.

4. **Go Slow**

You don't need to solve everything in one conversation. Take your time. Let it be a door, not a verdict. That kind of pacing creates safety and space for deeper dialogue.

Navigating Vulnerability and Building Confidence

Let's name the brave thing: asking for what you want sexually takes guts.

Especially for women raised with messages like "good girls don't," or "it's his job to enjoy, yours to endure." But God didn't write that script. He designed your pleasure on purpose. And He called it good.

It takes courage to let someone in. To be touched. To say, "This is what I want." But your vulnerability isn't a flaw—it's the doorway to authentic intimacy.

Body Confidence and Normalizing Your Anatomy

If you're not fully at home in your body, it can feel scary to invite someone else in. And that's okay. This is where grace meets growth.

Your vulva is beautiful. Your scent, your shape, your texture—it's all normal. You don't need to smell like a flower shop or look like a retouched photo. You are wonderfully made (Psalm 139:14), and your body deserves love as it is.

One simple confidence boost? Shower together. It's not just practical—it's playful and sensual. It gives you a fresh start physically and emotionally, setting the tone for ease rather than pressure.

The Right to Receive Pleasure

This might be the biggest shift of all: **you are allowed to receive pleasure**.

Not as a reward. Not as a duty fulfilled. Simply because you are worth delight.

Receiving isn't selfish. It's not a performance. It's a practice of trust. A sacred exchange that deepens connection. When you believe that your pleasure matters, you step into intimacy with openness—and that changes everything. Not just for you, but for him too.

What once felt like a tentative "Is this okay?" becomes a confident, "I want this." And that kind of invitation draws your husband closer—not just to your body, but to your heart.

You're doing holy work here, friend. One brave step at a time.

Your Personal Pleasure Map

Knowledge is powerful—especially when it's about your own body. Yet for many Christian women, their sexual anatomy feels like unfamiliar territory. Maybe you were never taught much beyond a basic health class—or worse, you were told more about what *not* to do with your body than what you *could* enjoy with it.

This section is your gentle, empowering guide to the sacred geography of your body. Not to overwhelm you with biology, but to give you the keys to your design. Because the truth is, you're not just *allowed* to enjoy your body—you're *invited* to.

Your Creator didn't make your body accidentally or ambiguously. He crafted it with intention. With joy. With layers of beautiful, intricate pleasure centers that are designed not just for reproduction, but for connection, delight, and intimacy. Let's get reacquainted with that gift.

Demystifying the Vulva: A Gentle Guided Tour

First, a small but important note: what many people call the "vagina" is actually the *vulva*. The vagina is the internal canal. The vulva is the outer part—the visible area—and it's full of rich, sensitive structures that respond to touch, pressure, warmth, and presence.

Let's take a tour:

- **Mons Pubis**: The soft, fleshy mound above your pubic bone, often covered with hair. During arousal, it becomes more sensitive and responsive to touch—like a gentle warm-up zone.

- **Labia Majora (Outer Lips)**: These are the outer folds that frame your vulva. They protect the inner structures and swell slightly with blood during arousal, making them more sensitive to kisses, caresses, and light touch.

- **Labia Minora (Inner Lips)**: Tucked inside the outer lips, these delicate folds vary widely in shape, size, and color. No two are alike—and every variation is normal. They contain numerous nerve endings and lead upward toward the clitoral hood, guiding you to the most concentrated source of pleasure.

Understanding this basic structure helps you become fluent in your own body—so you can explore it with confidence and guide your husband with clarity and kindness.

The Epicenter of Pleasure: The Clitoris

If your vulva is the terrain, the clitoris is the epicenter—the core of your pleasure landscape. And it is stunningly designed.

The clitoris has one purpose: pleasure. That's it. It's not for peeing, birthing, or menstruating. Just pleasure. God gave you over 10,000 nerve endings here—more than any other single part of the male or female body. That alone is worth pausing to consider. What kind of God designs a part of your body *just* to help you feel delight?

And here's what's even more amazing: what you see on the outside is only the tip of the story.

The External Clitoris:

- **Glans Clitoris**: This is the small, visible nub at the top of your vulva, where the inner lips meet. Because it's incredibly sensitive, many women prefer gentle or indirect stimulation—think more whisper than shout.

- **Clitoral Hood**: This fold of skin covers and protects the glans. It's a great place to start if direct touch feels too intense. Stroking the hood or tracing circles around it can bring deep pleasure without overwhelming sensation.

The Internal Clitoris:

Surprise! The clitoris is not just a tiny nub—it's a large internal structure shaped like an upside-down wishbone:

- **The Body**: Extends backward from the glans.

- **Crura (Legs)**: These two "legs" flank your vaginal canal, about three inches long each.

- **Vestibular Bulbs**: These soft, spongy cushions sit at the base of the vulva. During arousal, they fill with blood, causing the area to swell and become exquisitely responsive.

This deeper structure is why vaginal and clitoral stimulation often feel connected—it's all part of the same incredible system. When you hear terms like "G-spot," they often refer to stimulation that's activating the internal clitoris from inside the vaginal wall.

What About the "G-Spot"?

The G-spot is often presented like a secret magic button—but it's not a separate part. It's an area on the front vaginal wall, about two inches in, that presses against the internal clitoral network. When stimulated, it can create sensations that feel fuller, deeper, and more intense—especially when you're already aroused.

In other words, vaginal pleasure is often still clitoral pleasure—just accessed from another angle. Understanding that helps you avoid unnecessary pressure or chasing myths. You're not broken if you don't feel fireworks right away. You're learning your instrument—and every body plays a little differently.

A Pleasure Map at a Glance

Here's a quick-reference guide to the anatomy of your delight:

- **Mons Pubis**: Soft, responsive mound above the vulva. Great for massage or warm pressure.

- **Labia Majora**: Outer lips. Sensitive to gentle stroking, cupping, or light kissing.

- **Labia Minora**: Inner lips. Highly sensitive to touch and often overlooked.

- **Clitoral Hood**: Indirect access to intense pleasure—especially when arousal is building.

- **Glans Clitoris**: Extremely sensitive tip—responds to gentle, thoughtful stimulation.

- **Internal Clitoris (Body, Crura, Bulbs)**: Hidden powerhouse that reacts to both external and internal touch.

- **G-Spot Area**: The front wall of the vagina—especially pleasurable when combined with other forms of arousal.

You Are Not a Mystery—You're a Masterpiece

Understanding your body isn't clinical. It's *transformational*. The more you know about how you're designed, the more you can approach intimacy with courage, not confusion. With holy confidence, not hesitation.

You don't need to wait for someone else to unlock your pleasure—you already hold the key. And you're not greedy for wanting to use it. You're honoring the incredible, intentional design God gave you.

You are not a puzzle to be solved. You are a garden to be delighted in (Song of Songs 4:16). And every time you explore your body with reverence, curiosity, and joy—you echo the Creator's delight.

Starting the Conversation

Now that you've been building trust, body confidence, and a deeper sense of emotional safety, it's time for one of the most vulnerable—and powerful—steps in intimacy: *asking for what you want.*

For many women, especially those who were never encouraged to connect with their sexual needs, even the idea of bringing up oral sex can feel like stepping onto a tightrope. What if he feels pressured? What if I say it wrong? What if it gets awkward?

Totally normal questions. But here's the truth that will carry you forward: *when approached with warmth, honesty, and mutual care, talking about sex can become one of the most intimate, bonding experiences you share.* Seriously. Conversation is one of the most underrated forms of foreplay. This section will help you find your voice—and use it well.

Choosing the Right Moment and Setting

When it comes to tender topics like oral sex, timing matters. A lot.

You want a space that's calm, pressure-free, and emotionally safe. The goal isn't to drop a surprise announcement mid-makeout or spring it on him while you're brushing your teeth. You're creating a sacred space for curiosity—not cornering him into a decision.

Here's how to set the stage:

- **Outside the Bedroom Is Best**

    Conversations about sex go better when they happen *away* from the act itself. Why? Because the bedroom can carry unspoken pressure—performance anxiety, expectations, or fear of disappointing one another.

Choose a neutral moment: on a walk, during a cuddle session, or over coffee on a lazy Saturday.

- **Look for Natural Connection**

  You don't need a dramatic lead-in. The best conversations often flow from a sense of closeness already present. Maybe you've just laughed together, shared something vulnerable, or spent quality time. Let the emotional intimacy set the tone for the physical kind.

- **Protect the Space**

  Make sure you won't be interrupted. This isn't a "while the kids are occupied for five minutes" kind of chat. Give it the sacred attention it deserves.

Gentle Openers: Scripts to Help You Begin

Even if you're ready in your heart, finding the words can still feel awkward. That's okay! Think of these as gentle on-ramps—ways to express desire without pressure. Use them verbatim or tweak them to sound like you.

The Fantasy Approach

Playful and low-pressure.

- "I've been having this fantasy lately... your mouth on me. I can't stop thinking about how that would feel."

- "I was mentally sexting you today. (Don't worry, it was holy.) I kept imagining your mouth between my thighs..."

The Vulnerability Approach

Great if you're feeling tender or nervous.

- "I feel a little shy bringing this up, but I've been curious about exploring oral sex together. Would you be open to trying that with me?"

- "I don't have this all figured out yet, but I trust you, and I'd love to learn what receiving oral sex could feel like—with you."

The Direct and Loving Approach

Perfect when you already feel safe and confident.

- "I've been thinking about ways we could grow closer—and I'd love to try receiving oral sex. What do you think?"

- "I really enjoy being close to you, and I think this is something that could be beautiful and fun for both of us."

The Gift of Mutuality: Not a Transaction

If you've already enjoyed giving oral sex to your husband, it's natural to feel curious about receiving it, too. And that's a beautiful thing to share:

- "I love giving you oral sex—it's one of my favorite ways to connect. And lately, I've been wondering what it would feel like to receive that kind of attention from you."

Just remember: *this is not a trade.* You're not bargaining pleasure—you're inviting deeper connection.

Healthy intimacy doesn't keep score. It gives freely, joyfully, and generously. When your desire is framed not as a debt he owes you, but as a gift you want to explore together, it shifts the energy from pressure to play.

That's what mutuality is all about: not "you do this because I did that," but "let's explore this together because we want to grow, delight, and love one another more fully."

Next up is the practical guidance for helping him learn how to love your body well.

The Beginner's Playbook

So, you've had the conversation. You've opened your heart. You've even giggled a little at the awkwardness—and now, you and your husband are ready to take this next step together.

Let's be clear right from the start: your first experience with receiving oral sex doesn't have to be anything grand or cinematic. You're not trying to win an imaginary award for Best Orgasm Under Pressure. This is about connection, not performance. *Presence,* not perfection.

In fact, the best way to approach this is with the mindset of discovery. Think of it as a tasting menu at a fine restaurant—you're not rushing to the main course; you're savoring each new flavor, one delicious bite at a time.

Let's walk through how to set the stage, slow things down, and enjoy the beauty of sampling together.

Setting the Scene for Comfort and Connection

Creating a sensual, safe environment is half the magic. Why? Because our nervous systems need to feel calm and connected before we can experience deep pleasure. Especially for women, desire blooms best in the soil of emotional safety.

Here are a few practical ways to nurture that:

- **Create a Sensual Atmosphere**

Dim the lights. Light a candle. Put on a soft playlist with a soothing rhythm. Make the space feel cozy, beautiful, and undistracted. This tells your body, "It's okay to slow down. I'm safe here."

- **Prioritize Physical Comfort**

  Use pillows to support your neck, back, or under your knees—whatever helps you feel fully relaxed and held. When your body feels supported, your mind can let go.

- **Turn Hygiene into Foreplay**

  A warm shower together before intimacy can be both practical and playfully romantic. It's a shared ritual that builds anticipation, promotes confidence, and sets a tone of mutual care before you ever reach the sheets.

The Art of the Slow Start: Why Foreplay Matters

One of the biggest myths about oral sex is that it starts with a direct dive. But for most women, pleasure builds in layers—and those early layers matter.

- **Warm-Up is Wisdom**

  Start with what already feels safe and good: slow kisses, cuddles, full-body touch, or sensual massage. This increases blood flow to your vulva and helps your body say a slow but steady *yes* to the growing arousal.

- **Let the Moment Unfold**

  When oral sex flows naturally from connection—not from obligation—it becomes a continuation of your closeness, not a separate, pressure-filled act. It's not about "doing something to you." It's about *being with you*, in delight and discovery.

Remember: clitoral stimulation is the main route to orgasm for most women. So taking your time isn't just kind—it's strategic.

Beginner Techniques: A "Tasting Menu" of Touch

Think of this section like a sampler platter: small bites of new sensations, tried together in a spirit of play.

- **Map the Territory**

  Have your husband begin by exploring *around* your vulva—your inner thighs, belly, and mons pubis. These areas are sensitive and often overlooked, building anticipation and layering arousal without rushing.

- **Use Broad, Gentle Strokes**

  When he makes contact with your vulva, slow and wide movements using the *flat* of the tongue tend to be more comfortable than darting or poking with the tip. Think of it like painting—a canvas, not a target.

- **Try the Alphabet Technique**

  It's playful and built for feedback. He can trace letters with his tongue, and you can respond with encouragement: "That 'S' was amazing—can we try that again?" Suddenly, learning feels like flirting, not testing.

- **Mix Sensations**

  Encourage him to explore with his lips, the tip and flat of his tongue, even soft, warm breaths blown against your skin. Every texture brings a different flavor of pleasure.

The Supporting Role of Hands

While his mouth may be the star of the show, his hands are the supporting cast—there to add richness, grounding, and emotional presence.

- **Touch Beyond the Vulva**

  Gentle caresses across your belly, hips, or breasts help keep your whole body engaged. It reminds you that this isn't just about genitals—it's about *you.*

- **Ground You Gently**

  Placing hands on your thighs or hips—firm, but not forceful—can help you feel secure, anchored, and cherished.

- **Offer Access with Respect**

  As arousal increases and your body softens, he can gently part your labia to allow for more focused exploration. Always with sensitivity. Always at your pace.

This first experience isn't about goals or milestones—it's about memory-making. About being seen, savored, and known. So let curiosity lead. Let laughter be welcome. And above all, let love be the loudest thing in the room.

The Language of Pleasure

Let's be clear right up front: great lovers aren't born—they're built. Not by pressure or performance, but by communication. And you, dear reader, are the coach.

Your voice—both the words you say and the way your body responds—is one of your most powerful tools for transforming "meh" into magic. This section is your coaching manual: how to guide your husband with kindness, how to ask for what you want without shame, and how to turn feedback into the sexiest form of connection.

Verbal Guidance: Your In-the-Moment Toolkit

Talking during sex might feel awkward at first—especially if you're not used to hearing your own voice in the bedroom. But it's the express lane to connection and better pleasure.

And good news: it doesn't have to be complicated or clinical. Just real, warm, and kind.

1. Use Positive Reinforcement

This is your golden rule. Affirm what's working. Your brain—and his—lights up with affirmation. Even a whispered "yes" can be more powerful than a five-minute instructional monologue.

Try:

- "Mmm, yes—just like that."
- "That feels amazing right there."
- "Don't stop. That's perfect."

You're not faking anything—you're guiding. And when he feels confident, he'll stay engaged, relaxed, and eager to keep learning.

2. Try the Compliment Sandwich

If something needs to change, wrap it in warmth. Offer a praise, a gentle suggestion, and a confirming affirmation.

Like this:

- "That pressure feels sooo good... could you slow down just a little? Mmm, yes—right there, that's it."

- "I love the way you use your tongue... a little more to the left? Yesss, that's exactly it."

This tone keeps things collaborative, not corrective.

3. Let Your Sounds Lead

You don't always need words. Moans, sighs, and breathy "mmm"s are like holy breadcrumbs, guiding your husband deeper into what's good. Your vocal pleasure reassures him: "I'm with you. This feels amazing."

So if you're enjoying it, let yourself express it. Don't mute the music—let your body sing.

The Feedback Translator: Turning Criticism Into Coaching

Let's be honest—sometimes it's not amazing. Maybe it's too fast, too light, or just not hitting the right spot. But instead of shutting down or silently enduring, here's how to redirect with grace.

If It Feels Too Rough or Fast:

Try:

"Mmm, I love this... could you slow it down just a bit? Yes—like that. Perfect."

Affirmation plus suggestion = a smoother shift.

If He's Missing the Spot:

Try:

"That's so close... a little more to the right... yep, right there. Don't move."

You're helping him win—gently.

If It Tickles or Irritates:

Try:

"Could we try the flat of your tongue instead? That kind of pressure feels so good."

Reframe discomfort into invitation.

If You Want Him to Use His Hands:

Try:

"It would feel amazing if you touched my breasts while you do that."

You're not critiquing—you're co-creating.

If It's Too Much Tongue:

Try:

"I love how wet that is... can you try just the tip of your tongue for a moment? Ooh, yes—like that."

You're guiding, not grading.

The more you practice this kind of feedback, the more natural it becomes. Over time, you won't just be correcting— you'll be building trust and deepening desire.

Non-Verbal Cues: Letting Your Body Speak

Sometimes the best coaching happens without a single word.

Use the Pelvic Tilt:

Gently tilting your hips toward him says, "More of that, please." Pulling back or arching away signals, "Let's adjust." Teach him to read those cues.

Hands as Gentle Guides:

- **On His Head:** A soft hand at the back of his head can guide rhythm or pressure—without turning it into a wrestling match.

- **On Your Own Body:** Show him. Use your hand to demonstrate the rhythm or pressure you love. Ask, "Can I show you?" It's vulnerable, intimate, and bonding.

The Post-Game Debrief: Growing Together

Feedback doesn't stop at the finish line. A follow-up conversation—later that evening or the next day—can turn a good experience into a growing one.

- **Pick a Low-Pressure Moment:** Over coffee, during a cuddle, or while relaxing in bed.

- **Start with Affirmation:** "That was so good. I especially loved that circle motion with your tongue."

Then, if it feels right, you might add:

- "Would you be open to trying something a little different next time?"

- Or: "What did you love most about last night?"

This keeps the conversation open, collaborative, and exciting—like planning your next great adventure together.

Talking about sex doesn't kill the mood—it creates it. When you guide your partner with confidence, kindness, and playful honesty, you're not just building better technique. You're becoming co-creators of joy.

Leveling Up

Once you and your husband feel confident with the basics—and communication is flowing with more ease—you're ready to take things up a notch. But let's make one thing clear: "advanced" pleasure isn't about circus-level flexibility or mastering acrobatic maneuvers. It's about deepening connection, layering sensation, and turning already-good intimacy into something even richer.

You're not just chasing orgasms here. You're crafting textured, emotionally connected, holy experiences of pleasure—together.

The Symphony of Touch: Mouth + Hands + Heart

When you move from one-zone stimulation to multi-sensory, multi-touch engagement, something magical happens. Instead of isolating pleasure to one part of the body, your husband learns to treat your entire being as an instrument—and he's learning to play you like a symphony.

Internal + External Clitoral Stimulation

One of the most powerful combinations is external clitoral attention paired with internal stimulation. While his mouth gives consistent, rhythmic focus to your clitoral hood and glans, he can slide one or two well-lubricated fingers inside your vagina. With a gentle "come hither" motion or steady pressure on the front vaginal wall, he's activating the internal parts of your clitoral network—yes, that includes what's commonly called the G-spot. This dual stimulation engages your pleasure pathways from both sides and can lead to full-body, blended orgasms that feel expansive and soul-deep.

Whole-Body Touch

Don't let his free hand go to waste. As he uses his mouth and one hand for your core pleasure zones, the other hand can stroke your belly, gently cup your breast, or explore your thighs. These seemingly simple gestures remind your nervous system: you are cherished, not just touched. This is about the whole of you—body, heart, and soul.

Mastering Rhythm, Pressure, and Speed

Great oral sex isn't a one-note experience. Learning to vary rhythm and intensity is like composing a score: tension, release, crescendo.

Edging (Arousal on a Rollercoaster)

Edging is the practice of bringing you near climax, then easing off slightly—letting you hover at the edge. This cycle of build-up and back-off increases blood flow, heightens sensitivity, and makes the eventual orgasm dramatically more powerful. It's like savoring every bite of dessert before the final, satisfying finish.

Suction Play

When arousal is high, light suction (like a focused kiss) on the clitoral glans can feel electrifying. It's not about vacuum force—it's about intention. Paired with slow, deep tongue movements, it adds a layer of delightful surprise. Just make sure to check in; a little goes a long way here.

The "K" and "L" Techniques

The alphabet trick gets a glow-up. The "K" technique uses the broad, flat surface of the tongue for long, sweeping motions. The "L" technique taps the tongue tip for precise, flicking contact. Alternating between these sensations creates contrast—sharp then soft, fast then slow—and keeps your nervous system tuned in and delighted.

Positioning for Comfort, Access, and Empowerment

The way you position your body can totally change the experience. These setups are designed for comfort, deeper connection, and the occasional empowering role reversal.

The Elevated Receiver (Pillow Boost)

Place a firm pillow or two under your hips while lying on your back. This tilts your pelvis upward, giving your husband a beautiful view and easy access while supporting your spine and neck.

The Edge of the Bed

You lie back with your hips right at the edge, and he kneels on a cushion or sits in a chair below. This angle offers optimal range for him—and a grounding surface for you to rest into.

Standing "O"

You stand, supported by a wall or headboard, while he kneels. This gives you full visibility and control—and can be incredibly empowering if you're feeling bold.

Face-Sitting (The Queening Position)

You sit on his face, either fully or hovering. You guide the rhythm with your hips and determine the depth of contact. Trust is essential—so establish a simple signal (like a shoulder tap) to adjust or pause as needed. This position can be one of the most empowering ways to receive pleasure.

Creative Exploration: Sensory and Sensual Additions

Want to turn things up even more? With safety, mutual enthusiasm, and a sense of play, you can explore new sensory elements that heighten pleasure.

Temperature Play

He takes a sip of ice water and lets the coolness meet your warm skin. Or he traces your thighs with an ice cube, then follows with his mouth. The contrast jolts your nerve endings awake and adds a surprising spark.

Edible Additions

Whipped cream, flavored lubricants, or a drizzle of honey (used externally only!) can make the experience delicious in more ways than one. Just remember: sugar and internal genitals don't mix—so keep the sweetness on the outer vulva and clean up well, unless you want a yeast infection.

Vibrators as Companions

A small bullet vibrator can be a powerful addition. He can hold it against your clitoral hood while focusing elsewhere with his mouth—or you can guide the sensation while he stays attuned to your rhythm. The mix of vibration and oral stimulation can unlock next-level pleasure.

This phase of your journey isn't about proving anything. It's about deepening the dance, layering the pleasure, and letting your intimacy become a living, growing expression of love. It's not just about feeling good—it's about feeling seen, cherished, and fully known.

Cultivating a Lifelong Dialogue of Pleasure

You've journeyed through the sacred terrain of receiving oral sex—not as a technique to master, but as an invitation into deeper intimacy. This guide may have offered the map, but the real adventure? That belongs to you and your husband. Together, you're the explorers—charting new territory, uncovering hidden treasures, and learning to speak the language of pleasure one conversation, one caress, one shared smile at a time.

This chapter wasn't just about "how-to." It was about heart-to-heart. The real magic lives in what happens between the lines—between breaths, between bodies, between souls. The trust you build, the vulnerability you share, the joy you receive together—that's where intimacy truly thrives. Communication, curiosity, and collaboration aren't just tools for sex; they're the lifeblood of a marriage that keeps growing in delight.

And here's one of the most freeing truths about intimacy: it's never final. Your body will change. His preferences might shift. Life will bring new seasons—some vibrant, others tender, maybe even challenging. But that doesn't mean you've lost your spark. It means you're human. It means your love is alive. What excited you last year might evolve next month, and that's not a failure—it's a sacred invitation to keep discovering each other, over and over again.

Rather than viewing your sex life as a performance to preserve, think of it as a lifelong conversation to nurture. Set aside moments to check in—not with critique or pressure, but with curiosity and joy. Ask each other:

- "What felt really good lately?"
- "Is there anything new you're curious to try?"
- "What helps you feel most connected to me right now?"

These questions aren't just about better pleasure—they're about deeper partnership. They're how we keep intimacy tender, alive, and joyfully evolving.

By stepping into this space—by learning your body, voicing your needs, and receiving pleasure as a holy and healing gift—you're doing far more than trying something new in the bedroom. You're sowing seeds for a marriage that grows in intimacy and joy. You're choosing delight over duty, connection over confusion, presence over performance.

And that, dear sister, is an act of sacred courage. Your pleasure is not a problem to manage or a reward to earn—it's a gift. It's a blessing. It's one of the many ways God knits your hearts together, over time, into something beautiful and strong.

Wrapping It Up

This chapter has taken us on quite a ride—starting with the surprising and beautiful truth that oral sex shows up in the poetic pages of Scripture, and ending with a tender, transformational invitation to both give and receive with holy confidence.

We've uncovered that oral sex—when practiced in the safety of a loving, monogamous, Christ-centered marriage—is not only permitted by God, it's celebrated in His Word. From the Song of Songs to the sighs of mutual delight, the Bible shows us that pleasure and purity are not opposites. They are partners.

We dove into the joy of giving—learning how to approach oral pleasure not as a performance, but as a form of connection. With communication, curiosity, and compassion, we saw how giving can be deeply pleasurable for the giver too.

Then we stepped into the joy of receiving, which for many women is the braver, more vulnerable journey. We talked about creating emotional safety, understanding your body, voicing your desires, and receiving pleasure as a gift—not just for you, but for your marriage.

So what now?

Now it's time to keep going. Keep learning. Keep exploring. This is not a one-time experience—it's a lifelong conversation. And with every shared touch, every honest word, every moment of laughter or learning, you're building something sacred. Something worth celebrating.

And if you've done all this beautiful work and still feel something's missing—if desire feels flat, or energy is low, or your get-up-and-go has gotten up and gone—it may not be about technique or tension. It might be about hormones.

In the next chapter, we'll talk about testosterone: how a tiny, God-designed hormone can have a surprisingly big impact on your mood, your energy, and yes—your desire. Because sometimes, the thing that helps you feel sexy again isn't just emotional or spiritual—it's physiological.

Chapter 16: Testosterone & Tingles

The Spark That Went Missing

*E*mily stared at the half-eaten granola bar in her minivan's cup holder, wondering if it counted as breakfast—or lunch. Probably both. She glanced at the clock: 2:37 p.m. She was still wearing the same leggings she'd slept in, her toddler's applesauce pouch had exploded sometime after drop-off, and she had exactly three minutes before the school pickup line demanded her presence. Again.

She leaned back against the headrest and let out a sigh that sounded more like a deflated balloon than a human woman. Lately, everything felt flat. Not just her hair, which hadn't seen dry shampoo in a questionable number of days—but her spark. Her get-up-and-go. Her interest in... well, anything. Including her husband, who was still as handsome and kind as ever, and also apparently very confused about why his once-flirty wife now responded to shoulder massages with "I'm just so tired."

Which was true. She was tired. Bone-deep, brain-fogged, please-don't-touch-me tired.

And confused.

Because the intimacy part of marriage—the part that used to feel electric and playful—now felt like an item on a very long list she kept failing to cross off. She wasn't angry or closed off. Just... blank. Like the lights were dimmed and she couldn't find the switch.

So when her best friend mentioned something called "testosterone pellets" over coffee one morning—with the same reverent tone usually reserved for miracle serums or Holy Spirit breakthroughs—Emily perked up. "Wait, isn't testosterone for guys?" she'd asked, swirling her lukewarm latte like a nervous habit.

Turns out, it wasn't. Turns out, women need it too—just in different amounts. And sometimes, when that tiny but mighty hormone runs low, everything else starts to feel low too: energy, mood, desire, even joy.

Emily didn't make an appointment that day. But she thought about it that night. And the next. And when she finally picked up the phone to schedule a consult, she felt a tiny flutter of something she hadn't felt in a while.

Hope.

Maybe—just maybe—she wasn't broken. Maybe she just needed a little help finding her spark again.

Hormone Help & Holy Longing

Let's start with some holy honesty: when it comes to low desire, especially for women, it's rarely *just* about hormones. Sure, hormones play a role. But they're usually one thread in a much larger tapestry—one woven with stress, shame, disconnection, trauma, exhaustion, and spiritual weariness. The kinds of things that don't show up on a lab panel but still weigh heavy on the soul.

But sometimes? Hormones are the *missing piece*. And addressing them—particularly with low-dose testosterone therapy—can unlock vitality you didn't even know was possible.

Testosterone? Yep, the so-called "man hormone" is actually vital for women too. God designed your body with it in mind—just in smaller amounts. And when levels dip too low (which can happen due to age, stress, birth control, postpartum changes, or perimenopause), your body and brain can start sending distress signals: low energy, fuzzy thinking, flat mood, and yes—desire that feels MIA.

For some women, even after doing the emotional healing, relational work, and deep spiritual connection with God... there's still a sense that their sexual self is stuck in park. They *want* to want intimacy—but the spark just isn't there. That's where testosterone can be a gentle, effective support—not a replacement for healing, but a companion to it.

What It's Like

Low-dose testosterone therapy (often through tiny pellets placed under the skin near the hip) works slowly and steadily. No wild mood swings. No beard-growing drama. Just a subtle nudge toward balance. Women often describe it like someone quietly turned the lights back on. You may start to notice:

- A gentle return of desire—both in mind and body.
- More motivation to initiate or respond to intimacy.
- Stronger orgasms and deeper connection.
- A clearer head, more energy, and a sparkle you thought was gone for good.
- A confidence and assertiveness that helps you bravely explore new things.

And spiritually? Many women report feeling more *present*—more in tune with their own bodies, their marriages, and their sense of joy. That's not vanity. That's vitality. And it's holy ground.

The Process

The procedure itself is simple and quick. A numbing shot, a rice-sized pellet, a small bandage, and you're on your way. Most women begin to feel the effects within a few weeks. Some need a little dose adjustment (which your provider will help with through lab work), but when it's dialed in, the results can be transformational.

Now, let's talk money: pellet therapy usually isn't covered by insurance. And yes, it's an investment. But for many women, it's worth every penny—because life feels *livable* again. Like *you* again.

A Faithful Frame

Here's the key takeaway, friend: needing hormonal support doesn't make you broken. It doesn't mean you're weak, selfish, or "less Christian." It means you're *human*. And wonderfully complex. Remember—God designed your hormones, too. Caring for them is part of stewarding the body He knit together with love (Psalm 139:13-14).

Low desire isn't a spiritual failure. It's a signal. One that might be pointing to deeper healing—or, in some cases, a simple biochemical tweak. If you're curious, find a provider who respects your story, your values, and your faith. And if it feels like the right next step, know this: you're not alone. And you're not crazy. You're just ready to feel fully alive again.

Wrapping It Up

You've just explored one of the most overlooked—and potentially life-changing—tools in a woman's intimacy toolkit: testosterone. While it's not a magic bullet or a one-size-fits-all fix, for many women, low-dose testosterone therapy becomes the missing puzzle piece—the gentle spark that reignites energy, confidence, and yes... desire.

We've covered the basics: how testosterone works in the female body, what to expect from therapy, how the pellet procedure plays out, and how finding your "sweet spot" is more of a gentle dance than a dramatic transformation. It's not about becoming someone new—it's about reconnecting with the vibrant, pleasure-capable woman God created you to be.

So here's your gentle nudge: if something in this chapter resonated—if you've been feeling "off," foggy, or flatlined in the desire department—consider having a conversation with a hormone-literate provider. Ask questions. Get curious. Advocate for yourself. Because when your body is supported, your intimacy can flourish.

And speaking of intimacy flourishing...

Get ready to roll up your sleeves—literally. In the next chapter, we're getting hands-on. We'll explore the delightfully underrated art of manual pleasure, from hand jobs to finger play, and how using your hands (and guiding his) can become one of the most connected, confidence-building parts of your sexual rhythm. You in?

Chapter 17: Getting Handsy

"A Little to the Left?"

*J*essie stood in front of the mirror in her bathroom, tooth-brush in hand, wondering how she had gone from feeling like a goddess on her wedding night to Googling "hand job techniques" at 11:47 PM while her kids screamed over Goldfish crackers in the next room.

Her husband, Mark, had lovingly suggested that they "mix it up a bit" in bed last week. And bless him, he'd said it with such hope in his eyes—like she was the sexy heroine in a rom-com instead of a woman whose sweatpants had three-day-old pea-nut butter smudges and a strong opinion about bedtime bat-tles.

Jessie wasn't against it. In theory. She wanted to want it. She missed feeling connected, adventurous, awake. But now that they were finally alone, the house quiet, kids asleep, she felt the pressure creeping in.

What if I do it wrong? What if I grip it like a doorknob? What if I try something new and he makes that confused face again like the time I attempted dirty talk and accidentally sounded like a cartoon villain?

Still, she was trying. She lit a candle (why did she only do that when company came over?), found a clean-ish robe, and tip-toed into the bedroom like she was about to defuse a bomb in-stead of bless her husband with intimacy.

Mark looked up from the book he was reading and smiled. That smile—that goofy, heart-melting one—was why she was doing this. She wanted him to feel loved. Known. Desired. And maybe, just maybe, she wanted to feel that way too.

So, she climbed into bed, heart thudding, and whispered, "Okay. I don't know if I'll be amazing at this, but I want to try something... with my hands."

He blinked, surprised. Then nodded. "That sounds amazing."

And in that moment, Jessie realized—it didn't have to be perfect. It just had to be real. Honest. Connected. Maybe even a little funny. Because at the end of the day, it wasn't about techniques. It was about them.

Hand Jobs

Let's just go ahead and name it—"hand jobs" may not be the sexiest-sounding phrase in the English language, but don't be fooled. This form of manual intimacy is powerful, playful, and surprisingly profound. It's not just about "doing something with your hands"—it's about discovering a shared language of pleasure and connection that's uniquely yours as a couple.

If you haven't yet read the *Tongues of Fire* chapter, we highly recommend circling back. There's quite a bit of overlap in the principles, and rather than repeat ourselves, we'll build on that foundation here—shifting focus from your mouth to your hands as a source of life-giving touch.

So, why explore this? Because your hands carry a kind of intimacy all their own. They're strong and tender. Skilled and sensitive. They know how to soothe, spark, surprise. When invited into your sexual rhythm with intention and curiosity, your hands become instruments of worshipful connection—tools that not only bring your husband pleasure but also help you feel powerful and confident in your ability to love him well.

This chapter isn't about technique alone (though don't worry—we've got plenty of that coming). It's about cultivating presence. About learning how to attune to his body, read his responses, and co-create an experience that feels deeply personal. It's about offering your touch not out of obligation, but out of joyful generosity.

And perhaps most importantly, it's about reminding both of you that pleasure doesn't have to be complicated or reserved for "big moments." Sometimes, the simplest gestures—a slow stroke, a lingering gaze, a whispered "do you like that?"—carry the most meaning.

So take a deep breath. There's nothing to prove here. Just something to enjoy. You're not learning to perform. You're learning to connect—hand to body, heart to heart.

The Arc of Arousal: Reading the Rhythms of His Body

When it comes to sexual pleasure, knowledge isn't just power—it's tenderness. One of the most loving things you can offer your husband is your attunement, your willingness to learn how his body responds and flows. Male arousal may look straightforward from the outside, but under the surface, it follows a beautiful, predictable rhythm— what scientists call the four-phase cycle of sexual response.

Understanding these four stages can transform your experience together from guesswork into grace. It's like having a GPS for your hands: knowing where he is in the journey helps you navigate your touch, your pace, even your presence, with care and confidence.

Phase 1: Arousal (The Spark)

This is the ignition point—where desire starts to stir. Triggered by everything from your touch, your voice, a look across the room, or his own imagination, this phase kicks off when the brain sends signals that dilate the arteries in the penis. Blood rushes in, veins constrict to trap it, and voilà—an erection begins to form.

You'll notice his body becoming more alert: his scrotum might draw closer to his body, his breathing might deepen, and tension begins to rise in his muscles. This is the warm-up zone, where slow, broad, exploratory strokes are not just welcome—they're ideal. Think curiosity, not choreography. You're awakening his body, inviting him to relax into pleasure.

Phase 2: Plateau (The Climb)

As arousal builds, the body starts to climb the mountain. His heart rate and breathing spike, sometimes to levels near an intense workout. You might see his hips begin to move rhythmically, involuntary muscle twitches kicking in, and a small amount of clear pre-ejaculatory fluid (pre-cum) appearing at the tip of his penis.

This phase is the sweet spot for tuning in and adapting. Touch can become more focused, firmer, and targeted—especially to sensitive areas like the glans (head) and frenulum (the V-shaped underside). The key here is responsiveness: watch his reactions, listen to his breathing, and let your touch reflect what his body is asking for.

Phase 3: Orgasm (The Peak)

Orgasm isn't just a release—it's a crescendo of physical and emotional intensity. And yes, it usually happens quickly (thanks, biology), but it carries powerful meaning in your connection.

There are two parts to this phase:

1. **Emission** – This is the moment he feels that "point of no return." Semen is gathered at the base of the urethra, and he knows what's coming next.

2. **Ejaculation** – A series of strong, rhythmic contractions propel the semen outward. These contractions send intense waves of pleasure to his brain, creating that euphoric, often whole-body experience we call orgasm.

During this time, your continued rhythm and pressure are key. Most men benefit from consistent, unchanging stimulation to ride the wave through to completion.

Phase 4: Resolution and Refractory (The Exhale)

After orgasm, everything begins to soften—literally and emotionally. His erection will begin to fade, his muscles relax, and a wave of drowsiness might wash over him. This isn't him "checking out." It's biology doing its thing.

Enter the **refractory period**, where he's temporarily unable to have another orgasm. The length of this pause varies widely—from minutes to hours, depending on age, health, and other factors.

This is where emotional intimacy comes in. If you don't know what's happening, his quietness or lack of continued arousal might feel confusing or personal. But when you understand it as a built-in recovery system, you're freed to simply hold him, breathe with him, and let your presence be the bridge between pleasure and connection.

When you understand the arc of male arousal, you don't just "get better" at manual intimacy. You become a more attuned, empowered, and compassionate lover—one who can confidently meet your husband not just with touch, but with trust, timing, and tenderness.

The Art of the Hand

With a foundation of communication and a map of his body, you're ready to explore the practical art of touch. This section translates knowledge into action, presenting a variety of techniques not as rigid rules but as a creative palette. The focus here is on mastering core principles—pressure, pace, rhythm, and variety—which you can adapt to your husband's unique responses and preferences, making each experience a personalized dance of pleasure.

Essential Preparations: The Non-Negotiable Role of Lubrication

Before you begin, one preparation is absolutely essential for both his comfort and pleasure: lubrication. Using a high-quality personal lubricant isn't optional; it's a fundamental component of a good hand job. Dry friction from your hand against his sensitive skin can be uncomfortable, distracting, and even painful. Lube eliminates this friction, allowing your hand to glide smoothly and transforming the sensation from abrasive to exquisitely sensual. It prevents skin irritation and allows for a much wider range of motion and pressure, ultimately increasing his pleasure.

When choosing a lubricant, consider the following options:

- **Water-Based Lubricant**: Highly recommended for its versatility and safety. Water-based lubes feel similar to the body's natural lubrication, are safe for sensitive skin, and are easy to clean up with water, leaving no stains on sheets or clothing. Their primary drawback is that they can be absorbed by the skin or evaporate over time, meaning you may need to reapply during a longer session. Look for formulas that are free from glycerin, as this ingredient can sometimes cause irritation for some people.

- **Silicone-Based Lubricant**: Known for its long-lasting, silky glide. It's waterproof, making it an excellent choice for use in the shower or bath. However, it can be more difficult to clean off, often requiring soap and water, and may stain some fabrics. Note that silicone lube should not be used with silicone sex toys, as it can degrade the material.

- **Oil-Based Lubricant**: Options like coconut oil or massage oil are suitable for external-only manual stimulation. However, they're generally not recommended if there's any chance of transitioning to intercourse, as oils can damage latex condoms and may disrupt the natural balance of the vagina. They can also be messy and difficult to clean.

For a first experience, a quality water-based lubricant is the ideal choice. When you're ready to use it, squeeze a generous amount—more is almost always better—into your palm. Rub your hands together to warm the lube; applying cold lubricant can be a startling and unpleasant shock that breaks the mood. The very act of sensually applying the warm lube to his penis can be a beautiful part of foreplay, signaling the start of a pleasurable experience.

Foundational Principles: Mastering Pressure, Pace, and Rhythm

Before diving into specific techniques, it's essential to understand the three core principles that govern all forms of manual stimulation. Mastering these will allow you to adapt and respond to your husband in real-time, creating a truly dynamic experience.

- **Pressure**: The amount of pressure you apply is a key variable. A good starting point is a medium, firm grip—often compared to holding a can of soda. It should be firm enough to feel intentional and engaging, but not so tight that it causes discomfort or restricts movement. The beauty is in the variation. You can start with a lighter touch, increase pressure as his arousal builds, and then ease off again, creating waves of sensation.

- **Pace**: The speed of your movements should generally mirror the arc of his arousal. Begin with a slow, deliberate, and almost teasing pace. This builds anticipation and allows him to fully register the sensations. As you feel his arousal grow—his breathing quickens, his muscles tense—you can gradually increase the speed of your strokes. A common mistake for beginners is to start too fast and stay at one speed. Variety is key; alternating between fast and slow can be incredibly arousing.

- **Rhythm**: Once you find a pace and pressure he responds to, try to establish a consistent rhythm. Our bodies are naturally attuned to rhythm, and a steady, predictable motion can be deeply hypnotic and pleasurable. However, don't be afraid to break the rhythm intentionally to create a moment of surprise before re-establishing it. Pay close attention to his body's cues; his own breathing and the movement of his hips can give you a rhythm to match or complement.

Finally, ensure you're both in a comfortable position. A relaxed body is a more receptive body. You could have him stand in front of you while you sit on the edge of the bed, or you could lie on your back while he lies on his, allowing you to nestle between his legs and face him. Experiment to find what allows you both to relax and focus completely on the pleasure of the moment.

By embracing these principles and approaching each encounter with curiosity and attentiveness, you transform manual intimacy into a shared art form—a dance of connection, pleasure, and love.

Expanding Your Repertoire

Once you've got the basics down—lubrication, pressure, pace, and rhythm—it's time to have a little fun. This section is all about expanding your touch vocabulary. Think of these techniques not as a rigid routine, but like your favorite spice rack. You're not cooking the same dish every time—you're experimenting, combining flavors, and discovering what delights the senses. The goal isn't to find "the one move that works"—it's to keep things playful, personalized, and deeply connected.

The Firestarter

This one's a warm-up classic. With both hands well-lubricated, place his penis gently between your palms. Then, like you're rubbing two sticks together to start a fire, roll it back and forth with smooth, light pressure. It's not about speed—it's about awakening the skin, increasing blood flow, and easing both of you into a rhythm of shared anticipation.

Twist and Shout

Flip your hand so your palm faces you, and wrap it around his shaft. As you stroke upward, give a gentle twist with your wrist. When you reach the tip, loosen your grip just enough to let your palm glide softly across the sensitive glans. Then slide back down and repeat. This move creates a delicious contrast—firm twist, soft finish—and can be incredibly arousing when timed well during the build-up phase.

The Basketweave

Interlace your fingers loosely to form a sort of "basket" with both hands. Slide this over his shaft so the head peeks out between your thumbs. Maintain a medium grip and stroke up and down, adding a gentle twist at the top so your thumbs brush over the glans. The unique texture and combined motion create a layered sensation that's especially satisfying.

The Doorknob

Think tiny and targeted. With one hand holding the base to keep the skin taut, use your thumb and forefinger of the other hand to gently twist the glans back and forth—like you're turning a small, slick doorknob. It's best saved for moments of high arousal, when the head is ultra-sensitive and your touch can send waves of pleasure without needing much pressure.

Anvil & Milking

These two techniques rely on fluid, alternating motion. For the **Anvil**, start at the top and stroke down. As that hand reaches the base, the other takes over from the top, creating a steady, rolling flow. The **Milking** variation flips it—start at the base and stroke up, one hand following the other.

This creates a consistent, rhythmic stimulation that feels both grounding and intensifying.

The Cock Ring

Form a snug circle at the base of his penis using your thumb and forefinger, applying steady pressure. This helps trap blood flow, enhancing firmness and sensitivity. With your other hand, try any of the techniques above. The added pressure at the base can amplify everything else you do, turning even simple strokes into heightened sensations.

These aren't magic tricks—they're invitations to curiosity. Mix and match. Listen and adjust. Stay present, and enjoy the gift of exploration. When you're both tuned in to what feels good and what fosters connection, even the simplest move can become a holy act of love.

Engaging His Whole Body

A truly unforgettable hand job is never just about your hand and his penis. It's about his whole body—and yours. It's about attention, affection, and attunement. When you bring your full presence and curiosity into the moment, you create not just sensation, but connection. And that's where the magic happens.

Think of your hands as a team—one might be focused on the main event, but the other? It's your secret weapon. Your "roaming hand" has the power to awaken pleasure in places often overlooked but deeply responsive.

Start with his testicles—this area is rich in nerve endings and surprisingly sensitive to touch. Try gentle cupping, slow stroking, or lightly rolling them in your palm. Go slow and stay tuned in—what's delightful for one man may be ticklish for another. The key is loving curiosity and real-time feedback.

Move to his inner thighs, a tender zone that often gets skipped in favor of more obvious areas. Trace your fingers along the inner line of his thighs or press gently just above his knees and move inward. The teasing anticipation can heighten his arousal and deepen the experience.

You can even experiment with lightly tugging or running your fingers through his pubic hair—believe it or not, this can create a surprisingly enjoyable sensation when done with intention and gentleness. And don't forget the perineum—that soft area between the base of the scrotum and the anus. Applying steady pressure with your thumb here can stimulate deep internal pleasure and even intensify orgasm when timed well.

Now, let's talk about breath and lips—because your mouth isn't just for oral sex. Breathing warm air over the tip of his penis while your hands are working can create a delicious contrast of sensation. A whisper of warmth in just the right moment can be electrifying. So can soft kisses and tongue flicks on his belly, hips, or thighs—anchoring the experience with affection and surprise.

Eye contact, too, is its own kind of intimacy. Glancing up at him with a soft smile while your hands explore can speak volumes—saying "I'm here, I'm with you, and I delight in this." It's not about putting on a show—it's about letting him feel seen, wanted, and safe in your care.

This kind of whole-body engagement invites him into an experience that's more than physical—it's emotional, spiritual, and deeply connective. You're not just touching his body. You're honoring it. And when that happens, your hands become something far more powerful than tools of pleasure—they become instruments of love.

Feedback and Mutual Pleasure

Let's be honest—one of the biggest questions that hovers in the back of our minds when trying something new in the bedroom is: *Am I doing this right?* It's such a common worry, and it makes total sense. You care. You want to bring joy. You want him to feel amazing—and you want to feel confident while doing it.

But here's the truth that sets you free: this isn't a performance. It's not a talent show with judges holding up scorecards. It's a living, breathing, two-person dance. And the "music" that moves that dance forward? Feedback.

The goal isn't perfection—it's connection. When you learn to tune into your husband's cues—both verbal and non-verbal—you move from guessing to co-creating. From performance pressure to playful partnership. From "I hope this works" to "Let's find out what we love together."

The Language of Pleasure: Reading His Non-Verbal Cues

Before he ever says a word, his body is speaking volumes. And learning that language is one of the most loving, empowering things you can do.

Start by watching his **breathing**. Is it getting deeper, quicker, more uneven? A sudden inhale or held breath can mean, *That right there. Do that again.*

Pay attention to his **sounds**. Moans, sighs, groans—these are your green lights. They're not just expressions of pleasure; they're encouragement. They're his way of saying, *Yes, this is good.*

His **body movements** can also speak louder than words. Are his hips rising to meet your hand? Is his back arching, or his thighs tensing? These small shifts are his way of responding, inviting, and affirming.

And of course, if he does speak, take it as a gift. A simple "Right there," or "That feels incredible," is golden guidance. Receive it with gratitude—and keep going!

How to Ask for—and Receive—Feedback with Confidence

While learning to read his cues is powerful, the real magic happens when you get bold enough to ask. Not because you're unsure. But because you care. Because you want to co-create something beautiful.

Here's the key: ask in ways that move the moment forward, not in ways that make him feel like he needs to grade you.

Avoid questions like, *"Was that good?"* or *"Did I do it right?"* Those can feel like pressure to reassure, not invitations to connect. Instead, make your questions about curiosity, not correctness.

Try this:

- **The Compliment Sandwich**: Start with something affirming, then gently add a request, and end with more affirmation. For example:

  "Mmm, this is making me so hot... how's the pace and firmness for you... I love hearing what you like."

- **Ask for Specifics**: Say things like,

  "I loved trying that twist move—how did that feel for you?" or

  "Was there a part that really stood out to you?"

- **Use Sexy Check-ins**: Let your questions become part of the moment. Whisper,

  "Like that?" or

  "Tell me what you want..." or

  "Do you want it slower or firmer?"

- **Show, Don't Just Tell**: Invite him to guide your hands. Literally. Say,

- *"Put your hand over mine and show me what you like."*

  This isn't awkward—it's hot. And it can be one of the most intimate things you share.

When you lead with love, ask with confidence, and listen with your whole heart, you transform a simple act into something sacred. You turn feedback into foreplay and insecurity into intimacy. And that, my friend, is the real art of getting handsy.

After the Climax

The moment after orgasm is tender, sacred space. It's the quiet after the crescendo, the gentle return to earth after soaring heights of intimacy. And how you spend those next few minutes? It matters. A lot.

This is where *aftercare* comes in. And no, it's not just for intense or edgy sexual practices. It's for every couple who wants to protect their connection and wrap their physical intimacy in a cocoon of safety, warmth, and love.

What Is Aftercare, and Why Does It Matter?

Aftercare is the time you spend emotionally and physically caring for one another after sex. It's not about prolonging the act—it's about deepening the bond. It can look like:

- Cuddling or spooning in silence
- Whispering affirmations or playful giggles
- Holding hands while you debrief the best parts
- Rubbing his back or stroking his hair
- Simply breathing together, skin to skin

These moments are more than sweet—they're *stabilizing*. Neuroscience shows that the emotional systems in our brains are still highly activated after orgasm. Oxytocin (the bonding hormone) is flowing, dopamine is settling, and cortisol (the stress hormone) is recalibrating. It's a vulnerable window where reassurance matters, even if neither of you can put that need into words.

Protecting Your Connection—And His Heart

Surprise fact: research has found that many men—up to 41% in some studies—experience post-coital dysphoria (PCD) at least once in their lives. That's the wave of unexpected sadness, irritability, or anxiety that can follow an otherwise good sexual experience. For some, it's a blip. For others, it can be a regular challenge.

This isn't about you doing something wrong. It's about his nervous system. Orgasm is intense, and the neurochemical drop afterward can leave him feeling disoriented or exposed. That's why aftercare is so powerful—it grounds him emotionally, giving his heart a soft place to land while his body resets.

The reassurance of your presence—the way you stroke his arm or say, *"I loved that with you"*—anchors him. It reminds him he's not just desired; he's cherished.

Completing the Cycle of Connection

Just as the male sexual response cycle ends in physiological resolution, emotional intimacy needs its own resolution too. Aftercare is what completes the arc. It says, *"We're still us."* It's the relational exhale after shared intensity. And it makes the whole experience feel not just satisfying—but safe, sacred, and secure.

So don't rush to get dressed or scroll your phone. Linger. Breathe. Be together. Whether you're sharing a deep conversation or just lying in quiet affection, you're reinforcing the truth at the core of your intimacy: *This is about more than bodies. It's about love.*

And that, dear one, is the real climax.

Finger Banging

Let's talk about hands-on exploration—literally.

Manual stimulation, or what some cheekily call "finger banging," is a form of intimate touch that allows your husband to engage with your body in a deeply personal, responsive, and connection-driven way. But let's be clear: this isn't about becoming a "sex expert" or delivering a flawless performance. This is about discovery. About finding new ways to enjoy one another. About creating space for pleasure, curiosity, and play in the safe harbor of your marriage.

Think of this not as a checklist to master, but as an invitation to adventure together.

A Journey, Not a Performance

You and your husband are co-explorers. There's no map with a big red X and no points deducted for detours. The goal isn't orgasm (though if it happens, hooray!). The goal is shared experience—emotional closeness, mutual understanding, and physical delight. This mindset relieves the pressure and opens the door for authentic connection.

And let's be honest: it's going to be a little awkward at first. There may be moments of nervous laughter, clumsy angles, or too much pressure here and not enough there. That's not failure—that's real life. You're learning a new language together, and it's okay if you fumble some of the vocabulary. What matters is that you're speaking love with your hands and hearts.

Curiosity Is the Key

Approach this practice with the same energy you'd bring to learning a new recipe or exploring a scenic trail. Let curiosity lead: What feels good? What builds anticipation? What slows things down in the best way?

Invite questions and offer feedback—not as critique, but as clues: "Try softer here," or "I think I like that motion better." Your guidance is a gift, not a correction. And remember, your body is wonderfully unique, so what works for one woman may not work for another. That's why shared exploration is so valuable—it helps you uncover what's true for *you*.

Built on Trust, Framed by Love

This kind of intimate exploration works best when it's built on a strong relational foundation: mutual trust, a sense of emotional safety, and the covenant of a committed marriage. It's not about "spicing things up" to fix something broken—it's about celebrating what you already have, and discovering new dimensions of delight within it.

So take a breath. Let go of expectations. And step into this space not as a task to check off, but as a tender, sometimes silly, always sacred adventure of touch, laughter, and intimacy.

Because, sister, your body is worth exploring. And your marriage is worth the joy it can bring.

Setting the Stage

Let's be real: good sex doesn't start with fingers—it starts with intention. The environment you create, the care you show, and the thoughtfulness you bring into your intimate space are just as important as the touch itself. These aren't just practical steps—they're deeply meaningful, non-verbal acts of love that say, *"You matter. Your comfort, your pleasure, and your body are sacred to me."*

These simple, foundational preparations are more than checklists—they're a kind of foreplay all their own. They build trust. They communicate respect. And they signal to your body (and brain) that you're safe, wanted, and free to enjoy.

Hygiene Is Intimacy in Action

Yes, it's basic—but also essential. Good hygiene isn't about being clinical; it's about cultivating safety. It's a tangible, physical way to say, *"I care for you."* Before any intimate touch happens, these simple steps help set a sacred, comfortable tone:

- **Clean Hands Are Non-Negotiable**

  Our hands go *everywhere* throughout the day, and when it comes to your most sensitive parts, that's not a place to take chances. A good handwashing with soap and warm water is a baseline of care—it protects against infections like UTIs or bacterial vaginosis and shows that your partner's not just ready, but respectfully prepared.

- **Trim and File Those Nails**

  One hangnail. That's all it takes to turn a tender moment into a full-body clench. His fingernails should be short and *smooth*—no jagged edges, no accidental "oops." File them well. It might feel like a small detail, but it makes a massive difference in helping you relax fully.

- **Remove Jewelry**

  Wedding rings are beautiful, but not always in the bedroom. Rings, bracelets, and watches can scratch, pinch, or snag, disrupting the gentle, fluid movement your body craves. Best to remove anything that could get in the way—then get to the good stuff.

Lube Is Love (Seriously)

Let's bust the myth: lubricant isn't just for people with "problems." It's for people who want *great* sex. Using lube during manual stimulation isn't a backup plan—it's an enhancement. It reduces friction, amplifies sensation, and makes everything feel smoother, sexier, and more inviting.

- **Why Lube Makes Everything Better**

  Even if you're naturally aroused, skin-on-skin contact (especially fingers) can sometimes feel more draggy than delicious. A generous layer of lube creates glide, increases comfort, and allows for more sustained, pleasurable touch. Plus, it gives you better feedback—because when there's no friction, he can really feel the pressure and motion in all the right ways.

- **Choosing the Right Type**

  You've got options, and here's what to know:

  - **Water-Based:** The MVP for most situations. Safe, gentle, toy-compatible, and easy to clean. Just know it may need reapplying mid-session.

  - **Silicone-Based:** The marathon runner. Super long-lasting and silky-smooth—great for manual stimulation. Just skip it if you're using silicone toys.

  - **What to Avoid:** Oils like baby oil, petroleum jelly, or cooking oil might sound sexy in theory—but they mess with vaginal health and can destroy condoms. Save the coconut oil for your skincare routine.

- **Pro Tips for Use**

  - **Warm It Up:** Cold lube straight to your bits? No, thank you. Have your husband warm it in his hands first. The heat adds to the experience and tells your body, *"You're safe. You're seen. Let's enjoy."*

  - **Be Generous:** Don't skimp. Lube should be applied to both his fingers and your vulva—think inner and outer labia, clitoral area, and vaginal entrance. And don't hesitate to reapply. There's no such thing as too much glide.

Creating this environment isn't just about avoiding discomfort—it's about building anticipation. It's foreplay that begins before a single touch. When your husband takes time to care for the setting, he's not just preparing your body—he's nurturing your trust. And that, dear sister, makes all the difference.

The Manual of Manual Stimulation

This section is your guide to manual intimacy—not as a list of steps to memorize, but as a shared language of sensation you and your husband get to co-create. Think of it as a playlist of touch—a handful of techniques and rhythms you can mix, match, and adjust depending on how you're feeling. Because here's the truth: what feels amazing one night might feel too intense the next. Your body is wonderfully dynamic. And that's not a problem—it's a gift.

The real skill in manual stimulation isn't about mastering a single "signature move." It's about becoming attuned and responsive—learning to read each other, stay present, and dance with the moment.

Start Slow: The Power of a Gradual Approach

Sexual arousal is like simmering a pot, not flipping a light switch. Your nervous system and pleasure centers need time to unwind from the noise of the day and tune into the sensations of the moment. That's why a slow build isn't just sweet—it's science-backed.

A beautiful way to imagine this is through the gentle philosophy behind lymphatic massage: light pressure, rhythmic motion, and a movement from outer areas inward. The idea isn't to rush—it's to awaken. To coax. To invite.

- **Begin Far from the Center**

  Let your husband start by touching secondary erogenous zones with care—your arms, back, lower legs. Maybe it's a foot rub. Maybe it's just slow, affectionate caresses. As you both relax, he can begin exploring more intimate territory like your lower abdomen, hips, or inner thighs. The goal is anticipation, not acceleration.

- **The First Vulvar Touch**

  When he reaches your vulva, the first contact should feel reverent, not rushed. One wonderful way to start: using the warm flat of his palm to press gently over your mons pubis—either over clothing or directly on the skin. It's non-invasive and diffuse, signaling his presence with patience, not pressure.

Part I: Exploring the Exterior—Clitoral Stimulation

For most women, external clitoral stimulation is the most consistent and reliable path to orgasm. The glans clitoris, however, is highly sensitive—so a light touch over the hood is almost always a better place to start.

Techniques to Try:

- **The Classic Circle**

  With one or two fingers, he can draw slow, soft circles over your clitoral hood. Let him vary the size and speed as your body begins to respond.

- **Up-and-Down / Side-to-Side**

  A gentle slide across the hood—either vertically or horizontally—adds variety. These motions help him "learn the landscape" and discover what your body responds to.

- **The Gentle Tap**

  Light, rhythmic taps can feel playful and arousing—especially when the rhythm changes up like a flirtatious drumbeat.

- **The Peace Pinch**

  With his index and middle fingers in a "V" shape, he can gently straddle your clitoral shaft and slide up and down on either side. It's indirect, diffused stimulation that avoids overwhelming you.

- **Pressure Play**

  If you need a break from focused touch, his warm palm pressed firmly but gently over your entire clitoral area can feel grounding and comforting—a reset button that still feels good.

Part II: Venturing Within—Vaginal and G-Spot Stimulation

When you're deeply aroused and lubricated, you may feel ready to invite him inside. Internal touch isn't just about penetration—it's about exploring the hidden network of clitoral tissue that wraps around your vaginal canal.

Techniques to Try:

- **The "Come Hither" Motion**

  With one or two well-lubricated fingers inserted palm-up, he can gently curl them toward your belly button in a rhythmic motion. This targets the G-spot—part of the internal clitoral network.

- **Firm, Rhythmic Pressure**

  Unlike the glans clitoris, the G-spot often prefers steady, firm pressure—like kneading into a dense muscle. Think less flutter, more massage.

- **Mix Up the Motion**

  Some women prefer pulsing. Others like a gentle grind. Let him vary the angle and speed, and give feedback as you go. There's no "one right way"—just what feels best right now.

Part III: The Blended Approach—Double the Delight

Here's where things get symphonic. Combining internal and external stimulation engages the full clitoral structure and can lead to some of the most powerful orgasms a woman can experience.

Blended Techniques:

- **Thumb-and-Finger Harmony**

  While two fingers perform the "come hither" motion inside, his thumb circles or presses gently on your external clitoris. This two-point stimulation can feel deeply synchronized and overwhelmingly good.

- **Optimize Your Position**

  Lying on your back with a pillow under your hips gives him better access to both the G-spot and clitoral area. It tilts your pelvis upward and makes simultaneous stimulation easier and more effective.

In this stage of exploration, variety is your superpower. Switch between light and firm, fast and slow, deep and delicate. Let laughter have its place. Let curiosity lead. You're not just practicing techniques—you're creating a shared language of pleasure that says, *"I know you. I love you. I want to give you joy."*

Showing, Not Just Telling

Sometimes the clearest—and honestly, sexiest—way to communicate your desire is through physical demonstration.

Words are powerful, yes. But when you're both in the thick of intimacy, your body can speak volumes in ways that are direct, loving, and beautifully arousing.

Hand-Over-Hand Guidance

When he's trying to find the right spot or match your rhythm but isn't quite hitting it, you don't have to rely only on words. Try this: gently place your hand over his, and guide him. Show him the exact pressure, motion, or rhythm that feels amazing. This isn't criticism—it's collaboration. And it can be deeply connecting for both of you.

Touching teaches faster than talking. And when you guide with tenderness, it says: *I trust you to learn me. I want to be known by you.* That's intimacy at its best.

The Self-Demonstration Invitation

Here's another deeply powerful—and surprisingly magnetic—tool: showing him what you like on your own body. You might pause and whisper, "Can I show you for a second how I like it?" Then, with him watching, use your fingers to demonstrate. It's not about performing. It's about giving him a visual map—plus a kinetic sense of rhythm and pressure—to learn from. Many couples find this moment deeply vulnerable, erotic, and helpful all at once.

Remember, you're not saying "you're doing it wrong." You're saying "come learn my body with me." And that makes all the difference.

The Feedback Compass: Reframes That Build Confidence

Let's get practical. Sometimes you'll want to adjust what he's doing. And how you phrase that feedback can mean the difference between him feeling discouraged—or deeply encouraged to keep exploring.

When He's Touching the Wrong Spot

Instead of saying, "Not there," or "That's the wrong place," try guiding his hand and saying, *"Mmm, that's close. I love it when you touch me right here."* You're still being clear, but in a way that affirms his effort and builds connection instead of defensiveness.

When the Pressure Is Too Hard

Rather than blurting out, "Ouch!" or "That's too much," try, *"That pressure feels so good. Can you try just a little bit lighter?... Yes, like that—perfect."* This tells him he's on the right track and helps him adjust without losing momentum or confidence.

When You Want a Rhythm Change

Instead of saying, "That's too fast," or "Slow down," guide him with curiosity: *"Mmm, that's amazing... can we try going just a bit slower for a second?... Yes. That's it."* You're still leading—but now you're inviting him into the process with warmth and playfulness.

When Something Just Isn't Working

If a particular touch or technique just doesn't feel good, you don't have to power through or shut it down harshly. Try redirecting with something like, *"Hey, I really loved what you were doing a minute ago with those circles. Can we go back to that?"* That helps him know what does work—and keeps both of you emotionally and physically in sync.

This kind of feedback is what turns a hesitant experience into a confident, connected one. You're not giving a performance review. You're co-authoring a love story with your body. And the more you guide with grace and honesty, the deeper your shared pleasure will grow.

Wrapping It Up

In this chapter, we've explored the tender, transformative world of manual intimacy—how your hands, guided by curiosity, communication, and care, can become a powerful expression of love, connection, and sacred pleasure. From understanding the male and female arousal arcs to practicing techniques that are as playful as they are purposeful, we've dismantled the myth that sex is only about performance or penetration. You've learned that **pleasure is a shared journey**, not a destination—and that your touch can offer comfort, confidence, and even healing.

You've also discovered how **aftercare isn't extra—it's essential.** Those gentle moments after climax are where emotional connection is deepened, where safety is reinforced, and where intimacy becomes more than skin-deep.

So take a moment to reflect:

- What surprised or encouraged you in this chapter?
- What technique or insight are you curious to try?
- How might you invite your husband into this playful, pressure-free kind of exploration?

Whether this is your first time venturing into these waters or a long-overdue refresh of familiar practices, remember: **you're not doing this alone.** You and your husband are co-creators of a beautiful, evolving intimacy story.

And speaking of stories—what happens when you add movement to your magic? In the next chapter, we're exploring how **sexual positions** can open the door to variety, comfort, and deeper connection—not just for your body, but for your heart and soul, too.

Chapter 18: Sexy Twister

Spaghetti Legs and a Stack of Pillows

Maggie had no idea her core muscles were this underdeveloped until three minutes into the "spontaneous" sex position she found on Pinterest.

There she was—kneeling on the bed, elbows braced awkwardly on a stack of semi-firm throw pillows, knees slipping slowly apart on the comforter like a newborn giraffe. Her husband, James, was behind her, trying valiantly to look both supportive and turned on, while also adjusting his position for the fifth time.

"Is your knee okay?" she asked mid-wobble.

"I think it just popped… but in a good way?" he replied, clearly unsure.

They both burst out laughing.

Maggie collapsed into the pillows, limbs flailing, hair sticking to her forehead. This was not how the scene looked in her head. In her fantasy, she was wild and flexible and had excellent lighting. In real life? She was slightly sweaty, her hip was cramping, and she was about one thigh tremble away from calling it quits.

Still, she smiled.

Because even though her balance was questionable and she'd lost her dignity somewhere between the fourth and fifth pillow adjustment, she felt bold. She felt playful. And she felt... closer.

"I'm pretty sure this is not what Song of Solomon meant by 'your legs are pillars of marble,'" she snorted.

James chuckled, pressing a kiss to her shoulder. "Babe, marble's overrated. I'm here for spaghetti legs and that cute butt wiggle."

And somehow, in the midst of the mess and giggles, it felt holy. Not because they nailed the position. But because they were trying—together. Because Maggie was choosing to show up in her body, as it was, with curiosity and courage.

And that? That was sexy.

Spin the Arrow

Remember the game *Twister*? You'd spin the dial, laugh nervously, and contort your body into all kinds of wild shapes—half thrill, half chaos, and 100% fun. Exploring sexual positions can be a little like that. Playful. Unpredictable. Full of possibilities.

But here's the difference: in your bedroom, *you* get to spin the arrow. You decide what you want to try, what feels good, and what gets your curiosity going. You're not following someone else's list of "101 Positions to Try Before You Die." You're cultivating your own sense of sexual adventure—at your pace, in your body, with your husband.

And the real secret? The sexiest part isn't the position—it's your confidence.

When you say, "Let's try something new," or gently guide your husband into a different angle, or even just shift your hips into a new posture with a playful grin, that boldness is magnetic. It says, *I'm here. I'm curious. I'm in this with you.* And whether it leads to a grand success or a giggle-filled flop, you've made intimacy playful, connected, and real.

That's the heart of sexual adventure: confident experimentation. Every time you try something new, you learn a little more about your body, your preferences, your connection. And that process—full of grace, laughter, and a little holy courage—is what makes sex deeply satisfying and beautifully you.

The Key

Here's a little neuroscience-informed magic: your brain doesn't know the difference between *thinking* about something and *doing* it. That's right—when you mentally rehearse a new sexual position or imagine a bold, adventurous scenario, you're literally prepping your neural pathways. It's like strength training for your confidence. The more you fantasize or self-pleasure while imagining new sexual adventures, the easier it becomes to try them in real life.

So if there's a position you've been curious about or a scenario that excites you, start in your imagination. Picture yourself being confident, bold, and beautifully in charge. Let yourself feel turned on by the idea—not just by the act itself, but by who you become when you try it.

And here's the secret sauce: it doesn't have to look perfect to be powerful.

If you're caught up wondering how your body looks in a certain position, or worrying whether it's "awkward," you'll miss the very thing that makes it sexy—*your presence.* A woman who's turned on and enjoying herself is the most powerful aphrodisiac there is. Truly. Your pleasure is contagious. When you feel hot, you *are* hot, regardless of angles or lighting or choreography.

So don't let spectatoring steal your spark. Instead, see yourself—*in your mind's eye*—as the brave, beautiful, sexually adventurous woman you are becoming. Practice that vision often. Let it light you up inside. Because when your desire shows up boldly, your husband's desire will follow close behind.

Mental foreplay counts. And this kind of preparation? It's the key to unlocking your embodied confidence and rewriting the script of your sex life—one bold thought at a time.

Customize the Experience

At the heart of sexual confidence is *sexual intelligence*—the grace-filled ability to listen to your body, communicate openly, and creatively adapt any experience to suit your unique desires and needs. It's not about doing things "by the book," but about crafting your own adventure, with tools that help you feel both empowered and comfortable.

The Power of Props: Your Toolkit for Comfort and Creativity

Who says great sex has to stay on the mattress or follow a script? Sometimes the key to deeper pleasure—or simply staying comfortable long enough to enjoy yourself—is just a pillow away.

Think of props not as awkward add-ons, but as your personal support crew. They're not there to fix a problem—they're there to *enhance* your experience and free your body to focus on sensation instead of strain.

Pillows & Wedges

Let's start with the unsung hero of the bedroom: the humble pillow.

A pillow tucked under your hips in missionary or woman-on-top positions can shift the angle of penetration in delightful ways, bringing more targeted contact to the G-spot or simply making things feel more satisfying. In rear-entry positions, a few stacked pillows under your chest and belly can relieve the weight from your arms and shoulders, making it easier to relax and stay present.

You can also slip a pillow between your knees to ease joint pressure or under your lower back for extra support. Small shifts in alignment can make a big difference in comfort—and give you the freedom to enjoy new positions without distraction.

If you're feeling fancy, there are even purpose-designed sex wedges and cushions out there. But don't underestimate the power of your couch pillows. You probably already have everything you need.

Lubrication

We've said it before, but it's worth repeating: lube is not just for fixing dryness—it's for increasing delight. New positions often mean new angles and surfaces, and that can lead to unexpected friction. A good, body-safe lubricant keeps everything gliding smoothly, ensuring that pleasure—not discomfort—remains center stage.

Keep it within arm's reach. Make it part of the ritual. More often than not, a few extra drops of lube are the difference between "meh" and "mmmmm."

Furniture as Foreplay

Don't overlook the stage you're playing on. The edge of your bed can support positions like The Butterfly, offering ease and accessibility. A solid, armless chair is perfect for variations on The Lotus or woman-on-top. And if you're feeling bold, a countertop or even the back of a couch can turn standing positions into new adventures. Walls can support standing play. Rugs can cushion kneeling. And your whole space becomes a canvas for connection.

The goal isn't complexity—it's freedom. Customizing your space and your props lets you shift from "Is this going to work?" to "How can we make this even more fun?"

You're not stuck in a box—you're just getting started with the tools to make pleasure fit *you*.

Adapting to Your Unique Bodies

Every body is gloriously, wonderfully different—and that's part of the magic. What makes sex in a committed marriage so special isn't achieving a "perfect form," but discovering, over time, how your two beautifully unique bodies can move, shift, and sync together in ways that feel good, affirming, and real. Positions aren't rigid instructions—they're invitations to adapt, adjust, and explore.

Body Size & Shape

Let's bust a myth right now: your body size has nothing to do with your sexual worth, ability, or pleasure potential. What matters most is comfort, communication, and creativity. Different body sizes or shapes may require some extra finesse—but not less passion.

If one of you is significantly taller, broader, or curvier than the other, pillows are your best friend. In missionary, for example, a few pillows under your hips can lift your pelvis and make penetration smoother and more aligned. In woman-on-top positions, your husband can use pillows under his hips to adjust the angle and bring your bodies into better rhythm.

These aren't "fixes"—they're enhancements. The focus should never be on what a position "should" look like. Instead, ask: *What feels good? What brings us closer?* Props and small shifts can make a world of difference when you're tuned in to each other's comfort and pleasure.

Physical Limitations

Whether it's a sore knee, back stiffness, or a long-term condition, physical limitations don't disqualify you from a vibrant sex life—they invite innovation. This is not about pushing through pain; it's about choosing pleasure within the body's current capacity.

Borrowing wisdom from physical therapy and post-op care, think slow and supported. Avoid sudden movements, high-pressure poses, or anything that irritates sensitive areas. If kneeling is hard, skip it. If a shoulder is tender, try lying down instead of bearing weight.

Side-lying positions like The Spoon are often ideal, minimizing strain while still allowing for deep connection and intimacy. You're not failing if you need to adapt—you're thriving by honoring your body while staying connected to your spouse.

Pregnancy

As your belly grows, so does your need to adjust your sexual rhythms—and that's okay! Pregnancy shifts everything, from energy to body image to logistics. But it doesn't have to sideline your sex life.

As your pregnancy progresses, positions like missionary may put uncomfortable pressure on your abdomen or restrict your breathing. This is a wonderful opportunity to explore others. Woman-on-top allows you to control depth, pace, and pressure, all while protecting your growing belly. Side-lying positions like The Spoon remain gentle, comfortable, and safe throughout pregnancy—and they offer sweet opportunities for skin-to-skin closeness and emotional connection.

The key? Don't stop connecting. Communicate often. Laugh when something doesn't go as planned. And keep prioritizing physical closeness, even when your options shift.

Wrapping It Up

You don't need a list of 101 positions to be sexually adventurous—you need the courage to explore, the curiosity to adapt, and the confidence to follow your desire wherever it leads. This chapter wasn't about performing perfectly-shaped poses. It was about giving yourself permission to play, adjust, and discover what feels good for your *real* body, in your *real* marriage, right now.

Whether you're tweaking your favorite position with a pillow, fantasizing during solo time to build confidence, or trying something brand new with a laugh and a wink, you're cultivating something beautiful: a spirit of intimacy that's responsive, resilient, and richly satisfying.

So take a breath. You don't have to know it all today. You just need to stay open, stay kind to your body, and keep moving forward—one position, one pillow, one playful moment at a time.

And if you've ever found yourself wondering, *"Is it okay to want a little more edge, a little more kink, or a little more intensity?"*—then you're in for a freeing conversation. In the next chapter, we'll explore what makes something "kinky," whether that's biblically and relationally healthy, and how to tell if it might be something worth exploring in your own bedroom adventure.

Chapter 19: Kinky?

"What Would the Ladies' Group Think?"

*T*asha stared at the search history on her phone like it might catch fire. "Christian... bondage?" she whispered to herself, then flopped dramatically onto the bed. "Jesus, take the Wi-Fi."

It had started innocently enough. A flirty joke from her husband. A teasing "yes, sir" in the kitchen that made them both laugh—and then pause. That pause had turned into a late-night Google spiral, ending in a Pinterest board titled "Marriage Bed Ideas" and one very red face.

Now she couldn't stop wondering: Was it weird that she was turned on by the idea of being lightly restrained? Was she allowed to want that? Or was she on a slippery slope straight into a Proverbs 31 fail?

Her mind flashed to Bible study last Thursday. Karen had brought cinnamon muffins and a passionate warning about "the moral decline of society." Tasha had nodded solemnly while discreetly crossing her legs under the table, half-hoping no one could tell she'd been thinking about silk scarves in non-churchy ways.

She wasn't trying to be rebellious. She loved Jesus. She loved her husband. She just... wanted to spice things up without feeling like she needed to apologize for enjoying it.

She picked up her phone again, heart pounding like a middle schooler caught passing notes. There it was—another tab open from last night's reading: "Kink and the Christian Marriage: Exploring with Consent and Faith."

Her finger hovered. Then clicked.

She wasn't sure what she'd find. But for the first time in a long time, she felt curious instead of ashamed. Hopeful, even.

Maybe there was a way to be both holy and a little bit spicy.

Good Girl

Let's start with a quick disclaimer: If you're the type who was already clutching your pearls during the masturbation chapter—or if the idea of Christian women enjoying sex makes you start drafting a Facebook rant about the state of the church—this chapter might not be for you. Honestly, we bless you, but we're not writing this one with you in mind.

Now, for the rest of you—especially those who skipped straight to this chapter because the word "kinky" caught your eye? Girl, we see you, and you're safe here with us. Whether you're curious, excited, or blushing a bit (maybe all three), you're in the right place. No shame here. You're allowed to explore, ask bold questions, and enjoy being fully present in your God-designed sexuality. And yes... if you came here hoping for a little playful, grown-up conversation about spanking and power dynamics, we've got you.

Let's start by answering two foundational questions:

What is kink?

And is it okay for Christians?

The simplest definition of kink is *sexual behavior that's unusual or uncommon.* But "unusual" is totally relative. For some people, saying "yes" to oral sex still feels scandalous. For others, using a blindfold in the bedroom might be their Tuesday. Kink isn't a fixed checklist—it's more like a sliding scale of what feels outside the norm for you, your background, or your friend group.

So here's the real question: *Is kink biblically okay?* And the answer is found in our three-part filter:

- **Is it consensual?** Are both you and your husband enthusiastically on board, fully informed, and free to opt out at any point without guilt or pressure?

- **Is it monogamous?** Are you keeping the sexual experience between just the two of you—no outside participants, no porn, no OnlyFans?

- **Is it mutually pleasurable?** Are you both having fun, staying emotionally safe, and genuinely enjoying the adventure together?

If the answer to all three is yes—*congrats!* You're well within God-honoring boundaries, even if your Aunt Karen thinks rope play is a sign of the End Times.

Here's the deal: God is not threatened by your sexual creativity. He's not surprised by your desires. He's not ashamed of your curiosity. In fact, we believe He's delighted when a married couple plays, explores, and grows in joyful, wholehearted intimacy.

So whether you're ready to swing a flogger or you're just dipping a toe into "mildly spicy," this chapter is for you. If kink isn't your thing, that's also perfectly fine. There's no pressure to want what you don't want. But if your inner "good girl" is curious about coloring outside the lines... let's talk about it.

And while we're talking, let's be clear about something really important: coercion, manipulation, or pressure—especially around anything sexual—is *not* consent. It's not mutual. And it's *definitely* not okay. We want to dismantle shame around healthy exploration, but we're equally serious about dismantling distortions that weaponize kink or turn curiosity into obligation. If your spouse ever tries to use this chapter (or anything in this book) as a way to pressure you into something you're not comfortable with, please hear us: that doesn't reflect the heart of Jesus. That doesn't honor the safety and mutual delight He designed for your marriage bed.

You do *not* owe it to your spouse to explore kink. You are not less of a wife, woman, or sexual partner if this kind of play isn't for you. And if it *is* something you're interested in, that doesn't make you dirty or weird—it makes you a human with a body and a brain designed for curiosity and connection.

Here's another nuance worth naming: sometimes sexual experimentation—especially the kind that involves pain, intensity, or power dynamics—can be part of an addictive cycle. When sex becomes a substitute for emotional intimacy or a dopamine hit to escape deeper needs, kink (like anything else) can get distorted. So if there's unresolved trauma, pornography use, affairs, or emotional disconnection in your relationship, we encourage you to hit pause. Not because kink is inherently bad, but because emotional safety is foundational. You don't build a treehouse in a storm.

If that hits close to home, know that you're not alone. And there's help. We'd encourage you to reach out to a NICC therapist—like the ones at MyCounselor.Online®—who can help you and your spouse work through those deeper

JOSH & CASSIE SPURLOCK

issues before adding any new dynamics to your sex life. Healing makes room for joy. And joy is always the goal.

Dirty Talk

Okay, brace yourself—because this is your official soapbox moment from a Biblical languages major. (Yes, we exist. No, we don't all wear elbow patches or correct people's Greek pronunciation at parties. But we do have thoughts. And this one's about words. Spicy ones.)

Many of us grew up hearing that certain words—especially those infamous four-letter ones—were inherently sinful. We were taught to avoid them like spiritual landmines. "Watch your mouth" became the moral measuring stick. But what does Scripture *actually* say about language?

Let's look at **Ephesians 4:29**:

"Do not let any unwholesome talk come out of your mouths, but only what is helpful for building others up according to their needs, that it may benefit those who listen."

Notice what Paul *doesn't* do. He doesn't list off a naughty-word blacklist. He doesn't say, "Thou shalt not say that word that rhymes with duck." Instead, he points to *purpose* and *impact*. Unwholesome talk, biblically, isn't about syllables—it's about speech that tears down instead of building up.

In other words: You can be cruel with church-approved vocabulary. And you can be deeply loving with language that would make your grandma clutch her pearls.

It gets even clearer when we dig into semantics. Substituting "darn" or "freakin'" for their more direct cousins doesn't change the emotional payload. The heart of the matter is, well, *your heart*. Like Jesus said in **Luke 6:45**, *"Out* *of the overflow of the heart, the mouth speaks."* God's not just monitoring your mouth—He's listening to the heart behind your words. Are they flowing from love, vulnerability, joy? Or from bitterness, shame, or manipulation?

So, what does that mean for *bedroom talk*?

Let's be honest. The topic of "dirty talk" makes a lot of women feel like they're balancing on a high wire between prudish silence and full-on porno dialogue. But here's the truth: in a healthy, safe, Christ-centered marriage, using spicy words to express desire, playfulness, or passion is not only allowed—it can be downright sacred.

That's not hyperbole. That's **Song of Songs**. Just open your Bible to that poetic love letter and try not to blush. The metaphors? The sultry longing? The frank delight in each other's bodies? It's suggestive, bold, and beautifully erotic—and God put it in the Bible.

So here's the key question to ask about *any* word you want to use during intimacy:

Is this building connection or breaking it?

Is it loving or wounding?

Is it mutual delight, or veiled control?

If the answer is "we both feel loved, safe, and turned on"? Go. For. It.

Whether it's a cheeky compliment, a sultry suggestion, or a bold invitation whispered between kisses—your words can be a powerful part of your shared pleasure. The goal isn't sanitized speech. The goal is speech that builds trust, deepens desire, and reflects the joy God intended for your marriage bed.

So yes—talk dirty, if it's done in love. Say what you want. Say what you crave. Say it kindly, passionately, playfully. Just say it like you mean it—with a heart rooted in safety, honesty, and connection.

Now that's sexy *and* sacred.

Sexy Pain?

So... do people really get turned on by pain?

Well, have you ever visited a CrossFit gym?

No, seriously. Have you heard of a runner's high? Ask any marathoner or gym rat, and you'll likely hear about that euphoric, floaty rush that hits after pushing their body to the edge. They'll talk about how amazing it feels—how the burn turns into a buzz, and the sweat becomes a celebration. Sounds a little intense, right?

What they're actually describing is a totally real biological phenomenon: the release of your body's natural opioids, called **endorphins**. These little neurochemical ninjas flood your system in response to certain kinds of pain—especially pain that is controlled, intentional, and not overwhelming. And guess what? That rush doesn't just happen in spin class.

It happens during sex, too.

Here's how it works: when the body experiences a mild, sharp sensation—like a playful spanking, a firmer-than-usual pinch, or even the gentle tug of hair—it can trigger that same cascade of feel-good chemicals. These endorphins amplify sensation, reduce inhibition, and can actually *intensify* sexual arousal and orgasm. It's a delicious cocktail of tension, release, and reward—served up right inside your own nervous system.

Now, important disclaimer: not everyone finds this pleasurable. Some people (hi, it's me, Josh) will never understand the appeal of sore quads. And that's perfectly fine. There's no moral or marital virtue in pretending to enjoy something you don't.

But for others, a little exploration at the edge of sensation adds something electric. It can heighten anticipation, deepen surrender, or create a jolt of surprise that turns up the volume on everything else. Whether it's a firmer grip, a flick of a flogger, or the teasing prick of a pinwheel—if it's consensual, mutual, and pleasurable? It's fair game.

This isn't about pain for pain's sake. It's about discovering, together, where tension transforms into pleasure. It's about curiosity and communication. It's about playing with sensation—not punishment, not control, not shame. Just exploration, with a safe word.

So if you've ever been intrigued by the idea of a little sexy sting... you're not broken, weird, or rebellious. You're just human. And humans are delightfully complex.

And if that's not your thing? Totally okay. You're not missing out, and you're not less adventurous. You're just wired differently. The goal here is freedom, not performance.

Whether you're into pushups or pinwheels, the bottom line is this: if it's consensual, mutual, and brings joy to your marriage bed? It's in bounds. God made your body with nerve endings, chemicals, and the capacity for pleasure—including surprise and sensation. Explore as much—or as little—as you like.

The Forbidden Fruit Effect

Okay, asking for a friend: is it normal to get turned on by fantasies that involve embarrassment, humiliation, or even scenarios that feel a little... wrong?

Like being "forced" to behave in totally out-of-character ways, or imagining something wildly inappropriate—like being spanked in public, or caught doing something sexual and punished for it?

Yep. Totally normal. And no, you're not broken, shameful, or secretly twisted.

Let's dig into the *why* behind this, because the answer is as much about your nervous system as your imagination.

Remember how we talked about the body's natural response to pain—how endorphins can turn mild discomfort into pleasure? Well, your body does something similar with emotional intensity. When you feel embarrassment, fear, or that electric jolt of doing something "forbidden," your brain floods with **adrenaline, dopamine, and norepinephrine**—the same neurochemicals involved in sexual arousal. So when those heightened emotions happen in a *safe* setting—like during fantasy, self-pleasure, or intimacy with your husband—your nervous system reads them as *extra exciting*. It's like pouring rocket fuel on your arousal.

This is why a taboo or edgy storyline can light your brain (and body) on fire, even if the same scenario in real life would be horrifying. Your brain *knows* it's pretend. You're safe, you're in control, and you're not actually violating your values. You're just enjoying a playful, high-intensity remix of arousal and imagination.

So no, you don't actually want to be abducted or humiliated or bent over a desk in a real classroom. (Though hey, if you two want to reenact the *pretend* version in your bedroom—go for it.) The key difference is **consent and safety**. When those are present, your brain interprets the intensity as exhilarating. Without them, the experience would flip—becoming overwhelming, traumatic, or deeply distressing.

Which is why fantasy is just that—fantasy. It's a safe, private, imaginative space where your brain can experiment with intensity without crossing any actual boundaries. And just because you're aroused by something in a fantasy doesn't mean you *want* that thing in real life. Your body isn't making a moral judgment—it's just responding to the high-octane cocktail of chemicals that those scenarios trigger.

In God's design, your nervous system was built to feel. To crave intensity. To respond to pleasure, novelty, even danger in ways that stir your senses and awaken desire. That's not dirty—it's divine engineering. What matters is how you steward that gift in ways that are consensual, loving, and aligned with your values.

So next time a fantasy catches you off guard, you can smile and think: "Yep, that's just my brain doing what God made it to do." You're not crazy. You're not shameful. You're wonderfully made—with a powerful imagination and a beautifully responsive body.

All Tied Up

Handcuffs? Silk scarves? A soft rope under the bed?

The psychology behind why restraints can feel thrilling in the bedroom is rich and varied—more than we have space to fully unpack here. But we can explore a few core dynamics that make this particular spice so compelling for many women.

First, there's the novelty. Anything outside the routine naturally piques our interest and heightens arousal. Your brain thrives on new experiences—especially when they're just a little bit naughty. Trying something unusual, like being gently tied down or blindfolded, awakens curiosity and amps up your sense of anticipation. It's like your brain leans in and whispers, *"Ooh, what's happening here?"*

Then there's the power exchange. For some women, there's something deeply arousing about the idea of surrender—not in a creepy, coercive way, but in a chosen, playful way. When you allow your husband to gently restrain your hands or guide your experience, it can create a powerful sense of being desired, cherished, and fully focused on. That surrender, in the safety of trust, can feel incredibly intimate.

And don't overlook the thrill of unpredictability. When you're not quite sure what your partner is going to do next—whether he'll kiss your neck or trail his fingertips down your side—it creates a cocktail of excitement, vulnerability, and anticipation. Your body lights up, not just because of the physical sensations, but because your imagination is fully engaged.

For many women, this kind of play taps into a deep desire to *let go*. To stop overthinking, to release control, to be the one receiving instead of giving. In a world where women are constantly in charge—of kids, meals, calendars, emotions—being gently restrained in love can feel like a rare and sacred exhale.

Is it for everyone? Nope. And that's okay. If you try it and it's not your thing, you've still learned something valuable about your preferences. If you try it and discover it's surprisingly delightful, welcome to a new adventure in intimacy.

As with all forms of sexual exploration, the key ingredients are **trust, consent, and communication**. Restraints should never be about real control or coercion—they should be an extension of your shared play, where boundaries are respected, safewords are agreed upon if needed, and everything stops the moment someone says, "Pause."

If being "all tied up" sounds like something you want to explore, go ahead—talk about it, prepare for it, laugh through it. It might just unlock a new kind of closeness.

Spicy Books?

Okay, deep breath—we're going there. Let's talk about spicy books.

Not just talk about them around a coffee table in hushed tones or judge them silently from across the church foyer, but actually talk about them. The question of whether Christian women can or should read romance novels—especially ones with explicit sex scenes—is one that stirs up a lot of feelings. And opinions. And sometimes, full-on debates in mom groups and Bible studies.

We get it. This is one of those "everybody has a take but few people want to say it out loud" kind of topics. But around here, we'd rather take the risk of honest conversation than avoid the mess altogether. Because silence breeds shame, and shame has never healed anyone.

So here's the deal: we're not here to hand down a blanket "yes" or "no." This is one of those gray areas—what the Bible calls a *matter of conscience.* That means it's something you need to wrestle through with Jesus for yourself. Not your favorite influencer. Not your pastor's wife. And definitely not your Aunt Mildred with the "bless your heart" tone. This is between you and the Lord.

Paul put it this way in Romans 14: "Each of us will give an account of ourselves to God... so whatever you believe about these things keep between yourself and God. Blessed is the one who does not condemn himself by what he approves." (Romans 14:12, 22)

So before we dive into our thoughts, here's the most important thing: if you've sincerely prayed about it and feel at peace before God, then that's what matters. You don't owe anyone an explanation. And if your conviction is that spicy books aren't for you, that's just as valid. In fact, Paul urges us to be mindful of the "weaker brother" too—meaning, don't push your liberty in a way that wounds someone else's conscience.

Hear us clearly: we are *not* prescribing spicy books, and we're certainly not telling you what your conviction *should* be. What we *are* encouraging is this—have an earnest, open-hearted conversation with the Lord about it. Talk with your spouse, too. And whatever conviction you come to? Live it out with integrity. Hold it with confidence. But also—with grace. Especially when you encounter someone who lands in a different place. Because Jesus calls us to freedom, not fear—and to unity, not uniformity.

That said, let's walk through a few thoughtful angles you may not have heard before—just to help stir some meaningful reflection.

One common argument against reading steamy fiction is that it portrays scenarios—affairs, fantasy creatures, magical seductions—that would be sinful in real life. And that's true. But if we applied that same logic consistently, we'd also have to stop watching most movies, reading the Old

Testament (ever read Judges 19?), or enjoying any story where characters sin... which is, well, every story.

Others compare spicy books to pornography. And we get the concern—both are sexually stimulating. But they're not the same. Pornography, as an industry, is rife with exploitation, objectification, and real-world harm. It conditions the brain to associate arousal with images of strangers detached from emotional intimacy, often impairing real-life sexual connection.

Spicy books, on the other hand, are fictional narratives. They don't exploit real people, and they don't rewire the brain in the same ways. For many women, they serve as a safe space to re-engage desire, awaken imagination, and explore fantasy in a way that deepens—not diminishes—connection with their husbands.

Are they a healthy tool for everyone? No. Just like wine, social media, or dessert, anything can be misused. If you find that reading them is distancing you from your husband, replacing real connection with fantasy, or becoming a go-to escape from emotional intimacy, that's worth prayerful reflection.

But if you're using them mindfully, with your spouse's awareness, and they're producing good fruit—more desire, more confidence, more closeness—then maybe the Lord's invitation is not to shame yourself, but to steward that joy wisely.

We'll say it again: you'll answer to Jesus for how you walked this out. Not to us. Not to social media. And certainly not to someone else's Instagram theology.

So, are spicy books okay for Christian women?

Talk to Jesus. Examine the fruit. Respect your convictions and those of others.

And above all—walk in freedom, not fear.

Watch Yourself

Here's something you might not hear at your women's Bible study (but probably should): watching yourself during sex or self-pleasure can be deeply arousing—and it's not weird. It's actually quite common.

While culture often brands men as the "visual" ones in the relationship, the truth is, women are highly visual too. Many women find themselves turned on by watching their own bodies move, by catching glimpses of their hips in motion, or by seeing the play of light and shadow across their skin. Whether it's in a mirror, a short video clip, or simply imagining a past encounter in vivid detail, the visual side of desire is just as powerful for women. And it's okay to embrace that.

Watching yourself be touched, or seeing yourself in the midst of pleasure, isn't narcissistic or dirty—it's affirming. It says, "My body is good. My pleasure is good. And I can delight in both." There's something grounding and liberating about visually bearing witness to your own arousal. For many women, it helps them get out of their heads and into their bodies, anchoring them in the here-and-now instead of spiraling into self-doubt or distraction.

So yes—if you've never tried watching yourself in a mirror during sex or masturbation, give yourself permission to explore it. It might feel awkward or silly at first (many new things do), but don't let that stop you. You might just discover a whole new layer of connection with yourself and your husband.

And if video or photo feels more your speed (or you want to capture a moment to remember later), that's something many couples find empowering too. Just be wise with how and where those images are stored—safety and consent matter. But the act itself? Fully within bounds when it's consensual, monogamous, and mutual fun.

And don't underestimate the power of imagination, either. Replaying your favorite sexual memory in your mind or fantasizing about a future moment with your husband can amplify arousal and help you tune into desire. Your brain is your biggest erogenous zone—use it!

Bottom line: watching yourself or visualizing intimacy with your spouse isn't just "allowed"—it might be one of the keys to unlocking a deeper, richer connection with your sexual self. Your body is not something to hide from. It's something to behold—with wonder, gratitude, and maybe just a little extra sizzle.

Academy Girl and Headmaster?

Ever had your pulse quicken at the thought of bending over a desk while the Headmaster lifts your plaid skirt for a firm little spanking? Maybe it surprised you. Maybe it didn't. Either way—you are *definitely* not alone.

Role-playing is a form of sexual expression that many Christian couples find not only acceptable, but wildly fun, playful, and even emotionally connecting. At its core, it's simply imaginative storytelling... with a spicy twist.

Doctor and nurse. Pilot and stewardess. Knight and maiden. Pirate and captive. Cop and prisoner. Student and Headmaster. Maid and master of the house. These are more than just Halloween costumes—they're scripts for lovers' games, where both partners get to explore new dynamics and embody different facets of their sexuality. One day you're the shy schoolgirl. The next, you're the bossy CEO. That's the joy of play—you're free to explore without judgment.

And no, this isn't childish or silly. It's sacred play. It's stepping into a space where curiosity, safety, and passion get to dance together. When you and your husband choose to play out a fantasy together, you're deepening trust and giving one another a safe container to explore emotional themes like surrender, dominance, rescue, or rebellion—all within the safe, sacred bounds of marriage.

Plus, role-play can be a powerful tool for shifting out of stress and into sensuality. When you've been wearing the "mom hat" or the "professional hat" all day, it's not always easy to transition into "sexy wife mode." But slipping into character—maybe literally with a costume—can help bypass inhibition and open the door to boldness and fun.

So yes—if that little inner Academy Girl wants to meet the Headmaster after class, we say... show up for detention. Grab your husband. Let go of your grown-up self-consciousness. And enjoy the beautiful, brainy, blessed gift of sexual imagination.

The Forbidden Hole?

Let's start with a question many Christian women have silently wondered—but rarely felt permission to ask out loud: *Is anal play off-limits in a Christian marriage?*

Short answer? Not necessarily. If it honors God's design—mutuality, monogamy, and joy-filled consent—it's not forbidden. It may be unfamiliar, even intimidating, but that doesn't mean it's off-limits. Let's walk this out together.

The Bible doesn't give us a rigid checklist of bedroom behaviors labeled "acceptable" and "off-limits." Instead, it gives us a guiding framework for sexual intimacy that's rooted in relationship and love. In 1 Corinthians 7:3–5, Paul writes that husbands and wives each have authority over the other's body—not as a weapon or leverage, but as a tender, mutual offering. This passage isn't about obligation; it's about mutual delight, trust, and care.

Then there's Hebrews 13:4, which says, "Let marriage be held in honor among all, and let the marriage bed be undefiled." In context, this means the marriage bed is holy—set apart for mutual enjoyment, emotional safety, and joyful connection. It's not a space for shame or cultural fear, but for sacred exploration with the one person God gave you to know intimately.

So what does that mean for anal play? It means this: If both of you freely consent, if your shared exploration deepens your connection, and if it brings pleasure without coercion—then there's no biblical reason it's off-limits. Curiosity, when paired with communication and respect, is not sin. It's sacred discovery.

Now, if you're feeling unsure, squirmy, or just plain nervous—that's *totally* normal. This is often new territory, and with anything new, there's a learning curve. That's okay! Let's break it down together with grace and practical tips.

A Gentle Guide to Getting Started

1. **Start With a Conversation**
   Before anything physical happens, talk about it. This isn't a performance; it's an invitation. Share your curiosity, your hesitations, and your hopes. Ask him about his thoughts. Set

boundaries. This isn't a one-time conversation, either—it's an ongoing dialogue rooted in trust.

2. **Take It Slow—Like, Really Slow**

   The anal area isn't self-lubricating like the vagina, and it responds best to *relaxed* exploration. Start externally. Use light touch and lots of affirming connection. Breathe deeply. Patience is the name of the game here—this is about safety, not speed.

3. **Use Lots of Lube**

   We can't overstate this: *Lube is your best friend.* Silicone or water-based lubricants are essential. Never skip this step—it's not a bonus, it's a requirement for comfort and pleasure.

4. **Choose Tools Wisely**

   Start with fingers or a small, anal-safe toy—nothing with sharp edges or loose parts. And remember: clean everything thoroughly. Hygiene is part of honoring each other.

5. **Stay Present and Check In Often**

   Even if you've talked in advance, keep checking in. "Do you like this?" "Is this okay?" "Want to keep going?" These check-ins aren't mood-killers—they're love-builders. They say, *I see you. I care.*

6. **Clean Thoroughly—Always**

   This might not be the sexiest tip, but it's one of the most important. The bacteria around the anus belongs there—and only there. If it gets transferred to the vagina or mouth, it can cause infections (and no one wants that!). So be sure to wash anything that's been in or near the anus—fingers, toys, penis, you name it—*before* it goes anywhere else. Think of it as love-powered hygiene: caring for each other's bodies as sacred spaces.

7. **Invite God Into Your Joy**

   No, really. The Holy Spirit isn't afraid of your bedroom. God designed sex as a place of intimacy, trust, delight, and yes—playfulness. Joy doesn't scare Him. He delights in your delight.

The Bottom Line?

You are not broken, perverted, or sinful for being curious. You are not "less holy" for enjoying new forms of connection with your husband. You are a wonderfully made woman with a complex, God-designed capacity for pleasure and intimacy.

So if you and your husband are both saying yes, if you're respecting each other's boundaries and exploring with joy—not fear—then this isn't a forbidden path. It's just one more way to deepen your connection.

Let your story be shaped not by shame, but by grace.

Dominance & Submission

There's something undeniably thrilling about the idea of surrender—and the power of being the one surrendered to. That's the heart of dominance and submission (often shortened to D/s)—a consensual exploration of power dynamics that can stir up deeply erotic responses in both partners.

Let's be clear: in Christian marriage, this kind of play isn't about actual control or hierarchy. It's about trust. It's about creating a "scene"—a defined moment in time—where you and your husband agree to step into playful roles of giving and receiving direction, power, or pleasure. All of it happens inside the sacred framework of mutual consent, safety, and love. Think of it as holy improv with extra pillows and a safe word.

Safe Words Are Sacred

Before you begin any kind of power play, establish a clear stoplight system. A common approach is using the colors:

- **Green** – All good, keep going!
- **Yellow** – I need to slow down or pause.
- **Red** – Stop immediately, this is not okay for me.

You can also pick a specific, memorable word like *pineapple* or *mercy*—something you wouldn't normally shout during a hot moment, but that instantly signals, "This needs to pause now." A safe word is not a sign of weakness—it's a mark of maturity. It allows both of you to explore freely, knowing there's a safety net in place.

Curiosity, Not a Checklist

Dominance and submission is not a pre-packaged script; it's a co-written story. The key to safe, exciting exploration is communication before you ever start the scene. You don't have to try everything—nor should you. But it's worth having an open-hearted conversation about what intrigues you both.

Here are some areas you might explore, not as a to-do list, but as conversation starters:

Roles & Power Dynamics

- Who might enjoy being more dominant or more submissive?
- Would it be fun to play roles like headmaster/student, captor/captive, queen/servant, or boss/employee?

Sensory Experiences

- Curious about spanking, scratching, biting, nipple play, or hair pulling?
- Intrigued by tools like floggers, pinwheels, or wax play?
- Interested in temperature play—ice cubes, warm oils, or candle wax (only skin-safe, of course)?

Restraints & Control

- Want to try being tied up or doing the tying?
- Open to blindfolds, gags, cuffs, ropes, chains, or spreader bars?
- What feels sexy: being "taken" or "taken care of"?

Emotional Themes

- How do you feel about teasing, orgasm delay, denial, or control?
- Does the idea of "being at his mercy" or "being served" stir something inside you?
- What feelings do kneeling, obedience, or submission stir up—for better or worse?

Appearance & Atmosphere

- Would you enjoy dressing the part—lingerie, leather, a costume?

- Would photos or video be thrilling or uncomfortable?

- Is there something symbolic (a collar, a special necklace, an act of service) that could deepen the connection?

Remember, everything on this list is a *possibility*, not a prescription. Some things you may try and love. Others you might try and laugh through. And some you'll skip altogether—and that's perfect too.

A Game of Trust and Play

Exploring dominance and submission is ultimately about connection. It's about trust so strong that you can play with the edges of control and surrender. It's about saying, "Let's discover something new together," and having the courage to bring your whole self—desire, fear, faith, and fantasy—to the one person God gave you to be naked and unashamed with.

This kind of play isn't everyone's cup of tea—and that's okay. But if it's yours? There's room for it in the sacred, undefiled marriage bed.

Wrapping the Whip (and the Chapter)

So, what did we just do here? We opened the "forbidden" drawer—and found it wasn't so forbidden after all. From kink to consent, from spicy talk to spiritual freedom, we've explored how Christian couples can enjoy adventurous, playful, and even "unusual" intimacy without shame or secrecy.

We've discovered that what matters most is not whether something is considered kinky by your great aunt or your women's Bible study, but whether it's:

- **Mutual** – Do you both agree to and enjoy it?

- **Monogamous** – Is it shared only between husband and wife?

- **Meaningful** – Does it deepen your connection, delight, and trust?

If the answer is yes, then friend—you're in holy territory.

God isn't afraid of your curiosity. He's not shocked by your fantasies. He wired your body, your brain, and your bond with your husband for pleasure, play, and freedom. And that means you don't need to fear your desires. You just need a safe, sacred place to explore them—with wisdom, with love, and with a good dose of lube.

As you reflect, consider:

- What intrigued or challenged you in this chapter?

- Are there areas of sexual exploration you've felt ashamed of that may actually be safe and sacred?

- What's one playful experiment you and your husband might want to try—with full consent, clear communication, and open hearts?

Which brings us to the next conversation—because while your marriage bed is private, your journey toward sexual freedom wasn't meant to be lonely. In the next chapter, we'll explore why the Church desperately needs sex-positive spaces, and what it looks like to build a community that holds truth and grace in both hands.

Chapter 20: Sex Positive Church

The Text Thread That Started a Revolution

*J*enna stared at the blinking cursor in the group chat, thumb hovering over her phone screen like it might bite her. The chat title was "Bible Study Babes" and until now, it had been used for safe things like scheduling carpool pickups and sending prayer requests for things like Aunt Linda's surgery or Target deals on Chick-fil-A sauce.

But today? Jenna was about to change the game.

She typed, deleted, retyped, and finally hit send:

"Okay, don't judge me... but what if we talked about sex at group next week?"

There. It was done. No turning back now.

Instantly, her heart started pounding like she'd just confessed to shoplifting communion wafers. What was she thinking? These women had shared their quiet times and cried over their kids' temper tantrums. Could she really bring up bedroom stuff?

Bloop.

Maggie: "Like... with our husbands?? "

Bloop.

Tasha: "Girl, I was praying someone would say it. I've got QUESTIONS."

Bloop.

Lauren: "Only if we're allowed to laugh a lot and bring wine."

Jenna exhaled and laughed out loud. Relief and giddiness flooded her body like a fizzy soda pop. She wasn't alone. She wasn't crazy. And apparently, she wasn't the only one Googling "is it okay for Christians to read spicy romance books" at 1 a.m.

Later that night, as she folded laundry and half-listened to a podcast, Jenna whispered, "Okay, Jesus. I'll go first."

Because maybe it wasn't just about her marriage or her questions. Maybe this was about more than sex. Maybe it was about freedom. About women finally breathing again. About dragging shame into the light and watching it shrivel.

She smiled, imagining her living room packed next Thursday with candles, snacks, and the sound of women doing holy work—laughing, blushing, healing.

And maybe, just maybe… starting a revolution.

Revolution

We need a sex revolution in the Church.

The enemy has been wreaking havoc for far too long—twisting sex into something shameful, selfish, and secretive. He's distorted it in the culture, yes. But he's also stolen far too much ground inside the Church.

Let's be honest: many of us were handed two terrible options when it came to sex. One was the world's way—hypersexualized, self-focused, and empty. The other was purity culture—rigid, fearful, and full of silence. Both left people wounded, ashamed, and confused.

And it shows. Too many of God's sons and daughters are quietly carrying the fallout. Struggling with body shame, sexual anxiety, performance pressure, low desire, porn addictions, trauma, and secret questions they don't know where to ask.

Instead of dancing in the sexual freedom and joy God designed, many Christian couples are tiptoeing around landmines. We've lost our voice. Our joy. Our boldness.

But here's the good news: it doesn't have to stay this way.

Revival almost always starts with a whisper of honesty. With one brave voice breaking the silence. With one woman turning to another and saying, "Hey... can we talk about this?"

We're not saying you have to start a podcast or preach from a pulpit (though if that's you—go for it!). But we are saying this: every woman reading this book has the power to start a revolution. A quiet, underground, Spirit-filled uprising of truth, laughter, healing, and freedom.

And Jesus? He's all for it. He wants His Bride free. Unashamed. Radiant. Alive in her sexuality—not because the world taught her how to be, but because the Word did.

This chapter is a call to action.

Not the kind that wears sandwich boards or shouts on street corners—but the kind that brews coffee, opens her living room, and dares to talk honestly with her sisters.

Will you be part of the change?

The Spiciest Women's Group Ever

Okay, friend. Here's our big ask: will you help start the underground revolution by hosting the spiciest women's group your church has never seen coming?

You don't need a seminary degree. You don't need a perfectly clean house. You don't even need to know what you're doing. And you don't need permission, you have it from Jesus. All you need is a willingness to gather a few trusted girlfriends, read this book together, and talk honestly—like the world's most freeing, faith-filled, slightly blush-worthy book club.

Throughout these pages, we've beat the drum (and yes, occasionally the headboard) about a central truth of both Scripture and neuroscience: we need one another. Deeply. Desperately. Unapologetically.

We weren't designed to navigate life—or our sexuality—alone. We need safe, wise, vulnerable women around us. A Sage Circle. A few iron sharpeners who can say, "Me too," "You're not crazy," and "Let's grow through this together."

This is how we shed the false self. This is how we ditch fake joy. This is how we grow into the true self God created us to be—full of life, laughter, holy desire, and the kind of confidence that can't be faked or stolen.

So here's the invitation: Be the one who starts the circle. Or joins it. Be the woman who dares to say, "Let's talk about what no one talks about." Be the bridge to someone else's healing and freedom.

You don't have to be an expert. You just have to be real.

Jesus wants to use your story. Your tenderness. Your questions. Your freedom. He's not looking for perfect women—He's looking for willing ones. And when you show up, vulnerably and bravely, the Kingdom breaks in. Women rise. Marriages change. Shame crumbles.

So text the friend. Brew the coffee. Open the book. And start the conversation that might just change everything.

We're cheering wildly from the sidelines. You were made for this.

Righteous Flirting

Let's talk about something that rarely makes it into church bulletins but absolutely belongs in Kingdom culture: righteous flirting.

Now, before you clutch your pearls or start imagining awkward youth group "purity talks," let's define it. Righteous flirting is what happens when playful joy meets spiritual maturity. It's not manipulation. It's not seduction. It's the sacred art of speaking life—with delight and dignity.

Why It Matters

Men and women in the body of Christ need one another. Especially singles. Especially the widowed. Especially anyone who's been walking through a dry season where touch, encouragement, and delight feel like distant memories.

Doug Rosenau, a wise Christian sex therapist, described it beautifully: "Righteous flirting is affirming others with dignity and delight." Paul echoes a similar truth in 1 Timothy 5:2, urging believers to treat one another like family—older women as mothers, younger women as sisters, and by implication, men as fathers, brothers, and sons—with *absolute purity*.

But purity isn't cold. It's not withdrawn or self-protective. True purity is warm, full of light and goodness. And that means we don't hide our feminine radiance or pretend that kindness doesn't matter just because the world has misused it.

A Gift the World is Starving For

Let's be honest—affirmation is in short supply. Especially for men.

Many men go days, weeks, even months without a single kind, affectionate word from a woman that isn't either romantically charged or emotionally guarded. But you, sister, carry something powerful.

Your presence—your smile, your eyes, your "Hey, I see you"—can awaken something beautiful. You reflect God's nurturing, affirming heart. That's not "leading him on." That's leading him to life.

What the Brain Says

According to Neuroscience Informed Christian Counseling® (NICC), we are biologically wired for connection. Emotional attunement—when someone sees us and responds warmly—literally calms our nervous systems. It regulates our stress. It heals trauma.

So when you laugh with the single dad, thank the widowed elder, or cheer for the teenage guy who just ran the church tech board without a meltdown—you're not just being nice. You're helping co-regulate his nervous system in a world that often leaves men emotionally starving.

But What About Boundaries?

Yes. And amen. Boundaries are vital.

Righteous flirting is not recklessness. It's not an excuse to cross lines or stir up confusion. It's being intentional. Kind. Spirit-led. Pure-hearted.

It means knowing when to speak up—and when to stop. It means offering your kindness with wisdom and self-awareness, never to manipulate, always to bless. It also means trusting the Holy Spirit to guide you in how and when to offer that warmth.

And Let's Flip the Script

We need affirmation from men, too.

Not just from our husbands or boyfriends—but from spiritual brothers, fathers, mentors. Many women were never affirmed by their dads or safe male figures growing up. That's not a life sentence. It's a cue that the body of Christ has something healing to offer.

Receiving healthy, warm, non-sexual affirmation from men is not dangerous. It's not shameful. It's part of how God designed us to be whole.

Let's Be Women Who Speak Life

So let's practice this holy art. Smile at the worship leader. Thank the janitor. Crack a joke with the youth pastor. Compliment your married friend's courage or wisdom or sense of humor—without fear or weirdness.

You are not too much. You are not dangerous. You are a life-giver.

And the Church? She needs your voice, your presence, and your holy mischief more than ever.

Can I Get a Witness?

Can we just say it out loud? The Church is meant to be a witness to the *whole* goodness of God—including His glorious, joy-filled design for sex.

Our Creator is not embarrassed by pleasure. He invented it. He handcrafted intimacy not just for procreation, but for joy, connection, healing, and worship. Yes, worship.

So what if—stay with us here—the holy, happy, life-giving sex of God's people became one of the ways the world sees what abundant life really looks like?

Sex as a Light on a Hill

Jesus said we are the light of the world—a city on a hill that cannot be hidden (Matthew 5:14). That includes our sexuality. Not to flaunt, not to boast, but to *witness*—to show a watching, weary, sexually broken world that God's way is not prudish or oppressive... it's radiant.

When Christian couples live in freedom—laughing, experimenting, delighting, connecting—it creates a beautiful, powerful contrast. A world saturated in pornography, shame, hookups, and loneliness might just stop and wonder: *What do they have that I don't?*

That curiosity can open doors. Because embodied joy is one of the most persuasive forms of evangelism there is.

Lead the Revolution

This is the invitation: to be part of a sexual reformation in the Church. Not just in theory, but in real bedrooms, with real couples, and in real conversations.

Let's stop hiding behind silence. Let's ditch the shame. Let's be the kind of people who talk about sex with holiness and humor, with reverence and joy. Let's model marriages where trust and pleasure are growing, not shrinking.

There's a revival brewing, and it smells like freedom.

God is stirring something new in His Church—something bold, bright, and beautifully embodied. Will you be part of it?

JOSH & CASSIE SPURLOCK

Because someone out there—your daughter, your friend, your small group leader, your neighbor—is waiting for a witness.

Let's Light It Up

This chapter has been a call to courage—and to community.

We've explored what it means to be part of a sexual revolution in the Church. Not the kind that shocks for attention, but the kind that quietly and powerfully reclaims God's vision for sex as sacred, celebratory, and shame-free. You've been invited to help spark this movement in your circles—by starting the spiciest women's group ever, by engaging in righteous flirting that affirms and uplifts, and by letting your own joy-filled intimacy be a light in the darkness.

This isn't about being provocative for the sake of it. It's about being prophetic—living out the truth that God's design is *good*, and that His people should be the most free, most healed, and most joy-filled lovers on the planet.

So here's your invitation: reflect on how God might be calling *you* to help shift the culture. What brave conversations can you start? What groups could you gather? What light could you shine?

Because when we reclaim sex as worship, as connection, as a divine gift, the world can't help but notice.

And sometimes, the next step in that healing journey is getting some extra help. That's where we're headed next—into the world of Christian sex therapy. What is it? Who is it for? And how can it help bring even deeper freedom?

Chapter 21: Christian Sex Therapy

"Whispers from the Back Row"

*J*enna sat in the back row of her church's "Healthy Marriages" workshop, clutching her lukewarm coffee like it was a stress ball. The topic was emotional intimacy, and the leader was currently asking everyone to turn to their spouse and share one area of their sex life they'd like to improve.*

She stared at her husband. He stared at his coffee. She smiled. He smiled. Nobody moved.

Internally, she was screaming, I don't even know what I want to say, let alone how to say it out loud at 10 a.m. in the Fellowship Hall while Brenda from hospitality is two seats over.

Later, in the car, she finally whispered, "I don't think I'm broken, but something isn't working the way it's supposed to."

He didn't say much—just reached over and held her hand. It was the most connected she'd felt all week.

That night, after the kids were asleep and the laundry was half-folded (okay, not even close), she sat on the edge of their bed with her laptop and googled, "Christian help for sex problems." The results ranged from blogs that felt like they belonged in 1997 to articles that made her feel like she needed to repent for even asking.

She sighed, shut the laptop, and muttered, "There has to be a better way."

What she didn't know—what she was just beginning to hope— was that there was a better way. She just needed someone to connect the dots between her theology, her biology, and her very real marriage bed.

And maybe, just maybe, she didn't need to carry the shame or the pressure anymore.

The American Board of Christian Sex Therapists (ABCST)

Let's start with a big, important truth: there are many wonderful, wise Christian counselors out there—many of whom we count as dear friends and deeply respected colleagues. But here's something most people don't realize: **sex therapy is not part of the standard training counselors receive**. That means most licensed counselors, even very good ones, haven't been trained to navigate the unique and sometimes complex world of sexual concerns.

That's where Christian sex therapy comes in.

Christian sex therapists are trained counselors who've gone on to receive additional, specialized training in sexual health and intimacy—training that's grounded in solid theology and a biblical worldview. Think of it like this: just as a physician might complete medical school and then go on to do a fellowship in cardiology, Christian counselors can pursue extra education in sex therapy to become specialists in this sensitive and sacred area of human experience.

Josh, co-author of this book, trained through the **Institute for Sexual Wholeness (ISW)** and is board certified by the **American Board of Christian Sex Therapists (ABCST)**— the only certifying body specifically for Christian sex therapists. This certification signals that a therapist has completed rigorous academic coursework, supervised clinical experience, and demonstrated competency in both the science of sexual health and the art of integrating that knowledge with a biblical worldview.

Not every counselor needs to be a sex therapist. Just like not every doctor needs to be a cardiologist. But when someone has a heart issue, you want the right kind of doctor. The same is true when sex becomes a stumbling block or a place of pain. Competent Christian counselors will recognize when a client's concern requires the specialized help of a sex therapist—and they'll make a referral, not because they're not good at what they do, but because they love their clients enough to get them the help they deserve.

If you're wondering where to start, **the ABCST maintains a directory of certified Christian sex therapists**, making it easy to find someone who shares your values and has the training to truly help. And if you're open to online counseling—which is incredibly helpful for those living in areas without local access to faith-based sex therapy—**MyCounselor.Online®** provides Christian sex therapy to clients worldwide. It's one of the most trusted resources available and part of the same team that's helped bring this book to life.

You're not alone, and you're not without options. If you're running into barriers as you try to walk out what you're learning in these pages, Christian sex therapy may be the next faithful, freeing step.

Neuroscience Informed Christian Counseling® (NICC)

Neuroscience Informed Christian Counseling® (NICC) is more than just a therapeutic approach—it's a whole-person framework designed to bring deep healing, emotional maturity, and spiritual transformation. Developed by me (Josh Spurlock, MA, LPC, CST), and the clinical team at **My-Counselor.Online®**, NICC has been 20 years in the making and is delivering powerful results—with a client success rate of **93.6%**, which is virtually unheard of in the mental health field (where 70% is considered average and 80% is excellent).

So, what makes it so effective?

At its heart, NICC rests on a bold, beautiful premise: **the Author of Scripture and the Designer of your nervous system is the same person—Jesus**. That means when we study both neuroscience and the Bible, we're uncovering the same divine wisdom from different angles. With confidence, we can apply both to our healing journey—and watch incredible transformation unfold.

A Framework for Healing and Growth

NICC is a clinical, theological, and developmental model built to help people heal from trauma, repair developmental deficits, and grow into their God-given identity. It's grounded in the belief that humans are **embodied souls**—integrated beings of body, mind, and spirit—designed for connection, growth, and joy.

Central to this framework is the concept of the **Thrive-Drive**—God's life-giving impulse within us, calling us toward growth and wholeness. This divine spark pushes us to mature into our **Soul DNA**—the unique, God-breathed blueprint of who we were always meant to be. But life wounds us. Sin, trauma (wounds), neglect (gaps), and coping mechanisms (immature habits) shape a **false self** that keeps us stuck.

NICC helps us journey back to the **true self**—who God created us to be from the beginning.

The Five Developmental Domains

Healing and growth happen across five key areas of development:

1. **Connection** – Our ability to form safe, loving relationships.

2. **Independence** – The capacity to assert identity and make choices.

3. **Reality** – Accepting limits, grieving loss, and living in truth.

4. **Emotional Intelligence** – Feeling, understanding, and regulating emotion.

5. **Spirituality** – Integrating our relationship with God into daily life.

The Science of Change

NICC emphasizes that lasting change comes through **life-giving experiences**—moments of safety, attunement, and connection that contradict the pain of the past. These experiences activate your brain's natural capacity to heal through **neuroplasticity** and **memory reconsolidation**.

This is how NICC brings healing:

- It repairs **trauma wounds**
- It fills **developmental gaps**
- It updates the brain's internal map of relationships and self
- It leads to stable peace, joy, and hope—what NICC calls **true happiness**

Theologically, this reflects the heart of the gospel: not just salvation from sin, but **maturation in Christ**. God isn't just interested in making you forgiven—He's committed to making you whole.

Deep Roots and Broad Influences

NICC integrates insights from top-tier neuroscience and psychological models, including:

- **AEDP** (Accelerated Experiential Dynamic Psychotherapy – Diana Fosha)
- **EFT** (Emotionally Focused Therapy – Sue Johnson)
- **AF-EMDR** (Attachment-Focused EMDR – Laurel Parnell)
- **IFS** (Internal Family Systems – Richard Schwartz)
- **Schema Therapy, Interpersonal Neurobiology, Polyvagal Theory**, and **Memory Reconsolidation Research**

It also draws from rich theological sources—from evangelical scholars like Wayne Grudem, Dallas Willard, and N.T. Wright, to contemplative traditions like Ignatius of Loyola. It reads the brain as a theological reality—proof of divine design and a map to healing.

What Makes NICC Different

What truly sets NICC apart is its grounding in **neurotheology**—the belief that the brain's healing capacity is not just a marvel of biology, but a **gift from God**. This model doesn't just use therapeutic tools; it **invites the Holy Spirit** into every session, viewing transformation as a sacred collaboration between divine grace and human design.

NICC also scales beyond the counseling office. It's not just for therapists. It's also used in **Mental Health Discipleship**, equipping church leaders to walk with others through healing in spiritually and emotionally intelligent ways.

In short, **NICC is where biblical truth meets brain science**—and healing becomes a tangible reality.

MyCounselor.Online®

Hey friend, let's get real for a minute.

You've been doing the work—digging into your story, healing wounds, rethinking what intimacy really means, reclaiming your desire. You're showing up with courage. And yet… something still feels stuck.

Maybe your body isn't responding the way you hoped. Maybe your spouse feels unsure of how to join you in the journey. Maybe the shame is louder than the truth right now, and despite all the tools and insight you've gathered, you're not where you want to be.

That doesn't mean you're doing it wrong. It just means you might need some extra help.

That's exactly why we created **MyCounselor.Online®**.

Founded in 2007 by us—Josh and Cassie—**MyCounselor.Online® (MCO)** exists to bring expert, biblically faithful, neuroscience-informed counseling to people like you, wherever you are. With secure telehealth services available worldwide, you can connect with a Christian sex therapist from the privacy of your couch.

But MCO isn't your average counseling provider—and definitely not one of those "big box" therapy platforms. It's personal. It's pastoral. And it's proven—with a **93.6% success rate**, far surpassing the 70% industry average.

So, what makes us different?

1. NICC: Healing That Transforms the Whole Person

MCO is the home of **Neuroscience Informed Christian Counseling®** **(NICC)**—a groundbreaking model that weaves together Scripture, brain science, and trauma-informed care. This isn't generic "Christian counseling" where you get a Bible verse and a pep talk. It's deep, focused, compassionate care that meets you at the intersection of body, soul, and spirit.

NICC therapy creates space for Jesus to meet you in the parts of your story that ache most—and invites your nervous system to learn it's safe to come alive again.

2. Therapists You Can Actually Trust

Unlike platforms that randomly pair you with an independent contractor, every therapist at MCO is **an employee**. That matters—because it means they're thoroughly vetted, consistently trained, and held to rigorous theological and clinical standards. (Legally, contractor-based networks can't do that.)

Only the top **2% of applicants** are hired, and every counselor starts a **two-year post-graduate residency** in NICC before being entrusted with clients. That's after they've already earned a master's or doctoral degree.

They're not just Christian in name—they're trained to integrate faith and clinical skill in ways that actually bring healing.

3. Support That Complements (Not Competes)

Already seeing a counselor? That's awesome. MCO can come alongside your existing care to offer **specialized insight into your sexual story**—your body, your marriage, your intimacy roadblocks, your spiritual wrestling. Many of our clients continue their general therapy while working with a NICC therapist for a season of focused, expert care in this deeply personal area.

Especially if your current therapist isn't sex-positive, trauma-informed, or trained in Christian sexual ethics, this partnership can make all the difference.

Bottom Line?

If you've reached a point where a book and a prayer aren't enough, you're not weak or broken. You're wise. Healing isn't a solo project—it takes a village.

Let MyCounselor.Online® be part of yours.

You're not behind.

You're not broken.

You're becoming.

Is Sex Therapy Right for Me?

Here's the simple truth: Christian sex therapy might be exactly what you need if you've read through this book, nodded along with the ideas, believed in the truth—and still find yourself stuck.

Maybe your desire is still missing in action, despite all your efforts to rediscover it.

Maybe you can't seem to enjoy your body, even though you're trying.

Maybe past wounds keep rising up at the most inconvenient times, or your spouse seems resistant, confused, or just not engaging like you hoped.

If you're doing your best to apply the insights, practices, and encouragement in these pages, and it still feels like something's not working—**you're not failing.** You're human. And sometimes, we just need more support.

That's where Christian sex therapy comes in.

A skilled Christian sex therapist is like a wise guide for this journey—someone trained to help you identify where you're blocked, what's beneath the surface, and how to gently move toward freedom and connection. Whether the issue is physical, emotional, relational, or spiritual, sex therapy is a space where all of it gets to be seen, heard, and healed.

So if you're wondering, *"Is this for me?"* ask yourself:

- Have I hit a wall in this area, even after trying new things?

- Do I feel stuck in patterns I don't fully understand?

- Would it help to have someone walk with me through this tender part of my story?

- Do I want more joy and less fear when it comes to sex and intimacy?

If you're nodding yes to any of these, Christian sex therapy is a good next step.

Not because you're broken. But because you're worth it.

You were made for connection, for wholeness, and for sexual confidence that's deeply rooted in love—God's love, your husband's love, and your growing love for yourself.

Wrapping It Up

This chapter was all about bringing hope and help to the places where sexual confidence feels hard to reach. We introduced you to the world of Christian sex therapy—what it is, who it's for, and why it matters. We unpacked the NICC® model and gave you a peek behind the curtain at My-Counselor.Online®, a team passionately committed to helping people like you walk into freedom, healing, and joy.

If you're feeling hesitant, take a deep breath. Seeking help doesn't mean you're weak. It means you're brave. It means you're ready to move beyond the surface and into the kind of transformation that lasts.

God is not intimidated by your questions, your body, or your stuck places. He designed you with care and wired you for healing. If therapy might be the next right step, take it. And if you're not sure yet, that's okay too. Just don't believe the lie that you're too far gone or meant to do this alone.

You're not broken. You're becoming.

And speaking of becoming... the next chapter is going to explore how sex—like good wine, old cheese, or your grandma's cast iron skillet—is designed to get better with time. Let's talk about why your best sex can be ahead of you... all the way until one of you kicks the bucket. (Then sex should probably stop. Otherwise, yes, it gets weird.)

Chapter 22: Until Death Do We Sex

The Chocolate Milk Revelation

*E*llie was 38, wore fuzzy socks year-round, and had recently discovered a new spiritual gift: forgetting why she walked into a room.

That morning had started with the usual chaos—her 6-year-old had spilled chocolate milk all over the kitchen floor ("It was an EXPERIMENT, Mom!"), her husband had accidentally taken her keys to work, and the dog had vomited what appeared to be an entire crayon. Somewhere in the middle of that glorious circus, Ellie had paused, rag in hand, and thought: "Wait. Is this it? Is this just what life is now? Chocolate milk and missing keys and zero time to feel sexy?"

It wasn't that she didn't love her husband. She did—deeply. But between the schedules, the stress, and the surprise existential crises brought on by folding too much laundry, their sex life had... plateaued. Okay, maybe "plateaued" was generous. It had been months since she felt that flutter of excitement, that boldness in her body. And honestly? It made her sad.

But that night, something shifted.

They were both lying in bed, worn out and a little giggly from a late-night snack run gone wrong (never send two sleep-

deprived adults into a gas station with a sweet tooth and zero self-control). Ellie turned toward him, hair a mess, breath smelling vaguely of gummy bears, and said, "Do you ever think we'll get better at this? Sex, I mean. Or is it just... this?"

He looked at her, sleepy and soft-eyed, and said, "I hope not. I hope we get way better. Like, embarrass-our-grandkids level better."

And for some reason, that goofy, honest answer lit something in her. Not fireworks, not yet. But a warm little flame of hope.

Maybe they weren't behind. Maybe they were just beginning.

Life, Like Fine Wine

Here's a truth worth celebrating: God designed sex to age like fine wine—growing deeper, richer, and more satisfying with time.

Despite what movies, magazines, or even well-meaning Christian culture might have implied, honeymoon sex isn't the pinnacle. It's the starting line. The beginning of a long, beautiful unfolding. And honestly? It's supposed to be a bit clumsy. That's not failure—that's design.

Why? Because God didn't intend sex to be a one-time performance you nail right out of the gate. He intended it to be a lifelong dance of discovery, one that matures as you do. As you grow into your true self—confident, joyful, embodied, and spiritually anchored—your sexual self matures too. And that means you get to enjoy sex more and more, not less and less.

This isn't just poetic talk. It's the lived testimony of couples who've chosen to keep growing, keep laughing, keep trying, and keep talking. Whether you've been married for five years or fifty, the invitation stands: the best is still ahead.

Yes, bodies change. Yes, seasons shift. But with each new chapter, you have the chance to rewrite what pleasure and connection mean for you. No rush. No comparison. Just curiosity, courage, and covenant love.

And just to be clear—for theological accuracy and general decency—this promise holds until one of you dies. After that? Please stop. That would get weird.

But seriously: for as long as you both shall live, your sex life is meant to keep getting better.

So take a breath, take heart, and take the hand of your beloved. **The best is yet to come.**

About Josh and Cassie

Josh and Cassie Spurlock are a husband-and-wife team with a passion for helping Christians experience healing, wholeness, and holy pleasure—especially in the bedroom.

Josh is a Licensed Professional Counselor, Certified Sex Therapist, and the founder of *MyCounselor.Online®*, where he developed the Neuroscience Informed Christian Counseling® (NICC) model. With over two decades of experience in clinical practice, biblical scholarship, and trauma recovery, Josh is known for bringing together brain science and Scripture in a way that's both deeply wise and refreshingly practical.

Cassie is a gifted communicator, mentor, and creative force behind the Omazing® Intimacy brand. With her signature blend of warmth, wit, and gospel-grounded wisdom, Cassie loves walking with women through the ups and downs of marriage, motherhood, body image, and sexual confidence. Her gift? Making awkward conversations feel safe, funny, and life-giving.

Together, Josh and Cassie speak, write, and coach couples on the journey toward authentic intimacy—emotionally, spiritually, and sexually. They believe sex is sacred, laughter is holy, and no one is too broken for healing.

They live in Montana with their delightfully wild crew of kids, beautiful mountains, and more books than they can shelve. When they're not teaching about sex, they're probably sipping coffee, hanging out with friends, or sneaking off for a date night. **Learn more at JoshCassie.com!**

Back Cover

You love Jesus—but you're not always sure what to do with sex.

You're not alone. So many Christian women long to feel confident, connected, and actually look forward sex—but instead, they feel stuck in shame, confusion, or disconnection. Whether you're newlywed, seasoned in marriage, or somewhere in between, you've probably wondered:

"Is something wrong with me?"

"Why don't I want sex like my husband does?"

"Is it okay to want more... or to want something different?"

In Feeling Sexy, husband-and-wife team Josh and Cassie Spurlock offer a funny, tender, and unfiltered guide to cultivating sexual confidence and deep desire—without ditching your faith. Drawing on Scripture, neuroscience, and years of experience as a Certified Sex Therapist (Josh) and women's mentor (Cassie), they gently dismantle shame and help you rediscover holy pleasure as part of God's beautiful design.

You'll explore practical truths about arousal, fantasy, communication, healing, and creative intimacy—all with warm encouragement and laugh-out-loud honesty.

This book is your invitation to feel seen, understood, and set free to enjoy the kind of sex God always dreamed for you: joyful, sacred, satisfying, and gloriously fun.

Josh and Cassie Spurlock are a husband-and-wife team helping Christians experience healing, wholeness, and holy pleasure—especially in the bedroom. Josh is a Licensed Professional Counselor and Certified Sex Therapist, best known for developing the Neuroscience Informed Christian Counseling® (NICC) model and founding My-Counselor.Online®. Cassie is the voice behind Omazing® Intimacy, a gifted mentor who makes awkward conversations feel safe, funny, and gospel-rich. Together, they speak, write, and coach couples toward authentic, Jesus-centered intimacy. They live in Montana with their wild tribe of kids, beautiful mountains, and enough books to start a library.

Learn more at JoshCassie.com!

www.ingramcontent.com/pod-product-compliance
Lightning Source LLC
Chambersburg PA
CBHW060126130626
46556CB00006B/2246